The Scarecrow Press, Inc.
Metuchen, N.J., & London 1982

FILES ON PARADE

A Memoir by William B. Ready

Library of Congress Cataloging in Publication Data

Ready, William Bernard, 1914-1981
    Files on parade.

    1. Ready, William Bernard, 1914-1981.
2. Librarians--Canada--Biography. I. Title.
Z720.R4A33 1982   020'.92'4 [B]   81-23310
ISBN 0-8108-1516-8   AACR2

To Nora

An introduction to an autobiography is not an easy thing to
write. The writer has written of his life, and it should be
read by the reader with neither addition nor deletion by others.
Such supplements or excisions can smack of apology, or even
worse. However, Will Ready's sudden death in Victoria,
B. C. , just days after he had finished writing the manuscript,
robbed him of a proper opportunity to review the whole.
This brief introduction is intended only to apprise the pro-
spective reader of this and of other things that are germane
to his reading of the book.

Will Ready was a complex man. An Irishman, born
in Wales, he lived for the greater part of his life in North
America, retiring as University Librarian, Emeritus, from
McMaster University in Hamilton, Canada, to settle in British
Columbia. He lived for people and for books, and knew many
of both. He took a delight in libraries of all kinds and conditions, as they were the places in which the people and the
books came together. He regarded librarianship as an artisan's calling, and as only an artisan could, he thrived in the
environment of academic librarianship. Not always understanding the technology of a computer terminal or the legal
jargon of a contract, he unfailingly grasped the significance
of a new development or opportunity, and promptly enlisted
the willing support of others in achieving a goal. He swept
others along with him to reach the objective, whether it was
the application of the computer to library processing, or the
acquisition of an archive.

For ten years I worked under Will Ready as Collections Librarian and succeeded him on his retirement. I
probably saw as much of him during those years as did most
members of his family, and we travelled thousands of miles
together to inspect and acquire books and archives. During

v

this time I came to know through his eyes many of the people and events that he has now described. His hatred of sham and pretence joined with his natural wit to afford him the gift of the born raconteur. He had much to tell: of his childhood and family in Cardiff, the Depression years of his youth; of his encounter with military service, of LIAP, LILOPS, and LOLLIPOPS; of his progression from Minnesota, to Berkeley, Stanford, Milwaukee, and finally to Hamilton; of the people he knew, the writers, the collectors, the booksellers, the wise men, the knaves and the fools; of the books and collections that he brought safe to libraries.

This book is not part of the "library literature" that he loved to hate. It is the relation of a librarian and writer who left his mark on the library world, and for whom the joys always outweighed the sorrows. He is missed by all who knew him.

Graham R. Hill
Hamilton, Canada
March 1982

1

Whenever I recall my life as a librarian I get around to the clatter of horse hoofs in the Harvard Yard.

It was my first visit to the Widener Library, about thirty years ago. Keyes Metcalf was the great librarian there in those days. I had written from Stanford where I was employed, asking whether, when I was passing through Boston, he could spare me time for a visit. He not only agreed, but invited me to lunch. That was a lesson that I never forgot: always welcome aspirants who want to visit. Cancel a committee to do so.

Keyes took me to the Faculty Club for lunch. I ate horsemeat there for the first and last time in my life. I had eaten camel once, when it came up to us in the Sinai Desert with the rest of the Army rations. It was labelled as sausage, and turned and smelled into donkey and camel droppings, into sick pustular dollops, when it was cooked. It was much worse than the Abyssinian old goats that had become our fresh meat staple during that World War II time when the Suez was closed, and the Mediterranean Sea had become a Fascist waterway.

The horsemeat at Harvard was palatable, and of a different colour to camel. It was rather dark and tough, but edible enough. There was a French cook in the kitchen, they alleged: hence the horsemeat. I made a good meal of it, having but that morning arrived non-stop by bus from San Francisco, a trip that scarred more than my soul and shrivelled my stomach.

Now whether I did hear the steaks-to-be clatter past at a canter is a moot point. Perhaps I dreamed it, or have told it as the truth so often that I have ended up believing,

1

as is my wont. That happens to all of us, believe me. We
are all in search of an audience or a friend, and so we tell
the tale. We never can recall the past exactly. This generally makes for a better story than those bare and unrelated
facts that fill the notebook of a constable. The reminiscence
can be far more pertinent and revealing than any linear data
or statistics.

That visit to Harvard, long ago, clinched my future.
Keyes Metcalf was a darting oak. He remains a landmark
man. There is concrete evidence of his nutmeg, pumice,
and apple ideas in the libraries that he has planned all over
the world. We are very different people, Keyes and I, the
long and the short of it. We could not see eye to eye if
we wanted to, and our ideas are divergent. I care more
for books, he for the libraries to house them, but he has
been a teacher and friend since I've known him. Good
friends, good teachers are jewels, the more so when they
are all in one. I owe more than I can say to him and his
two younger colleagues, Phil McNiff and Ed Williams, who
joined arms with me in that and all the other later visits.

The Widener I would have sunk below ground even
then, and I would have trebled the size of the Lamont. The
House libraries would have been none of my concern. I
stocked a library, not comfort stations.

It was the care and more that Metcalf gave to the
ablest of his staff that impressed me. He used them as
outriders; they guarded his weak flanks, they protected his
rear, and remained on the field to top off his work while
he flew off to Tokyo or Dublin to plan another library, and
try to shape it with his ideas. They held the fort at Harvard, and thrust out his encroachments further. They were
a band of brothers, and to anyone who has kinfolk that does
not mean beaming sweetness and light, with little cute say-
ings, but shouts, yells, even darkness and flames, but all
within the family.

Above all I was marked for life by Metcalf's unwaver-
ing devotion to the library. He lacked any academic pretensions, those pretensions that have so debilitated our action. He left that to some of his outriders and rear guard,
realizing that the library requires a mix of human element
that combines part reader, part scholar, and part administrator. Librarians belong to an old profession, art, craft,
and trade, so that we are only a part of all the other insti-

tutions and agencies of the University, a puzzle and often a target. We are neither their flesh, nor fish, nor fowl. The library is our job, and anything else we do around the university is ancillary.

The faculty and research teams can look after themselves; they do, often too well. The administration is well padded also. The salaries and privileges of these groups constitute a danger to the library, as does the growing clout that the students have obtained, by threats and guile as a rule, in University Affairs. And worst of all are the permanent officials, the civil servants, and their masters the politicians. They know, in some inchoate and aliterate way, the time-bomb element of the library. Some of them openly question why the library contains so many books in foreign languages, books that have dirty words, or present ideas of government that are not their own. Somehow the politicos realize the threat that learning contains for the likes of them. It was always a part of any colonial policy to keep the subject peoples illiterate, to keep them away from the books. Never underestimate the politicians, nor dismiss them with an easy sneer. They are smarter than we are, and they control the Purse. They need to be courted, like a cobra with a whistle. I have never met one, nor heard of one who could be depended on when the chips were down.

Librarians are loners, and they had better believe it. There have been several salient factors in my life as a librarian. They are strung like stepping stones across a mossy pond, and now that I have declared my creed I must go back and relate them: they are all related.

I got my first job in a library when I was sixteen, in 1930. Cardiff, where I was born and raised, was the biggest town in Wales. It never has been a capital city, like Edinburgh or Dublin, and while its establishment dates back to Roman times it achieved size and stature only with the advent of King Coal. Then, when the industrial world switched to oil from coal for its energy and power, in the early 1920's, and the world suffered the Great Depression, Cardiff and the surrounding valleys whence they had cut the coal that Cardiff shipped, became a Distressed Area. Nearly every able-bodied man and boy that I knew was on the unemployment lists and survived somehow on the meagre dole. My father, a coal-trimmer, a difficult and dangerous job, was on the dole either part or full time from the late '20's on. The trimmers and colliers were on strike for ten months in 1922. There was a General Strike in 1927 and a desperate long strike again to follow it, leaving the coal unmined in the pits or stacked in huge piles around the docks at Cardiff and at the other shipping ports, Newport, Barry, Aberavon, and Swansea, as far west as Llanelli.

I was lucky to get a library job. Nearly every Cardiff boy who had finished high school applied for the position or for a job also advertised in the Burial Registration District of City Hall. I was able to take home £1.7.10½d. a week in a cellophane envelope. My mother gave me back half a crown and the rest went into a jug on the dresser to tide the family over. We were better off than most of the families whose children I had gone to school with. Coaltrimming paid good money when Coal was reigning, up until the early 1920's. Then Cardiff and district, the Valleys, that triangle that ran in a rough line from the base line Cardiff-Swansea up to the apex of Methyr Tydfil, all the coal trade grew feebler and feebler until it was nearly all gone.

Had it not been for the social reforms of Lloyd George in the 1900's, and their subsequent development, things would have been far worse for us. There would have been Revolution, I am sure. As it was it was a close-run thing.

Our family was better off than most of our neighbours, nearly all who depended on the Coal for their living. We lived on the fringe of the Dowler's Cottages, street after street of workers' houses that were built to house the dock workers. Our house was a bit better than the others, with four rooms up and down and an inside bathroom and a small back yard where there were two bushes of lilac, a stand of rhubarb, some mint and other herbs. There was a chest-high stone wall separating our back yards, but the whole block of houses presented one block to the world. There was even a glass conservatory added to the middle room downstairs and a good fireplace. For years our Mam used to rent that middle room downstairs and the one upstairs to young married couples for ten shillings a week, with kitchen privileges. They were all decent quiet folk as I remember them, and they stayed for a year or so before moving on to a council house that they had been waiting for since their marriage, and the rent was adjusted to their income.

In between times we had members of the family staying there and for years Willie Welsh, a cousin from Aberavon, lived with us a member of the family paying his whack and going home to Aberavon every weekend. He shared the back bedroom with me and was a teacher at St. Cuthbert's, the dockside parish, waiting for a job nearer home.

The Readys and the McCarthys were two of the Irish families that sort of laced the whole community together. John Ready, my great grandfather, was one of the six Aberavon Irish who brought the first priest from Italy to function publicly in South Wales since the Reformation. He was killed in the Morfa Colliery disaster on Easter Monday 1890. Somehow he was able to pull his eldest son William out of the pit and dock work to learn his trade as a carpenter and joiner. Unlike the rest of the Irish my grandfather, apprenticed in a Welsh yard, learned to speak that language fluently. The Welsh had, still have, a passion for music and education so that my grandfather became an organist, a choir leader, and was dedicated to the education of his children. He married Joanna Mahoney who grew up in one of the few Irish families who became agricultural workers, ploughmen, hedgers, thatchers and ditchers. She was a compact, red-haired woman with a twin sister Ellen who looked just like her. All her life Ellen lived in a grace and favour thatched cottage near Fonman Castle. She was a widow whose husband had died in the service of one of the great and wealthy shipowners, and this rent-free cottage on land and market garden was given to her as solace. One of her brothers, Jeremiah, a very big and gentle man, had to leave hurriedly in his youth for the States. I never did know what sent him on his hurried journey across the Atlantic, or whether it even reached the courts, but by the time I knew him he was back an older man, older than Gran or Aunt Ellen or Uncle Charlie, the first-born of the Glamorgan Mahoneys. He was well liked by all around, and given great respect. At once, upon his return he began to work in the cement works in Aberthaw, and there were some children with Irish names, but who had been absorbed into the prevailing Welshry, who went to Non-Conformist Chapel, and called him Grandpa, although their surname was not Mahoney but another family name, like Purcell or Nash. Many a night when I was there he used to carry me on his shoulder to the local inn, the Morganwg Arms, a very old and historic tavern, and set me down with a soft drink while he went into the bar for a while with his brother Charlie, a short, round, jolly man who was much in demand as a thatcher, and colloque with the ploughmen, the stablemen, the small farmers, and the cement workers. Then, as night was falling he and Charlie would make their way home across the fields with the smell of buttercups, clover, hedgerows, and sweet grass in the air. I will never forget these days at the thatched cottage. I slept under the thatch with my two uncles, while Ellen and Gran slept in a curtained wall bed in the room off the flag-stoned kitchen.

I do not know about her brothers and sisters, but Gran could not read nor write. I was nearly grown up before I realised this.

When she went out to meet Will, my grandfather, with me of a Saturday morning, she would ask me to read the destination cards on the electric trains. "I've left my glasses home, Will," she would say. "Is this a Number 7 for the Pier Head?"

"No, Gran" I would say, peering at the two-decker clanging electric tram. "It's a Number 9 for the Sophia Gardens."

Gran would peer at that as the tram came swaying to a halt. "Ah, so it is. We'll wait for a Number 7." And she would purse her mouth affectionately and rest a hand on my head.

I spent a lot of time at my grandparents' who lived in a house on St. Peter Street just across from the large church that occupied a whole city block and was built in Pugin Gothic, with the school occupying the next block and spilling out behind. Their two children Annie and Charles had both graduated from Teachers College and were employed there until they both became principals of other schools at quite an early age. My grandfather had begun to fill the house with books for them. He added more for me, subscribing to a smudgy reprint of the complete works of Dickens that came in a blue and gilt cloth binding and standing in its own bookcase, that came with the set. Newnes and other subscription publishers were responsible for large illustrated books upon the War, the History of England, and others. They were handsomely illustrated and were good for browsing over and dreaming about, curled up on the sofa in the front room on a sunny day. It was a very quiet street, the church and school making a near cul-de-sac out of it. Mr. Higgins, the previous principal of St. Peter's School, had raised his family there until their growing up and increasing social life had led him to move to Richmond Road where the houses were larger and more elegant.

But the house on St. Peter Street has always remained

6

dear to me. As the eldest of a growing family, in a time
of Depression, I spent most of my time there--the quiet,
the solid furniture made by a master craftsman and his son
Will, my uncle, who followed his father in the woodworking
trade and became a teacher of the craft as well as a good
wood carver and had his own business now and then. I often
accompanied him in his hand card to custom jobs that he had
undertaken. He and his son John Bernard, who died of a
mastoid infection while growing up, were good friends of
mine and Uncle Will's affection for his brother John, my
father, was good to see.

I would be working at the table doing my homework
as the five o'clcok hooter went. Gran would look up from
her armchair by the fireplace and look at the clock, although,
as I learned later, it was the hooter not the clock that gave
her the time.

"Five o'clock. Your grandfather will be home soon."
True enough. Every weekday he would come in through the
front door where the latch was on a string, down the passage
and stand in the doorway, his tools in a straw and rope bas-
ket over his shoulder, secured by a claw hammer whose
shaft he held in his right hand. He always smelled of fresh
wood shavings and was dusted with sawdust. He wore white
coveralls, stained and worn by the end of the week, under-
neath his coat. He would stand in the doorway of the kitchen
silently enjoying the peace and quiet of it. The Mount Stew-
art Dry Dock where he worked for so many years was a
noisy place, with the riveters, the smiths, the riggers all
plying their trades in the confined space.

Grandpa would stand in the door enjoying it all.
There was a deep dark Welsh dresser alongside the wall
facing the window with Swansea ware, gaily coloured dishes,
cups and saucers on the open top half shelves of it. On the
sideboard was invariably a shining cut glass and silver cruet,
a large covered cheese dish, the carving knives and forks,
a silver tureen, and the low small bowls of flowers, all
shining and flourishing. The sloping drying sun at early
dark would be coming through the window where his wooden
slatted armchair backed to it with the gaslight to the side
door leading out to the scullery, the bathroom, and beyond.
There was the garden where he kept his chickens, a few
ducks now and then. In the back yard he grew all our vege-
tables. There were some berry bushes, rhubarb, and herbs
and the lilac tree.

7

At the back of the garden was Grandpa's tool shed where over the years he had collected as prime a collection of tools as any master carpenter could obtain. They were all well ordered, and shone with use. He had built every piece of furniture in the house, framed the pictures--there was a large coloured print of Daniel O'Connell the Liberator on the wall facing the fireplace. I sat at my homework on the side of the table that was a polished oak, a wall bookcase behind me, and Gran sat waiting in her armchair that backed on to the wall beside the Welsh dresser. This was in the days before radio, and the only regular sound was of the moving coals glowing in the tiled and metalled fireplace and now and then a bubbling from the pot of simmering beef and onion that was Grandpa's invariable supper on every working day save Friday, when he had a sort of soufflé of eggs and cheese.

"Well, Joanna?" Grandma, her eyes faintly lighting, would reply "Well, Will?"

Grandpa would then look at me, writing or reading by candlelight. "That's it, bachan, keep at the books. You'll be a £5-a-week man yet." At the time his income, after forty years of work, was less than £3 a week, and the two teachers, Charles and Annie, made about £7 a week between them. It was enough, in those days, and my father was making all that income together with more besides, until the bottom dropped out of coal. So well-to-do were the coal trimmers' wives, they used to say, that they paid for their groceries in sovereigns, and tested the huge slab of butter in the store of Williams the Grocer with a gold piece.

Grandpa would go out to the scullery to wash under the cold tap, take his white apron off, and hang up his scarf, cap, and bag of tools. He would sort of brush his scant white hair, put on his old black coat and come into the kitchen again. The rest of us had our dinner at midday. Grandma would have set the table cloth half way and there would be a steaming deep soup plate of beef and onion on the table. As he ate Grandma would regale him with the gossip of the day. He would have lit the gas light on his way back from the scullery and I would have blown out my candle.

While he drank his large cup of tea that topped off his meal he would quickly peruse the Western Mail and the South Wales Echo so that he was all primed by the time that Gran had cleared the dishes, washed them up in the scullery, and folded the white linen table cloth and put it away in one of the Welsh dresser drawers. She sat back, in semi-darkness while Grandpa read the news to her, with comments that would send them off into reminiscence and discussion. Grandpa enjoyed reading aloud. His voice sometimes had a hwyl to it as when he recalled a speech made by David Lloyd George on his last visit to Cardiff before World War I.

I enjoyed listening to both of them for about an hour. Then, like as not, I would light my oil lamp on my bicycle and cycle home into the lighter, noisier Carlisle Street, about two miles away across the bridge into Splott where we lived on the fringe of the Dowlais Cottages. Nearly all of Splott has been levelled since those days, all within the past decade. The Dowlais Cottages, street after street of them, have been levelled for a large park, a green belt between the docks, steel works and freight yards and the belt of Splott Road nearby where our house still stands.

But when I was riding back on my bike so long ago it was a time of great contentment, a sartorial situation, all to do with Dad's overcoat and that of his fellow coal-trimmer and lifelong butty, the Usher. They, like all the trimmers, the longshoremen, the riggers, tippers, watermen and colliers, had begun to shrivel in the cold wind of the Great Depression. Both of them lacked good overcoats for the coming of the Parade. In those days, long ago, the Irish used to parade, parish by parish, behind their bands, through the high streets, something, on a smaller scale, like do the Italians in New York on Columbus Day. The Cardiff Irish marched, just the men and older boys, through Queen Street to the Castle on the Sunday within the octave of St. Patrick's Day, all of them in their good suits and, because it was in the middle of March, wearing their overcoats.

Topcoats were rarely worn around the dockers' parish of St. Alban's. Coal-trimmers wore reefer jackets to work, torn and ragged raincoats, oilskin slickers, now and then, with moleskin trousers, dark gray flannel shirts, singlets and drawers, mufflers, stiff with coal and sweat, broken-peaked caps, and heavy steel-capped cleated boots.

They bought overcoats only for the formal occasions of weddings, funerals, wakes, and the Parade. Since the toppling of King Coal neither the Usher nor Dad had renewed their wardrobe. The inevitable had caught up with them; they were at a loss for overcoats.

9

Forty years before, on the first Parade, Grandpa and the Usher's father had been the stewards. There were pictures in the South Wales Argus of the riot that followed, one of the rare occasions of Irish-Welsh fracas that was now old history. The Usher's father and Grandpa were plainly to be seen with police thrusting them into a black Maria. They were wearing fine heavy topcoats. They had remained as chief stewards for twenty years. Their conservative dress style had set the Parade fashion, and now their sons were taking over. I can still see Dad shaking his head about it as the time of the Parade drew near. Mam would look up from her ironing and just look at him over our heads who were eating or reading around the table. Dad's favourite place was standing up by the fireplace resting his elbows on the mantelpiece between the two brass horses that Uncle Ted had cast for us at the Dowler's blast furnace. This chair was at the table adjacent to the fireplace and he used to read The Echo and Thomas Hardy with his stockinged feet on the fender around the fire. That fire never went out. Every morning the first job around the house was raking the embers and taking out the ashes. It was a big cast-iron stove that heated the water to a certain amount, not very much, never enough for Dad's two tubs every time he came home from work. It was big enough for Mam to do the cooking on and dry the clothes before. It was the only working fireplace in the house and we went to bed by candle light. Then, just as a cloud had settled over us because of Dad's lack of an overcoat the sun shone through. A miracle happened. We never had to worry again about Dad's topcoat. The adage was proved that it is darkest just before the dawn. Just a day or so before I can still see Johnny Fortnight, the credit draper, in the kitchen with Mam and Dad sadly shaking his head. The family's credit was pledged already far above the limit allowed by his organisation in order to outfit us for school. Even then Mam had had to take for me an overcoat that was far too big for me and seemed to have been designed for a fat and gangling Billy Bunter. It had been returned by some indignant and affluent parent from Plas Newydd, so Johnny Fortnight was able to get rid of it at a knock down price. Strangely, over the years, I and the coat grew into one another and in the final, the third year, that I was to wear it the comment and derision about me in it ceased.

I have told the story of Dad's topcoat for the Parade so often, and because it is a revealing part of my autobiography, in a way preparing me for what I was to face through

10

the years of my life. I present it here in a more formal structure with some explanatory notes woven into it. Every word of it, I am convinced, is true.

When they were on the day shift, even when the shifts were becoming fewer and fewer, there was a general stirring around our block and the adjacent ones. About a third of the houses were those of men in the coal trade, the coal trimmers, the tippers, and the watermen. The trimmers worked in the holds of the ships, using their broad, peculiar shovels to spread the coal as it crashed down, to pack the hold and preserve the ship on an even keel. Since many ships carried 20,000 tons or more of coal, and the coal crashed down into the hold from railroad trucks that tipped from dockside steel platforms 50 feet high, the coal trimming was difficult, skilled, hard and dangerous work. The tippers graduated in those days from watermen, on their way up, some of them to being coal-trimmers. The watermen were employed, as were the tippers, by the trimmers, and the watermen were in the hold spraying water on the coal to lay the dust and they did to some extent. Most of the coal-trimmers, the contemporaries of my father, died in their 40's and 50's because of the arduous nature of the work in the coal-dust-ridden and confined space. We were never allowed near the ships as they were being loaded but sometimes, pretending that I had a message for Dad and recognized by nearly all the dockers, I was allowed through. I could see the coal crashing, the thunder and the clang and shouts within the hold that was lit by long tallow candles that flickered away what else would have been prevailing darkness. Sometimes I would see coming ashore some trimmers, making their way to their lodge made of railroad sleepers where they would warm their tea and eat their food. There were no baths supplied. The shipowners and the Marquess of Bute, who owned all of Cardiff land, refused as adamantly to build bathhouses for the coal trimmers as did the tycoons up the valley refuse to build pit-head baths for the colliers. All of this was in the working lifetime of my father. Until he finished work, into the 1940's, he still bathed in front of the kitchen fire after cycling, his face coal black, from the docks that were miles away. I seem to remember a special coal trimmers' tram that drove them from the Pier Head early in the morning as they came off the night shift. They were too filthy dirty for ordinary trams. These special ones had wooden slatted benches that were engrained with coal dust, and there was a small coke stove in the middle of the tram, with its chimney poking through the roof. The coal

11

trimmers, like the colliers, had small pocked blue scars over their hands and faces, inflicted by the flying flakes of coal. They were badges of honour to me and I wished I shared them, but even in those early days I had developed a prudent attitude towards the hard life and danger that has remained with me ever since.

On the great day that they got their coats the Usher was on the day shift in the Queen's Dock. Dad was laid off at the Roath. The Usher woke up about five o'clock and having a deep and justified distrust of all clocks in his household--Jim, his eldest son, had a fascination for fixing things, was always working on the clocks to make them better so that none of them worked--he would roll out of bed, pull his cricket cap the more firmly on, and stumble across to the window that looked out on Railway Street, around the corner from us. He would sit in a chair, with his head quivering and shivering like a hunter poking out of the open window.

The Usher would be a hunter and his voice would be the gun. Along the road outside would come some gently whirring cyclist on his way to work until the Usher's voice would knock him off his bike.

Then, as the cyclist picked himself up, a more conversational tone from the dark and open window would ask for the proper time. When he had got that information monosyllabically from the cyclist, who remounted and rode testily away vowing to get to Splott Bridge in future by Inkerman Avenue, a quieter street, the Usher started to get ready for work. As he went downstairs in stockinged feet--it is a singular fact that all Britons not born west of Wales invariably wear their socks to bed--the Usher started to me-me-mee quietly to himself to see if his singing voice was in good order. He did have a good baritone, was the mainstay of the parish choir, but he was inordinately fond of it, and he knew it but cossetted it as his only gift beside the amateur plastering that he did on the side to augment his income in the hard times that had come upon King Coal.

By the time the ashes were emptied, the fire going, the bread and bacon frying the Usher would be in full voice. There is a tremolo in a Vivaldi Mass, at the Ave Virgo Virginum that the Usher liked full well. He gave it all he had, with a rumble from within him that set the crockery to dancing on the table. Like Dad, like most of the dockers, the Usher ate standing up in front of the fire with his plate, cutlery, and cup balanced on the mantelpiece. His working clothes were snug and warm, having been suspended all night from the rack above the fireplace.

He looked critically at his moleskins as he pulled them on. They were getting worn at the waist, the knees and the shins, and beyond all that he was lacking a topcoat for the Parade. He swore an oath at that and made a decision. It was about the same time as Dad, staring at the ceiling, made his decision also. It was of a Tuesday, March 15, and it was a day somehow that seemed to be the turning of the ways for both of them and, indeed, it was connected with the stirring that very day of Cardiff from the dead, although they did not know it at the time, nor was it to be apparent for years to come. A little breeze was blowing the dust off the coal piles. Grass was growing along and amid the railroad tracks, and the pit-head slag heaps in the Valleys were turning green and brambled.

Dad had been at the local Splott branch of the Public Library all the afternoon reading the papers and magazines in the reading room before coming home for tea with a copy of The Mayor of Casterbridge that he had borrowed from the circulation desk. It was one of Thomas Hardy's books that the branch librarian had got for him from the Central Library: the Splott branch was not very strong on its Hardy collection; Nat Gould, Zane Grey, Ethel M. Dell and Edgar Rice Burroughs were more popular. There was a good selection of children's books and lots of P. G. Wodehouse for all ages, but Dad had been waiting for months for The Jungle by Upton Sinclair, and Dreiser, any Dreiser at all.

After tea he turned to Will who was reading the week's tuppenny school story, The Magnet, about the doings of Harry Wharton, Billy Bunter and Co. "Are you coming up to your grandmother's tonight?"

"Aye. I left my exercise books there, for doing my homework."

"Well, come on then. I'll walk up with you." He said it over-casually, as if he had made a decision.

Mam and Will both looked at him, a question in their eyes.

Mam said: "It's only Sundays, after Benediction, that you go for a walk to there. It's Tuesday."

Dad stirred a little. "Aye, aye. I-- I--" he swallowed. "There's something I got to see to. Talk to my father about."

Mam persisted. "Is it the door on the chicken-run again? You ought to leave that to your father, like he says. You're no carpenter, Jack, no matter what your mother thinks. She likes just having you around to talk to. It's quiet up there during the day. All we can talk about here is what I'll tell the policeman next time he brings the summons for the rates, or how I'll pay Duggan the grocer for last week's order. God help us, Jack. You go with Will. Who knows? Grandma might have some idea about a topcoat for next Sunday. It's a pity Charlie is a foot taller than you are. You could wear his coat, and he could wear his Burberry. After all, he's not leading the parade, and he'll be walking with St. Peter's anyhow. Your father is much too wide in the shoulder for you to borrow his coat, and he's got to wear it anyway, for being the staff man on the Dry Dock banner. Go ahead, you can have a good talk anyhow, and walk home with Will about nine, when he's finished his homework. I'm going to the Mothers Meeting anyhow, and Nora and Sheila are going to a school play rehearsal. What's it called?"

Sheila, cheeky, the young one of the family. "The Colleen Bawn, Mam. We keep telling you." She appealed to her sister, who was enjoying it all, and waiting for Mam's next line.

"The Colleen Bawn. That's it. It's the same play we did at St. David's when I went to school. Better than that old Maid of Cefn Ydfa they did here last year. I'd have had your part, Sheila, in the play when I was in school. Got the same colouring we have, and the same gift of the gab. But I left school when I was in Second Grade to go fer a help at The Merthyr and Dowlais." She pushed her tea cup away with a small sigh. "Ah well. It was just as well. I learned to read, anyhow," and she looked around with her slanting grin that was never far away. "I was not so much at school but I've met the scholars." She turned to Will:

"Get along with the pair of you now. You'd better do your homework in the middle room up there unless your Auntie Annie has a meeting of the Truth Society, or Charlie of that Football club he manages."

14

It was a pleasant walk most nights from our house to
St. Peter Street.   The bridge that linked us, one of three
bridges, with the rest of Cardiff, was near enough for us
to be out of Splott in a few minutes, passing by the Splott
Cinema where I went at least twice a week and, like The
Movie-Goer from Louisiana, I was influenced for life by my
movie-going.

My mother was a great movie-goer too.   She took
me as like as not, whenever she wasn't partnered by our
nextdoor neighbour and her life-long Love Lane friend, Anas-
tasia Phelan.

They were born within weeks of one another, they had
raised the same sort of families, although one of Stasia's
sons was a secular priest, and she was to have a nephew
who was to be a Benedictine monk.   Her husband, Scrummy
Phelan, was a coal-trimmer in Dad's gang.   He had been a
great rugby player in his youth and had turned professional,
Northern League, to lead the Wigan pack, but had grown
homesick for Love Lane, Cardiff, and the docks, and had
come back to get his father's job on the coal.   Once, I remember, when I was very young, Mam and Stasia went all
the way downtown, to the Capitol super cinema to see the
Welsh première of Lillian Gish in Way Down East.   I trailed
behind them like a jackal instead of doing my homework,
and found them in the queue.   With a light cuff from Mam
and a hug from the buxom Stasia I joined them to see Lillian
Gish crossing the river on an ice floe.   That picture Way
Down East remains clearly in my memory still, along with
the silent comics of Laurel and Hardy, Charlie Chase, Harold Lloyd. . . .   I never cared for Chaplin save for The Gold
Rush and Shoulder Arms.   Buster Keaton did nothing for me
ever either.

All through the 30's I was a regular movie-goer.
The light comedies and the musicals from Hollywood played
a greater sociological role all through the world than has
ever been really analysed.   The Western Movies presented
the image of Roland at Roncesvalles, and the holy folly of
Don Quixote, that is our civilisation's contribution to a world
hopefully still in the future.

I have meandered away from that walk that Dad and I
took to St. Peter Street.   That walk, every Sunday, was the one
time, going and coming, that Dad discoursed to me.   He
loved reading, and as long as we could get by on the dole

15

and the family contributions, the rent from the middle rooms, he was glad of the opportunity it gave him to use the Library. He was the most intelligent of his brood, was recognised throughout the family compact as such. When he was still in his early 'teens he had passed the examination for the junior civil service, but had to give up any idea of a civil service white collar job, to earn enough to pay for his brothers and sisters to get through college, or what passed for certificating institutions for primary school teachers and the like in those days. As a result of his financing that education, they rallied around, with Grandpa helping, so that we never experienced the dark poverty of many of our neighbours.

Dad was well read in nineteenth-century European history. No professor better discoursed to me than he did on these walks, about Bismarck, Gladstone, Disraeli, Parnell, the Land Wars, the English property laws and such novelists as Hardy, Arnold Bennett, Melville, Upton Sinclair and, most of all the American, Theodore Dreiser. He had almost a reverence for Tolstoy and Turgenev and for Flaubert. It was his talks, conversations really, on history that made me include it as one of my university subjects when the time was come for decision.

Auntie Annie was using the middle room for the Truth Society, and I wanted to be in on Dad's conference with his father, so I followed him into the kitchen on St. Peter Street after pulling the string that opened the front door and following him down the hall.

Gran's eyes lighted when we came in, but she did not move from her position, her hands folded across her lap and seated in her arm chair beside the fire.

"Well, John," said Gran, and Grandpa repeated it, taking off his glasses and laying down on the table that morning's Western Mail that he was reading from.

"Well, John," he repeated the welcome with those words, and Grandma's face was questioning right behind.

"How's the family, John? It seems months, it must be all just in the New Year that we saw them all last. And how are the children? How's that Miss, Sheila?"

It was the same series of questions that they had

16

asked him on Sunday last, but it was the best they could do, taken by surprise at Dad's visit. There must be something up for him to visit in the middle of the week.

Dad answered them perfunctorily. He was anxious to get on with his decision:

"Father, you know that I am the lead in the St. Alban's Parade on Sunday. Me and the Usher. Neither of us have a topcoat we can wear, and well...." He waved his arms a little, a rare sign of emotion for him. "Our credit's all gone with Johnny Fortnight. There are the rates overdue and I was thinking.... I hate to say this, but your topcoat, Father. Do you have to walk with St. Peter's on Sunday? Then I could wear your coat."

Grandpa stirred in his chair, took a deep breath. "Better than that, John. Do you remember seeing a picture of that coat that I was wearing when I was arrested, on that first parade? Me and Con Driscoll?"

Dad nodded, so did Granny with a question in her eyes, and the same sort of look that Mam was to show later that same evening. "Well, I never wore that coat again. It's been lying on top of the wardrobe in the front bedroom ever since.

"John, that coat is made of Irish frieze, and when I took it to Poultenay the Tailor to have a rip in the collar repaired, that the police gave it pulling me into the Black Maria, he said it was the best material he had ever handled. That the Bishop himself, Bishop Medley it was then, could not have got that coat made of it. It had been off the looms and the market ever since the textile mill at Omagh had closed down years before."

Grandpa took off his glasses to beckon with them the better. I looked up from my book, Martin Chuzzlewit it was, not one of Dickens' finest: I had only been pretending to read it anyhow, taking in the rare scene in the kitchen.

"I put it away when it came back from Poultenay. It had been a present, for a start, from my grandfather Purcell. When he died in Waterford he said the coat was to go to John Ready. He had hoped that my father would have stayed with the firm. He had always hoped to have seen him back with the firm, but your grandfather married Mary McCarthy in Taibach and here we are."

17

"I had meant you to have it, John, after I've passed on. But," he sighed "you'd better have it now, and turn it over to Will there when your time comes."

Grandpa got up heavily and clumped upstairs. Grandma still sat in her armchair, her eyes glinting now with anticipation and, I suspected, with some apprehension too.

We heard Grandpa's feet go up the stairs, the scraping of a chair across to the wardrobe in the bedroom and then his descending the stairs with a large brown parcel in his arms. The smell of camphor nearly took our breath away, but he carried on out to the back. We could hear the heavy paper wrapping being torn off and then the beating of the coat with the bamboo carpet beater that hung up in the scullery.

Grandpa came back in breathing a little heavily and carrying the coat across his arm. There was still a strong smell of camphor in the air but not enough to take our breath away, and the coal fire ceased puttering forth blue flames.

He helped Dad on with the coat. I noticed Gran's eyes fill with tears. Grandpa stood back and looked at Dad with pride and admiration. Dad looked back at him, working his shoulders, stretching his arms. They both looked strangely innocent and relieved.

The coat was far too big for my father. The velvet collar and the heavy frieze shoulders were greening with age. The coat was cut in a very old-fashioned style and Dad's head protruded from it, like a turtle's.

"There" Grandpa nodded. "It's yours from now on. And now that it's over I'm glad of it. Somehow I never felt easy about leaving it on top of the wardrobe for so long. You'll have to keep working your shoulders a bit to stop the coat from slipping off you. Maybe it's a bit on the long side for you. What do you think, Johanna?"

He did not turn his eyes to look at her but carefully, proudly, looked over at Dad in the coat.

Grandma did not speak. She just nodded and put her large lawn linen handkerchief to her face. This coat was a man's world that she could hardly believe.

Grandpa went on earnestly. "Walk on the balls of

18

your feet, John, like you were springing, or playing like a fullback against a Kick High and Folley Up team. Then the hem of it will keep off the ground. " He looked anxiously at Dad. "Will I wrap it up again, John, so you can carry it home? Or would you rather leave it here and take it fresh, on Saturday? "

Dad nodded his head slowly. It was his coat now and nothing would ever part them.

"I'll wear it home now, Father. " He looked at me, pretending to be crouched over by Chuzzlewit.

"Are you ready now, son? Or are you going to stay on and come home on your way to school for the rest of your books?" There was always a bed for me in Uncle Charlie's room, and he enjoyed my company. We stayed awake for hours sometimes, talking. He used to subscribe to John O'London's Weekly, a literary periodical, and some of the articles in that, or the reviews, would set us off for hours.

I would not have missed walking home with Dad that night for a year's subscription to John O'London. It was dark outside, and St. Peter Street was not very well lit. We passed nobody until we crossed City Road and then people stared hard at Dad as he came along, slowed down and halted, looking after him as the waft of camphor caught them and momentarily tranfixed them as we went on our way. Dad was so concerned getting the hang of wearing his heirloom of a topcoat, working the shoulders, keeping his head above the collar, swinging his arms and walking on the balls of his feet that he did not notice that I had dropped behind a pace or two to watch his progress. By the time we had crossed Splott Bridge he had mastered the navigation of the coat. He stopped in at the Usher's house to show him, pulling the string and making for the kitchen. His wife cast one quick look at Dad and hustled into the scullery, grabbing Joseph, who was my age, by the scruff of the neck before he could say anything, and shooing the two girls and Jim in front of her, closing the door behind them.

The Usher was at the table wearing his cricket cap, his glasses perched on the end of his nose, practising an Offertory motet for the Sunday morning Sung Mass. He faltered to a halt in the middle of it as he saw Dad, adjusted his glasses and gave a good warm grin that had respect in it.

"Bedam, Jack. So you got the coat! You know, Jack, God has been good to the pair of us. On my way home from work, still coal-black, I stopped at Brother Joe's office. I haven't put the bite on him since Christmas. He's been doing well with the fuel business, better than ever. He was expecting a meeting with his Board that afternoon and to get the look of coal out of his office he gave me his topcoat and five quid besides. The coat's a bit snug for me, and lively too, a sort of loud herringbone. But you'll compensate for the pair of us. "

The pair of them led the Parade that next Sunday. It was Saint Alban's turn to lead the Parade. With their white wands festooned by ribbon and shamrock they marched proudly in front of the Silver Band, the Usher shrivelling a little to keep his overcoat from bursting out of its buttons, and Dad navigating, as if to the manor born, his full-bodied covering.

He never wore it again. It was wrapped up and camphorated and lies on top of the wardrobe in our old home, where my brother still lives. He is coming to visit over here one day and I'm thinking of getting an old Lithuanian tailor down the street to make a reefer jacket of it, for me to wear on my morning walks along the shore. He works crosslegged. We often talk together. The parishes were beginning to scatter after that Parade and soon ceased to be as the Cardiff Irish merged into the prevailing society.

2

The April after that Parade I got my first job in Cardiff Public Library where I was to learn my apprentice craft in my old profession.   I am glad that I missed out on the job in the Graves Registration Bureau in City Hall.   I would not have been enthralled by it, and would have probably ended up in Teachers College as did my Uncle Charlie and Brother Jack.

From the morning, at ten minutes to nine, that I walked up the steps of the Cardiff City Central Library, turned left through the STAFF ONLY door, and signed my name and time of arrival in the book on the high old-fashioned desk, I knew that I was entering into a new phase of my life.

Until then all my life had been spent with my own kind, the teachers who taught in our own state-supported separate schools, the coal-trimmers, watermen, and tippers, my high-school mates.   Our high school was the only one of its kind in Wales, separate and state-supported.   I was taught by university graduates who were Christian Brothers imported from Ireland.   They hammered into us some rudiments of the subjects we would need for college, university, or the professions.   Very few of us survived the course.   The Brothers were off the farm generally, the first generation that grew up under the Free State that followed the Irish Troubles that had started with the Rising of Easter Week 1916.

They were strict and heavy-handed with a fairly large turnover, many returning to the secular life as schoolmasters in Ireland or Britain after a decade or so with the stern Brotherhood.   There were a few remarkably gifted and devoted men among them who spent their lives in the Order. One of them, Brother Gilbert, was the most exciting teacher of English that I ever had.   He remained within the Order, eventually achieving a chief administrative rank.   Another was

21

a near-genius, also a teacher of English, who went mad. He
wrote to me years later excoriating me savagely when he
read my first Atlantic Monthly story "Barring the Weight. "
It was largely a tribute to another Christian Brother, John,
a fine history teacher with other interests, Rugby Football
above all. He had coached the likes of me from the time we
were eight or nine years old until we graduated. Then he
travelled with us when we were free of the School on all our
hard-fought Rugby games up and down the Valleys, loving the
tipple, the singing, and the fun, drinking with the colliers
who had been our opponents and spectators. They crowded
around him in our carousing after the games. They had never
even heard of a clergyman like Brother John before, certainly
never in their Capel Zion which was still a centre of their
lives, and where the clergyman was never seen in a taproom,
the spit and sawdust bar, or in the saloon lounge where
Brother John held court until we helped him onto the bus for
the long ride back to Cardiff. Their own reverend clergy
preached to them the evils of the flesh, a major Celtic fault,
and choral singing like nowhere else in the world.

    We had become an alumni team--Old Boys they are
called in Britain--and because of his long years of coaching,
and he was a great coach, we remained an undefeated team
for years until we won the honour of opposing a Cardiff team,
the greatest rugby club in the world, and we were soundly,
and completely defeated. We were the losers, happy and
proud of it, and brought thereby the great occasion to Brother
John. All through his teaching he had tried, how he did not
know, to tell us that losing should be the target, not success,
that we should be one with Christ, Don Quixote and the Celt.
Losers, if we were to be the keepers.

    All that fell from me as I entered the world of the
Library, a land I never knew, save as a suppliant at the circulation desk of the Splott branch library and as an ill-
directed but voracious reader.

    I was a stranger to the staff as they were to me. The
public libraries were enjoying a time that they never had before nor will ever have again. Books and reading had become,
with the enforced leisure of the Great Depression, one of the
great solaces of a vast audience that had never read before
for anything but basic information, transportation schedules,
government orders and instructions, the prices of goods,
labels, and what passed for newspapers in those days. There
were largely large simple headlines full of scare and scandals,

cartoons, photographs, betting results and sports scores and gossip. Public education had created an aliterate society, such as, for technological and social reasons, we are enjoying today. For one penny plain or for two pence coloured there were comics for sale, or Mutt and Jeff, animated animals like Felix the Cat, Winnie-the-Pooh. There was Marzipan the Magician, Little Orphan Annie with its strange ugly overtones that were so popular. Good newspapers, like the London Times, the Manchester Guardian, the Yorkshire Post, save for their politics, maintained a high level of journalism as they do today, much too high, but then, as now, few read them.

The thirties were lacking, save for the movies and public spectacles of sport, any relaxation for the fearful, troubled, and hungry masses. There was nowhere for them to go from cold, crowded, or squalling homes save the Public Library. Since their book stock was largely intended for learning, education, and the enjoyment of the literate few there was an amazing demand for popular reading of the thriller adventure and detective kind, and for romances. Authors like Edgar Wallace became so popular that it was hard to get enough of his works. Vacant stores became rental bookshops, a nine-years-wonder, where thrillers and chillers of the popular kind could be rented for a few pence. Boots, a national drugstore chain, added a large rental library to most of its stores where, by means of a quick turnover, books of better quality could be rented cheaply and often were available on demand, often at the very date of publication and in advance of the reviews. For about £1 a year a reader could get advance copies for rent, and although I worked in a public library six and one-half days a week, nearly engulfed by books of all kinds, I found it to my advantage to take out a subscription. There was the London Library that loaned books, of good quality, to rural areas, and The Thriller and similar magazines published weekly on newsprint a whole new novel for two pence.

Nevertheless the Library was the haven of the scholars, the students, the enquiring, and the poor.

Cardiff Public Library had begun as the National Library of Wales, but under David Lloyd George and his Welsh-speaking establishment that was moved to a new life and condition in Welsh Wales, in Aberystwith, where had been established the University of Wales that later was joined by constituent colleges and universities in Cardiff, Swansea, and

23

Bangor, where English became the language of instruction and neither the faculty nor the students were truly Cymric.

The old National Library thereupon became the Cardiff Public Library with all its considerable and significant Welshry removed, leaving a building that presented an imposing façade, situate in the heart of a booming City of King Coal, that was largely an empty shell. But this was in the prosperous days of Cardiff and under the leadership of Harry Farr, a bookman of the old school with no pretensions to professional librarianship but a respect for learning coupled with a liking for erotica, that was kept locked up, the shelves were filled with the basic books of a good Victorian/Edwardian library, shelved on a classification system that was unique, as were many, before Dewey conquered.

It has remained something of a bane to me all my life, for I shelved books based on it for six years, for hours every day. Come what may, despite Bliss, Dewey, UBC, Ranganathan and the Library of Congress systems, the poems and prose of William Butler Yeats will always first be in my memory under 798. 4.

The Depression changed all that. Hordes of people began to frequent the library. There was a force of uniformed attendants who ordered them peremptorily to obey the rules that were posted everywhere and were not very clear or concise. Most of the readers--they were anything but patrons-- were directed and readily made tracks for the Reading Room. Most of them had been waiting, often in the cold and rain, to get to that very place that was controlled by a little, fearless, uniformed tyrant called Feeks. He wore a wig that he must have come by through inheritance. It was far too big, dark and smooth. When he turned his head sharply if he heard the slightest sound of voices raised above a whisper, a smuggled laugh or grunt, his eyes would flash through his pince-nez in search of the offender and he would be glaring out from under the sideburns of the wig that only more slowly slid around. I frequented the Reading Room to observe this singular phenomenon far more often than my duties required.

It was a fine large room, wide and long, that now has become the main bookstacks and circulation area of the library while it waits, as it has waited for many years, to be located in a modern building some place else.

The influx of readers hit the old regulars hard. This

was before there were any library schools in the U.K. The national qualifying examinations of the Library Association were but beginning to bite, and the Old Guard, with few exceptions, hastened in the mornings in tidy and clerkly fashion to the lower environs of the basement Senior Staff Room where they reminisced, played solo, blued the air with their tobacco smoke, and rarely moved upstairs into the library proper save for a constitutional before returning for their bag lunches and more cups of the gallons of tea that they drank each day. The window of their dark and austere lounge was level with a graveyard. An old tilted tombstone leaned against it. It was a scene from Edwin Drood; it moved, muttered every day.

Around three o'clock they would in turn frequent the men's washroom and lave vigorously, wet and part their hair, polish their shoes and watch chains, and those whose day at the Library was over would pay a short visit to their office desks above, ask their inferiors keen and probing questions about events that had occurred and been resolved some time before, dust off their briefcases that they carried home once or twice a week filled with magazine discards for their wives to read, who were generally former librarians who had once served under them when they were younger and perhaps more hopeful.

Those two or three who were on charge duty until the library closed at 8 p.m. would open the staff room window to clear away the fug of the tobacco smoke and take their places at their desks, standing respectfully should an alderman or other member of the City Library Board be known to be in the building. Something of a challenge would now and then send them on a tour of the Reading Room, the Circulation Desk and the bookstacks, inspecting with practised eye and hand the cards being mailed for book recalls or advising readers that a book they had requested was now available, borrowed from the Public Library at Pontypridd. One of their own had secured the plum of the Chief Librarianship there, and spent a large deal of his time visiting his friends that he had left behind in the Senior Staff Room, regaling them with the intricacies of local government that he had to master in order to justify his appointment. Regularly he attended meetings and committees of the County at the splendid Glamorgan County Hall and invariably came into the Public Library, to his old office off the circulation desk where he had made a name for himself establishing a Cardiff-Pontypridd joint catalogue. He was something of a likeable rascal, ideal for a successful career in local government politics. His place had been taken by a neat little man who had avoided social relations with his peers. A semi-military man, he used to bewilder me by asking how many buttons there were on my waistcoat, and how many of them I fastened in the morning. I was always wrong. I still am at a loss about this although I wear a waistcoast rarely enough for the answer to sink in.

"Good man, good man," he would say to me, peering eye to eye through his sharp glasses. "Keep it up. Let your mind register. It was for want of a nail...." He would nod his head curtly. "That was the question that Sir Idwol Thomas asked of me when he was chairman of the Library Board on the day that I was appointed, and why I got the job, I feel sure. I answered smartly at once, and while the other nine candidates--we were all interviewed together in the Council Room, the same room where they saw you when you got the job--they were all counting on their hands or trying to run their fingers up and down their front, their lips moving.... Sir Idwol got impatient and proposed my name for the job in front of the rest of them. The Library Board agreed, and appointed Iorweath Llewellyn as runner-up. Mr. Llewellyn wasn't wearing a waistcoat at all. He had a pullover on instead. That's why he stayed calm during the question: there was nothing he could do. He got a job too, about a month later when Mr. Probert left here to go to the National Library to work in the Manx department."

Within a year, as the demand for library service grew and grew, with the opening up of libraries in the new housing estates that had begun to ring the old city. Tremorfa used to be the City Dump and vegetable allotments, where nearly every family had a perch or two to grow their potatoes, cabbage, kidney beans and vegetable marrows in--every Welsh family, that is; the Irish were never any good on the land, in Cardiff or in Canada or the States for that matter. Tremorfa was the first of the housing estates that I got to know, since that was really an adjunct to Splott. The Elias housing estate on the way to Cowbridge, was much bigger, and posed far more problems. Expanding the Splott schools and the branch library was able to cope with the Tremorfa development, but Elias needed new schools, a branch library, churches, playing grounds and a bus route. I was in on the expansion programme from the beginning. Some of the older branches, like the one at Cathays, were built with Carnegie money, and were quite Gothic and grand, dreadful for library

service but a builder's and a politician's delight. There was
another housing development at Rhymney where there was a
grass-grown quarry that we used to slide and tumble down in
the summer when we were children, and an old pottery that
had been going for hundreds of years. A lot of money went
into public housing and other public works, for there were
all the willing workers. The whole City work force was
seeking employment, and the families benefitted from being
taken off the dole and given much better housing at a rent
that was regulated by their income. It was the best housing
development that I have ever seen, then, before, or since.
There were no high rises, no townhouse development, but
each house had a small lot, with a garden of its own. Somehow, despite the Depression and attendant unemployment and
the end of Cardiff as a great port, there was a change for
the better in the standard of living. It was a rare sight to
see a coal-black coal-trimmer wearily cycling home. Men
sat in the parks and talked to one another. The women were
not so bound to the tub and stove at all hours. There were
school lunches for the children, with food more nutritious
than they ever got at home. Milk before was used in tea
only. Fruit and salads were by no means staple diet. There
was a general improvement in health. There was the dole,
so there was no destitution, a public health programme, and
every park was filled and some attempt made to expand them,
while all sorts of bands, bazookas most of all, marched,
counter-marched and performed all over South Wales.

The miners' leaders did what they could to keep the
flame of protest burning. I can recall Harry Pollit, the Communist leader, doing what he could to arouse the colliers,
the trimmers, and the idle dockers with his speeches. A.
J. Cook, the Miners' Leader, was flogging a dead horse.
Coal was dead. New steel strip mills began to develop along
the coast of South Wales stretching well-nigh from Newport
to Llanelli. The Miners Welfare Scholarships began to send
high school graduates to college rather than down the pit, and
as Hitler strutted his stuff there began to arise, so quietly
that we did not equate them with the violent times that were
to come, so-called "shadow" factories, and a call for youth
to join the Air Force, the Navy, that in the '20's had been
nearly "axed to death" by the economy, and a Territorial
Militia was beginning to train, house, and equip men for sum-
mers at camps and winter evenings in the Local Drill Hall.

All of this had an effect upon the librarians. While I
still did my four hours a day shouldering and pushing through

27

to the shelving, hauling the books from the bins where they were flung by the girls on Circulation, separating the books that needed mending of all kinds and carrying the loads of them down a winding stair to Tom Rees's area, the Bindery, I was being joined more and more by young men of an age or little older than myself. They often had come to the library not as a job of last resort, but because they saw a future in it. Their emoluments, when they were qualified, would be similar to those of elementary school teachers and city hall clerks, and the job seemed more interesting to them. Opportunities for employment as librarians were opening up. The Junior Staff Room became a talk place about the professional examinations. Correspondence courses were being offered by the Library Association. The new County Library Programme, an American Foundation, meant the establishment of an entirely new system of library service. The grant was only available to those education authorities that employed University graduates as Librarians: these were the only ones acceptable for employment, and since the grants were dependent upon adherence to this decision there were B. A. 's, even some M. A. 's new to the public library scene.

The University of London expanded its library programmes into a full time school. After a year's full time successful attendance the University granted a diploma that, after some years' service in the field, was recognized as a professional qualification.

By this time, three or four years after I had started, I was still the only aspirant librarian from across the Splott bridges. We young librarians-to-be enjoyed one another's company on the job. Mr. Edwards, to cope with the new influx, extended his questions that he asked us so curtly and in such a military manner. No longer was it just about the numbers of buttons on our waistcoat, but about the number of holes that we had to thread for our shoe laces that varied so, and were altogether different if we wore boots. He even started to ask us how many teeth we had in our head, the whorls in our ear lobes and the distance between our eyes. These searching questions must have occupied him considerably and when he began to ask us how many columns there were in the main portico of the library, the number of outside steps, and the extent of the stairway to the Reference Reading Room it became evident that he sensed a change in the pattern of library development and wanted to make sure that he would be able to cope with it.

Our replies grew more and more courteous and perfunctory. We devised crazy answers among ourselves to startle him, in between our conversations and informal workshops we held about the contents of the professional examinations. The failure rate was depressingly high in those days. The examination that gave chartered and professional status passed only about 15 per cent. It was mainly concerned with classification and cataloguing and technical services generally. The various classification systems bored and distracted me. I failed the examination several times, and finally only qualified in my final year, 1939, that I was to spend in public library service. I remember that I received the letter advising me of this success in the same mail that contained a letter from the University of Wales advising me on my success in the Honours Degree with History, English, Archeology, and Latin as my main courses, and awarding me a diploma in Archives and Palaeography.

There was also a letter on His Majesty's Service ordering me to report for summer training with the 242nd Battery of Royal Artillery, the militia or Territorial Unit of which a group of us had joined a month or so before when it seemed likely that a war with Hitler was very much a possibility. So altogether it was quite a mail. I recall with what relief I found that at length I had passed the professional qualifications that were to allow me to become a chartered librarian. The University letter was one that I expected, but it was rather more promising than I had hoped for, bringing a scholarship to Oxford, even to Balliol within view, although frequently out of sight because of the scudding clouds of circumstances.

We still thought, we group of rugby players who had joined up together in the 242nd Battery Royal Artillery, as militia, that the summer camp would be a time to dance and skylark as we had heard that it had been in past years. We had been organised into an Officer Producing Unit, and went to camp on full pay from the banks, offices, and various government agencies that employed us. Such generosity should have aroused our suspicions more than it did, or at least more than we confessed to one another. We looked forward to a month under canvas in the open air, with plenty of hand gunnery instruction and work during the day, and with all the nights our own. Our camp was to be at Manorbier, very near the seaside resort town of Tenby. We even had dress blue uniforms that had been individually tailored and needed but a few additions to become the evening garb of commissioned officers.

I remember that when I reported for work that morning I was greeted affectionately by my colleagues who already had passed their professional examinations. One of them, I recall, Ken Davies, rubbed his hand hard in congratulation across my cropped round head. I was the only one of them who had even attempted to graduate from University as I had done. This, particularly, the fourth, Honours year, had been a rough time for me, for my pay in the library had ceased during that year that needed all my time and more that I had to devote to University studies. It would have been impossible had not the family rallied around again to finance me, but this was easier than the first time when it seemed quite unlikely that I would make it at all through University. During the '30's more and more of the likes of me were going to University, generally to Redbrick, but even so Britain had fewer students, in proportion to their population, attending University than any other country in Europe. We who were of the proletariat family made up less than 2 per cent of the 6-7 per cent of the possible candidates who ever got into the halls of learning.

Moreover I had been out of school for six years, awaiting my time in a Teachers Training College. These were largely supported by the State. The high school that I attended had no tradition for any further career future. It was, I have grown to realize, a dexterous ploy that kept us in our state, teachers among our own kind and not beyond, unless we were needed for some extra skill that we possessed, generally in the field of physical education or athletic performance.

My six years in the library had saved me from that. Now that I was a professional librarian I had found another career. Although I was the first, several were to follow me, enough to make a significant breakthrough and, some decades later, they were beginning to be considered for senior administrative posts, something that could never have happened in my time. Already, in the late 1930's the young were taking over more and more of the Library economy. Mr. Edwards by this time was stressing his experience and seniority by asking brusquely the number of staircases in the library, how many steps it took to proceed from the Binding Area to the Shipping Dock. This particularly concerned me for the growing number and activities of the branch libraries meant that every Friday morning the books that had been repaired, new books, books that had been requested, all kinds of library materials, were shipped out to them on a truck that also took forth the weekly toilet supply needs and other items that had been requested. The return voyage brought back the books in need of repair and binding and passengers from among the maintenance staff to get their instructions for the closing hours and coming weeks of clean up from their commander, Mr. Feeks. Somehow or other Feeks had got outfitted with a uniform that could not possibly be mistaken for anything less than Chief Custodian. The only two other employees in the City that I ever saw so well garbed as he were the Chief Custodian of City Hall, and the Chief Porter of University College. These were men of substantial size and girth, former Regimental Sergeant-Majors at the very least, with their multi-coloured ribbons for the medals of their military campaigns brightening the jackets of their custodian attire.

Mr. Feeks was a rare one, a character I always recall when I remember my early library days.

3

This entering into a new world, as I did when I went up those stairs of a Monday morning, with a regular job for the first time in my life, was no dramatic breakthrough. It had been waiting in the wings, waiting for me, had I known. The library staff, Feeks in his uniform, the older librarians, civil servants who had become atrophied by the system, were but the start of it.

They were all as new and strange to me as I to them. There was small blame if any, and pleasant enough reasons for our lack of knowledge of one another.

From the very first day I started work in Cardiff Public Library I began to learn the value of apprenticeship as a way of learning. Really there is no other. Within the first hour I was tidying shelves, putting books on them in their places, setting books aside that needed repair, replacement, or binding. I was learning to cope with the eager readers who crowded around me as I shelved, plucking the Sabatinis, the Ethel M. Dells, the Edgar Wallaces from my hands before they had even reached the shelves. By noon, my first break, I was smelling and sweating of books, my hands were stained by them, and the ping of the unwashed readers had entered my pores.

The only way of learning how to do a task is to do it. There is a lot in that tough saw: "Those who can, do. Those who can't, teach. "

I have spent whole years of my life and other times away from the books and my own writing to teach about them, and have returned to the library and my own writing the worse for the experience.

I consider the most important library work that I have

done was to serve as secretary of the committee that was responsible for that vast bibliography, the National Union Catalog of the U. S. This was achieved through John Cronin, the Chief of Processing at the Library of Congress, and six or seven others of us, all working librarians, steadfast librarianating throughout, running our libraries as we fought it through. We would have turned into a Commission that would still be delivering reports, hiring consultants, giving the opposition time to muster and delay had we been otherwise.

Apprenticeship is a process that never ends. Nor is it confined to the present task in hand. Lately I have taken up carpentry, and after learning under good instructors who have tools in their hands, and who can handle power saws, I am now building a Welsh dresser. Yet I am writing more fluently than I ever have, and about a subject that is difficult: Myself as I think I am and have been.

The dreadful Squeers of Dothesboys Hall was a better teacher than Nicholas Nickleby or he himself knew. When he instructed his class of poor little castaways he taught them the wrong spelling for window. "Winder" he said. "W-I-N-D-E-R, Winder. Now go and wipe it. "

That is a way of learning what a window really is, putty, glass, frame and all, the very bitch of a thing often even to open or close or to replace a shattered pane. It is something we all would like to know and to hell with the grammarians who think they are teaching us by explaining the derivation of the word.

Dickens, like all of us, was an apprentice all the days of his life. He died of being too hasty. Had he put himself in the hands of a voice teacher, like all singers and actors do, he would have learned to conserve his energy. An amateur performer on a public stage for any length of time needs to conserve his energy, to use it only when and where it will do the most good. Great singers, great speakers and actors go to voice and sometimes breathing lessons all the years of their lives.

Applause and praise can be killers. Most enthusiasm is passing anyway. Who remembers tomorrow the great performance of today?

I learned this the hard way, very soon after I was hobbled and spancelled for life in a collar and tie and a neat suit. By the time that I qualified as a librarian in 1939, there was not one base job in the library that I did not know about, and was learning by experience and observation, questions and study to handle, if not to master. There are several aspects of my profession that still remain a closed book to me and there are tasks that I have shirked or not had time to master, or have failed because of fearful ignorance about machinery of all kinds.

We were lucky, at Cardiff Public Library, both as being at once the National Library which left us with a large stock of books in an imposing building downtown and also by the fact that Cardiff University College and the Technical College had but fledgling libraries. Also, and this is something that has always puzzled me, access to these libraries and use of their resources have generally been denied to non-University readers. It gives me the impression that were this ban removed and the use of these publicly funded or privately endowed resources made available to the public the libraries would be crowded with crowds seeking knowledge with such fervour that the scholars and would-be scholars would be left at a loss for books. In all my experience nothing is further from the truth. Also, the universities, especially during these times, remove themselves so far from the city centres that they are difficult to reach, and when one of them is reached the parking lots are filled.

It is people who have given me most pleasure, the best part of my life. Were it not for other people I would have foundered long ago. It is not that I particularly like people, I don't; only some of them. Sometimes I have found a nugget amid the slag hill of shale. Fool's gold has glittered all along the way. Yet every day I wake up wondering about people, how old acquaintances are going to react to the events of the day, who among the many dullards that I will encounter will, by my intended or inadvertent turning over the stone in him, by accident or by design, start a wing.

I did not know then that, once I left home, I was going to become so involved with people the rest of my life. Had I become a Graves Burial registration clerk, a part of the permanent local bureaucracy, or taken the examinations for the higher branches of local or national civil service, I would have had a reasonable chance of temporal success. The law attracted me. Some of my best friends, one of the very best, went into medicine. Others became accountants, others teachers. Many remained among the acquaintances I could understand the most who were working men, whether they had been apprenticed to a trade or not.

One great thing about a library is that all sorts of people visit it, for one reason or another. Some of them are or become quite regular users.

From the time I started work in the library my circle of acquaintances began to widen and spin at almost dizzying speed. Let alone among the librarians, with some of whom I formed lasting friendships, but among the readers especially. They were of all kinds and they appear in the vision of my memory still. I owe a great deal to them.

Turn but a stone, the poet says, and start a wing. There were no stones for me to turn over. They were turned over already into slippery, scattered and smelly people, waiting for me, following me, and standing between me and the bookshelves.

They were all shapes and sizes and I saw them in my shelving every day for years. Some among them didn't have the tuppence for the books in the rental library shops, but they had their library cards, and used them to the full.

As I grew more experienced at it I could line books up at the counter, bring them together in a single line and swing them up by dropping my right hand at the same time, so that I served off the arm, like an old-time waitress in a Baltimore boarding house.

I started off each morning with my hair slicked down with brilliantine, wearing a suit, a shirt with a white collar and a neatly knotted necktie. The hair parting of my brilliantined hair was called a dawsey. After my first few loads the dawsey was gone and my hair was sticking up in spikes like the hair of Jeremy Cruncher, the bank messenger and body snatcher in A Tale of Two Cities. Jeremy had always been my favourite character in that rather fustian novel, but at least he did not have a white collar to grow smirched and crumped from the books that took more than the starch out of it, and the necktie was slipped around my neck like a hangman's noose. My hands were stained with the book bindings, especially on rainy days. My suit was rumpled and smelled of book as did all of me.

Most of the eager readers who surrounded me to the

shelves--sometimes there was near a hundred of them--were
snatching the escape literature, nothing more. Edgar Wallace, rarely if ever read now, was a great favourite of
theirs. So was Nat Gould, who wrote novels about dirty
deeds at the horse track. They read Sabatini, Marie Corelli
and a few of them found P. G. Wodehouse funny.

We could not get enough books of their taste to come
near satisfying them. The original case bindings soon wore
out from their hard use and they were very sturdily rebound
by Cedric Chivers of Portway, Bath, England. The bindings
then outlasted the books. There was such handling, housing,
charging and discharging of the books from the shelves to the
readers, to the circulation desk, home and back again, that
every day, bar Sunday, there were not hours that I did not
have books in my hands or pressing against me.

These readers that I met first every morning spent
the rest of the day around and about the newspaper and magazine reading room. There were no conveniences in the libraries in those days so they stepped across to the Hayes
Market to relieve themselves. They were handsomely provided for in the public conveniences there, with goldfish
swimming in the high glass flush tanks. Just across from
the Hayes Open Market, that housed the underground conveniences, were the covered arcades that were a peculiar feature of downtown Cardiff. There were stores along dry and
glass-roofed pedestrian walks. Some of the stores featured
a large fizzling glass of burdock root and dandelion, or a
large mug of tea plus a thick slice of jelly roll for tuppence.
Nearby was the Pavilion cinema that featured matinée films
at a cut rate and served tea and biscuits in between features.

Between the library, the conveniences, the arcades
and the movies our well-nigh daily readers spent their time
before returning at night to the rooms in Tiger Bay. The
long long street of Bute that led by tramline to Pier Head
had been built up handsomely during the 1890's around the
Coal Exchange. So handsome and solid was this edifice constructed that it still stands solid today and should Wales ever
win any political independence it will become the Parliament
Building. The area was built up handsomely at the same
time with grand houses set in crescents, parks and gardens,
with fine hotels and maritime supply stores. Yet for some
reason or other the coal barons, the brokers and other men
of business never took to the area at all. The hotels were
boarded or closed up, with just the spit and sawdust bar

open for business and the houses became warrens with fugitive
unemployed or otherwise landed seamen from all over the
world (hence called Tiger Bay) renting rooms among them.
Otherwise the houses were split up for housing for those who
could make the rough and rigorous life of the coal trade.
Their lot grew even worse with the coming of the Depression
and it was from among them that the Library received its
first readers of a morning.

The main rush of this traffic began to dwindle after
the first two hours and the reader pattern changed. There
were all sorts of readers then and some I remember clearly
fifty years later....

There was Laird the dentist. He was always writing
letters to the South Wales Echo. Nearly every day he was
in the Library searching books about anthems, finding by
chapter and verse from the books that "Land of Hope and
Glory" and not "God Save the King" should be the national
anthem. If he pulled your tooth successfully he asked you
to sign a petition urging this. He kept greyhounds in his
back yard, and his wife played "Land of Hope and Glory"
loud enough while he pulled out teeth. He was also a great
reader of other books on greyhounds and whippets. Laird
was a small bustling man with a remarkably strong right
hand and forearm that he had developed from pulling teeth.

There was one who read fiction of the better kind and
books about the sea. He was a big burly man, always elegantly attired. He wore a well cut suit always, a meticulously laundered shirt, his good shoes shone. Should the
day be a rainy one he carried an umbrella besides the at-
taché case that he always had beneath his arm for his books.
He had such a respect for books, for library use and management that he was an ideal patron. His wife, when she accompanied him, was as well-dressed, as quiet and as pleasant as he was. Yet he was no scholar and was barely a
book man. The desire to read had come upon him as the
Depression brought him more leisure and empty days to fill.
Somehow he took to books and found in them a source of
pleasure that surprised him and he grew more and more to
be a reader. He had been ashamed of his ignorance until
he met me one day in the stacks, browsing through books as
I stacked and shelved them away from the hurly-burly of the
circulation desk: this was the most pleasant and rewarding
part of my day.

Somehow or other Olsen--that was his name; I never

knew his first one--had realised that I was the son of a coal-trimmer and that I had been raised in Splott. He hesitantly asked me about a book, any book, preferably American, that had to do with the sea and I showed him one book that has also been my favourite of its kind, Moby Dick. He actually grasped it in his large well-cared for worker's hands. The more I talked about the book the more did his feelings show, and month after month, then year after year, we got so that we looked out for one another through the stacks of a late morning and the more and more secure and settled did his reading habit grow.

The elegance of his attire, the bulk of his body, the rather rolling gait and his working class voice and vocabulary were a puzzle to me, and have remained so until this day. Olsen was one of a kind.

His family was one of the few Norwegian families that settled in Cardiff. They were seafarers to a man, to the second and third generation. Later Willi Oskar Christian Gotaar, a grandson of a Finnish ship's master, was to become a close friend of mine in College. Olsen himself had gone to sea, had sailed all over the world, even making the run to Australia and back on the four-masted windjammer the Herzogen Cecilie, but the Depression had caught him and the likes of him flat footed before they were able to consider moving aft of the mainmast as mates and skippers to be with their certificates from the Board of Trade. Then, however, without slouching off from the sea, Olsen set himself up as a water carrier and at the Pier Head loaded and delivered parcels, boxes, and gear to the ships that anchored in the Barry Roads as fewer and fewer of them incurred the dock dues of tying up at the Cardiff docks that were silting up with mud from the sliding coast line anyhow, as the two dredgers, the Duchess and the Countess were too costly to run full-time as they had when King Coal was lording the waters.

There were about a dozen boats like Olsen's. They were powered by the boatman at the stern, standing up, steering and rowing by means of one large stern oar. It required seamanship of a high kind to ship supplies, crews, pilots and others to the anchored ships in the Barry Roads. It has remained a wonder to me how Olsen became such a reader in those circumstances.

There was a wide and friendly couple who visited the library daily, both for their reading and for the pleasure they obtained from other people like them who at that time made the library the focus of their lives. In his youth and later the man of the couple had been a sailor. He had visited every port and obtained both carnal pleasure and more from his times ashore. He could tell me vivid stories about the high, wide, and handsome main avenues of Rio. Pelorus Jack of Melbourne was known to him. The Missions for British Sailors all over the world had been his hotels when he had decided to jump ship and spend further time in Baltimore or Alexandria. His stories were not of dockside carousing. Like the Ancient Mariner himself he knew how to enthral me with his memories of people and places all over the world. Almost daily, certainly several times a week while he was looking for books and I was posing as assisting him, we would get together and I would listen to him.

The unemployment irked him to his bones. At the time nearly every ocean-going ship bound east or west from Cardiff would carry as focs'le crews and stokers men with the Extra Master's Certificate or their credentials as first class engineers. There was no chance of his getting sea-going employment at all, and Cardiff was a barren area in the 30's now that the coal bonanza was over. Believing, both of them, that two can live as cheaply as one, he had established relations with a gusty free woman whose husband had left her, died or had been kicked out--I did not enquire-- and she accompanied him daily to the library, one of the few of our regular women readers. They dressed in a style that reflected their frugal buying from secondhand stores yet they gave the clothes a style, a style that reflected the gypsy in them. Their appearance stopped just short of being theatrical. They were rubicund, kind, and clean, revolutionaries almost against the drear dead Cardiff docks, unemployment and puritanism. They went everywhere together as man and woman. They grinned and more at their unwed state.

They were greeted every morning with a clench-fist green of Llewellyn, an excitable Welsh-speaking active member of the Communist Party. Llewellyn had been a collier in various pits. He had been fired regularly for his polemics and worse against the Capitalist Society. He was well known as an orator. Mardy, a town called "Little Moscow," was a favourite centre of his to perform his fulminations. He was so good at them that he could always draw a Cymric crowd with his oratory. He would rear back on his soap box on the slag heap and let this hwyl possess him. The hwyl was a joy to hear. It possessed few men, and always in

40

Welsh. One day he was speaking on the Common, outside University College--about the only place in Cardiff where Welsh was common parlance, among the students from the Valleys, and Myfanwy Jenkins caught my eye--she was a pretty girl from Blaenrhonda. "Better than the Reverend Matabele Jones he is" she muttered to me. That was praise indeed, for the Reverend Matabele, the son of the great Welsh Missioner to the Africans, had won that year the Oratorical Chair at the Gymanfu Cymry.

Llewellyn was always asking me for books, filling up forms requesting, nay, demanding, that the library obtain more Marxist Literature and many more copies of Tressall's Ragged Trousered Philanthropists, a book much in demand by Llewellyn and his like but seemingly always lost or at the binder's.

There was a big black man from Tiger Bay who brought in with him often several wide-eyed stranded black sailors to show them pictures from The Mad Mullah of Somaliland, a book greatly in demand by the library's black patrons. They were few in number, yet readers of all our Africana, and this book was kept for them on perpetual reserve.

An elegant vicar of one of Cardiff's oldest churches spent at least three mornings a week among the stacks of books on ecclesiastical history and the like. He wore a monocle for reading and disliked being disturbed by the likes of me shelving around him. He eventually made bishop, one of the few of The Church in Wales as the Anglican Church was known. This gave rise to some good political verse by G. K. Chesterton and to the longest word in the English language antidisestablishmentarianism. The novelist David Mathew was also a frequent visitor, most amiable and pleasant. He had been a midshipman on HMS Tiger at the Battle of Jutland, later went to Oxford and the Beda College in Rome. His historical work, The Celtic People and the Renaissance in Europe won him a doctorate from the University of Glasgow and at about the same time his novels Steam Packet and The Prince of Wales' Feathers were published. He was the first library reader to encourage me to make Librarianship my career and to persevere with my writing. I was composing poetry about this time and it is much to his credit that he never winced at it. Later he went on to become an Archbishop in Africa and returned home to a rural retreat where he ended his days in pain and in poor health.

41

He wrote to me every year and I always recall him as the
bubbling and kind curate. Gwyn Jones the novelist and Norse
scholar was another regular visitor. We had long talks about
books together. Every Tuesday night he had a regular book
session on the B. B. C. and one evening he said "When I was
talking today to Will Ready, at the Public Library, the question of the importance of Maria Edgeworth the first woman
novelist arose...." He said it quite casually. I was working and never heard it, but the rest of my family did, and
many others.

It was the first time that I received what can pass
for publicity. It was a year or so later that I received any
public notice and that was in the Welsh Rugby Times report-
ing on a game against Aberavon Green Stars: "Will Ready
fielded the kick of Tongynglas Jones at mid centre and ran
half the length of the field to plant it between the goal post
for a try that was unfortunately not converted." I can still
recall that notice, while nearly all others of a more professional and library kind send me to the indexes of library
literature to look up.

During the last two years of my apprenticeship I had
picked up a lot of know-how about handling books. The circulation desk and the open book stacks were where the action
was but just as I grew quite adept at sorting, sliding, and
stacking books I was moved upstairs to the reference reading
room where the books were kept on reserve, to be used only
in the library. The action was quiet here during most of the
day. My first task every morning was to check and to re-
plenish the journals. The library, because of its nature and
because Harry Farr, the City Librarian, was quite a bookman, took more literary journals than usual. The London
Mercury was in its heyday then. J. C. Squire was the editor of this beautifully produced magazine and H. L. Mencken
edited The American Mercury at the same time. There was
enough in these two monthly journals to keep me reading them,
between answering questions and serving the straggle of readers who came in to use the encyclopaedias and dictionaries.
I would read them every morning for days. There was little
to disturb me, for the large idle staff there were just waiting for elevation to the Senior Staff room, and there was
none of the busy buzzing of books that was present in the
circulation reading room below. My brilliantined hair kept
its dawsey, my shirt collar remained white and starched and
my necktie stayed properly placed and knotted. Glyn Jones,
the short story writer, Jack Jones, the novelist and play-

42

wright, were constant visitors. Jack Jones was a self-taught miner who used to cycle in from miles away to use the library or to give talks either upstairs in the Research Room or at the University. He always dressed very tidily, always wore bicycle clips around the ankles of his trousers and enjoyed a measure of more than local fame for decades. He used the library a lot, was always browsing through the encyclopaedias or talking to Jones the Welsh (in charge of Welsh books) about local history that later featured in his novels and his plays. Gradually, very gradually, over the years he began to assume a more literary appearance. His necktie hung looser around his neck. Whereas before he wore only a cap when the weather warranted it he began to wear a felt hat whose brim kept growing wider, and he cultivated a beard. Later, after I had left the library and was serving in the Army, Jack Jones served on the Lecture Force of the British Information Services. He had a good lilting Valleys voice and became extremely popular on his lecture tours overseas, especially in the U.S. Actually he was awarded a considerable civilian decoration for his war work and became the complete man of letters, wearing a cape, bearded, his hat in its black fur velour approaching both the style and shape of a Toulouse-Lautrec fedora. He also affected a walking stick that could have been the crook of a Basque shepherd in Arizona. All this was burgeoning within him before the war had started and I was still attached to the Special Collections Room of the Public Library. His fame began to wane by the '60's, but it was good while it lasted and added a dash of colour, even excitement, to the Reference Reading Room where his employment might have saved him from extravagance and added very greatly to the style of the staff.

I must have read thousands of first lines of poetry. Very strangely a first line of a poem by May Sarton has remained with me ever since I read it in the poetry pages of The London Mercury in the Reference Reading Room of the Library:

> Do not think that I will bear your pity
> Across my mouth like a soft January rain....

I can almost feel the fine paper it was printed on, and I can recall that occasion well.

By afternoon the students from the Medical School, University College, and Technical School had begun to arrive.

There were about eighteen copies of Gray's Anatomy and a similar number of Cunningham and other medical texts, along with the journals and other books that the Medical School students kept going in and off and on and out. The library was equally as well stacked with science books and journals. The editions of Shakespeare, Chaucer, Milton and the other poets were in equally rich and well-maintained profusion; there was an excellent non-circulating Library of the Classics and of European and British history.

Every so often some scholar, some writer from the University would pass by the desk into the private quarters and make his or her way up the winding marble stairs to the Research Room and Special Collections where were his working papers, peace and quiet. There was a flat roof adjacent where they could stroll and take their ease. Catherine McLean, always dressed in a delightful and most feminine style, the author of Born under Saturn, would visit and write there. David Williams, the historian, was a constant visitor and reader up there. There was generally a group of them, including amateur historians, some writing doctors, the odd lawyer and lecturer, who had embarked on some project of their own and on a sunny day there would always be a group of them lounging on the roof where I would inevitably join them as more and more I was assigned to care for their book needs in the Research and Special Collections Division.

The students would take a break and a smoke while they were waiting for a Gray's Anatomy to be returned, or just to give themselves a rest from too much delving into Chaucer, Shakespeare, or Catullus. I sought good company among them too and, save for my more formal garb, I could have been mistaken for one of them.

One of them I did become when I entered into terra incognita, into the babel of the Common Room as a freshman in September 1935. A stranger I was there, because nearly all of the students in those days came from the Valleys, both boys and girls, on Miners Welfare Scholarships.

Many of the girls lived in Aberdare Hall, the only residence on campus. The rest, and some of the boys, lived in strictly controlled lodgings around the campus. Others, hundreds of them, made the trip up and down the Valleys by Western Welsh bus. Save for the families of the doctors, the mining engineers, and the divines who ran the chapels, they were all, like me, children of parents who had never made it even to high school.

The babel of sound that greeted me like off-beat bells, was a mixture of English and of Welsh, the usual Valleys talk. There were few Cardiff students. Offspring of tradesmen and the like, they were not even eligible for the Miners Welfare Scholarships. If they were good enough, and a surprising number from Cardiff High School were, they became eligible for some grant to Oxford, Cambridge, or London and that is where they went, most of them being lost to Wales forever. All the students wore brief black gowns. I felt at home and quite easy in this new milieu. It did not take me long to pick up the Valley Welsh and English and I began spending more and more of my time at the University and less and less at the Public Library save for my book needs.

I realised very soon, and to learn this it must be experienced, that university life is different from all kinds of life before. It is not so much the learning and the classes but the company. Age, sex, courses--they do not matter as much as the company. It is not necessarily a better company. Often it is worse than the outsider experiences and generally less deserving. Yet, like Catholic education used to be, it imparts a stain, good or evil, that colours the rest of life. Among the writers that I have known, the good ones, those who never made it to college have felt that they missed out. The great Irish writer, Frank O'Connor, was always conscious of it. So was J. F. Powers, whose novel Morte D'Urban won the National Book Award and whose stories, collected in The Presence of Grace and Prince of Darkness are American classics. They both confided in me that they had lost out by not getting to University. It is an intangible that I cannot touch or explain, yet I know how they feel.

It was a time for me of swimming out of the aquariums or elevated glass flush bowls into a larger lake or a wide river like the Severn that ran out to the Cambrian Sea.

J. B. S. Haldane, with an open-necked cricket shirt and sandals, with socks on, of course, his bald head shining in the sun, and a Hindu lady in a sari standing behind him, lectured us from a portable pulpit on the patch of waste ground next to the University. It was a time of political unease with Hitler and his armies marching ever closer to a showdown with the fumbling democracies.

45

Books and reading, people, library service--seemed far away, over a dark hill that grew bigger, darker and more menacing with the years.

Haldane was lecturing and recruiting for the Spanish Republic. Many of my student friends enlisted in the International Brigade and many more talked big about it. Christopher Hill, the seventeenth-century historian, a friend and teacher of mine and a committed Marxist, organised students and relations like my brother Jack, to scrub and clean out a building in Caerleon to house Basque refugee children. The student unions generally swallowed Vera Brittain whole and resolved that not on any account would they fight for King and Country, as if their brave mock parliamentary declaration would stop dead in their tracks the rumble and the crash of Hitler and his legions.

4

There came six years after my early library years when I
was in the Army. Myself and a group of us volunteered for
military service in the Spring of '39 when we realized that
Hitler's war would soon be on us. By this early enlistment
we intended to learn a military skill that would give us an
edge of preference over those more laggardly in enlistment.
Events moved too fast for us. We were trained enough as
gunners by the beginning of the war that we could not be
spared from the arduous task of firing off thousands of rounds
of shells weighing over 50 lbs each to rid the casings of ex-
plosive used for training, so that they could be refilled with
a live ammunition that might shatter into fragments of shrapnel and bring down in flames low-flying enemy aircraft, or
break up the advance of infantry by firing shrapnel that would
shred their ranks. As a result when the war did come in
September we were too badly needed on the ranges to be
spared. The offer of a commission that was given freely to
us in June was made in September to untrained university
graduates. Jones and Evans and scores of others who had
graduated with us were getting their swords sharpened and
their uniforms tailored to measure without having even seen
a gun. Meanwhile myself and the companions of my folly
were firing on the range large guns, 3.7's, comparable to
the better German 88 mms., hauling these monsters to hastily prepared gun sites along the shores of the Cambrian Sea.
When we were not firing or hauling these vile weapons we
were busy setting up tents for our housing, stuffing palliases
with straw for our bedding, and learning how to cook and
serve the rations that were delivered by trucks from Cardiff.
What uniforms were available were needed for the draftees,
so we wore shapeless fatigue coveralls over our civilian
clothes. When we were through with the firing and the tent-
ing, we were digging latrines and trenches, those of us less
adept at gunnery learning to kindle reluctant flames in the

47

base of Crimean-type huge kettles, wherein to boil the water
for the morning tea. We sliced hundreds of loaves, frying
bacon by the flitch. There was no more gormless bedraggled
outfit in the Army than this Officer Producing Unit. There
was a certain macabre humour to it all. The regular Army
N. C. O. 's who were brought in from Woolwich, the H. Q. of
the Royal Artillery, from Aldershot and from regular units,
even from India, to make soldiers out of us, were at a loss.
Some jumped up and down, all brassed, trim, and shining in
their parade uniforms, screaming, foaming at us on parade.
We all had been issued with good boots, steel-toed and stud-
ded, a World War I cache that had turned up at Cardiff Barracks. They were thick with a grease that had preserved
them, and they were so heavy that they rooted at any halt,
so that the sharp smart stamp of a military parade was denied
us. Some N. C. O. 's requested an immediate transfer back to
their parent units, even if it meant a drop in rank, others
physically or mentally suffered a break-down when they tried
to impart to us a spit and polish. Eventually the N. C. O. 's
consisted of the dregs of other units who refused to take them
back, even as non-striped gunners. Some downright thugs
remained, and a warrant officer, a Sergeant-Major from the
Royal Horse Artillery, who must have had such charges pend-
ing against him if he failed to make a military unit out of us
that he did so. He was smart enough to take me and others
like me off all parades. We became permanent orderlies,
tending cookhouse fires, cleaning and digging latrines, and
spending all our other waking hours in the gun park. I recall
hope flickering for the first time in his battered face when a
gun sergeant brought him to the gun site and showed me actually being able to open a breach. This was the first time
that the crew were ever able to put a round up the spout
with myself at the breach. It was middle October by that
time, and we were growing pelts for lack of uniforms. We
had not been away from the guns since the war had been declared. We were very different from the group who had
danced and skylarked in the tailored dress uniforms through
most of the month of August.

My friends began to pass me by. With the advent of
draftees they were spending their time on the gun parks teaching the new young soldiers how to set a fuse, how to handle
from their perches the elevation and direction of the projectile
missiles. More and more I spent my time on orderly duties
around the cookhouse and latrines. Many and many a day did
I spend peeling potatoes, chopping onions, carrots, and cabbage. On off kitchen-orderly days I began to command as

orderly-in-chief the latrine cleaning and digging squad. For months deep into winter I squatted on my hunkers and scraped potatoes most days every week.

Finally, as the clothing mills began to switch into the making of military clothing, they issued us originals with uniforms. They allowed us off the gun sites. At the time we occupied a gun site on the Cardiff docks, the docks that had been revived by becoming a main port for the shipping of men and material for the British Expeditionary Force that was assembling in France. Moreover the docks were ports for food, fruit, and materials to make up for the war economies of the nation. We were housed in a derelict coal washery, where coal, in Cardiff's heyday, was run through washers if it was the best Welsh steam coal, all intended for overseas domestic consumption.

There were some blithe spirits at some sort of H. Q. (maybe it was our colonel in the fastness of his valley H. Q.) who believed that the uniforms of enlisted men could be better expended on the draftees than upon us, who one day would be ordering uniforms from military tailors. They were both thriving and expanding, and already had our measurements from the dress blues that we had ordered and paid for, and worn for a few times during July when we were already swaggering our sticks as officers to be. So the Army issued us with long pre-war uniforms, designed when the artillery was horse-drawn. I wore knee-high puttees, breeches and spurs. Our jackets were buttoned in brass, and were riding coats, while our top coats were fully skirted for the saddle.

They were real riding spurs, nothing fancy about them. The clank and jingle of these, along with the clatter and scraping of our steel-shod boots that after months of wear and polish were beginning to show something of a shine, made us a cause for comment. With our skirted topcoats and outdated peaked hats, as we waited for the Pier Head tram to take us downtown, people stopped and hailed us, as if we were ghosts, like Drake's drum, come back from the previous World War, to save our country once again.

Lizzie Coughlan, who had taught me in my childhood, ran up through the waiting line to hug me and kissed me with tears in her eyes. She was a contemporary of my Auntie Annie, and had been in and out of the house in Peter Street on school and Truth Society business ever since I could remember.

"Good God, Willie! What have they done to you?"

You could not blame Lizzie. She was emotional and excitable at the best of times, and there was I at the tram stop, looking like a deserter from Fred Karno's Army, especially as my puttees kept unwinding and wreathing around my boots until two old veterans lifted me up on a low wall and while my legs dangled wound up my puttees securely. The tram just came in time to stop them from adjusting my knapsack and lacing my boots so that they could fit securely and snugly into the stirrups.

The one thing that I did not lack during all these months monastic on the gun site was reading matter. We had been permitted visitors every Saturday and Sunday afternoon, and while they were not allowed on the gun site they talked to us through the high barbed fence that, as Gunner Nash, one of my fellow soldiers with smouldering eyes did say, was meant rather to keep us in than to let people in and out.

Our visitors had a long and tiresome walk to get to us, and they brought us parcels galore, food and clothing generally. Nearly always the parcel included a Penguin, one of the new paperbound series of books that were to make such a great change in book production, in distribution, and in the trade of publishing. They relieved the public libraries very considerably and were largely responsible for the close-down of the tupenny book rental shops.

My two sisters visited me regularly along with my mother and father. Somehow Mam used to bring me warmed cooked meals and more clothes than ever I could wear beneath my coveralls. I used to get every Saturday large boxes of Welsh bakestones and teesen lap, a large flat Welsh griddle cake. Nor did Mam ever forget the draftees from Liverpool and Glasgow who were my co-orderlies. She always had food and cigarettes for them. My brother was long gone in a destroyer, landed either in Gibraltar or Spanish Morocco on some secret communications deal. Most of the families and friends who came visiting included a Penguin or another book for me, most of the literary journals so that I could spend hours in the quiet huts reading and writing every day since I came off duty every day after the midday main meal was served and the pots and pans left boiling for the morning, and I became Cinderella again at 5 a.m.

There were two chief drivers of the heavy gun-trucks.

50

These huge vehicles not only towed the gun, carried the crew of ten, five tons of ammunition, and all the repair and replacement gear, but we always kept the wagon lines in tip-top condition. They spent a great deal of time at the local Cardiff Army Motor Vehicle Workshops and Bombardier Wellaway and Bombardier Chapman, the two drivers, were devoted to my mother. They visited her in their truck for tea and a chat whenever they came into Cardiff, their vehicles taking up nearly the whole block of the street, from sidewalk to road centre. They brought me in via Mam anything I needed. As a result I had a circulating library going and a literary group of sorts that met every night in the Wet Canteen. There was one table there that was always reserved for me, and the draftees even used to squat and listen to us while we quaffed our beer and argued or agreed about D. H. Lawrence, Somerset Maugham, and women writers.

The despatch rider, the Don R. in military parlance, was a particular pre-war friend of mine. He was as hard and bouncy as a golf ball, a rugby scrum-half infamous for his trickery and worse on the field, even in the Cardiff and District Rugby League. Every day he visited on his Army motor-bike every gun site in the Regiment and all-related units up to and including Brigade H. Q. on Penylan Hill. He was often questioned about his bike being propped up outside Cardiff Rugby Club but his answers were always immediate, justifiable, and meaningful to his uncomfortable prosecutor. He and Mam were very close; he was like a brother to me. Daily he called on Mam, acted as courier and kept me and my friends in other gun sites closely in touch.

He knew all the officers on one particular gun park very well, either from school, rugby, or elsewhere. They were entertaining that night the new Battery Commander, a stranger, a Major, who lived some place else, on Penylan Hill most likely, where the Regiment had a requisitioned comfortable old house for the brass, the experts, and the clerical workers. It was 7 p. m. when Puff the Don R. put his bike away, pulled off his outer snug clothes and hurried to join me and a few others in our heated hut where we were alone, the other gunners who slept there being away on duty or in the wet canteen.

As he passed by the officers' quarters a Catering Sergeant who had been brought in by the officers for the preparation and serving of the meal--from Penylan Hill most likely; he was wearing a white mess coat anyhow, according to Puff-- found himself lacking a waiter. He called out sharply to Puff

51

as he was passing and curtly pressed him into service. Puff washed hurriedly, pulled on a white coat, and served the first course, the hors d'oeuvres, on a tray. Instead of turning right however from the kitchen to the officers quarters, he turned left and served us with the course, returning with his empty tray for the next course, and the next. With the final course he wrapped up the dishes in the white coat and threw them over the cliff. We were all replete and sipping at some brandy that Dewi's mother had brought us on the previous Sunday when there were sounds of a hue and cry. Somebody had swiped the entire dinner so carefully planned for the Major. He was so puzzled, hungry, and angry that he joined in the quest for the culprits. The Catering Sergeant was not even in the Regiment. He had been borrowed from Signals and had only seen Puff in the gloaming and then for the first time. There was a hut-to-hut search, led by the Sergeant-Major and N. C. O. 's with bewildered and very embarrassed officers in their wake. They burst into our hut without ceremony to find us squatting and sitting around the fire, playing bridge. Puff and I were playing chess and there was an air of such calm among us that the Sergeant-Major would have apologised to us had he known how to.

By this time we had become very adept and mobile at gunnery, the Radar system was working and we were able to get to cities, rail centres and depots in time to hear the bombers overhead. We even shot down some of the enemy by mistake.

5

The raids lessened following the Battle of Britain victory in
the sky, the Canadian troops were arriving in force and the
Dunkirk survivors were soldiers again.   Churchill thereupon
decided to send a large part of the Army overseas and we
were among the first to go of our kind.   The convoy held
more than 100,000 men.   We would have suffered great losses
from the German wolfpack submarines had not the U. S. decided to conduct extensive anti-submarine manoeuvers all
around us across the Atlantic and then down the American
coast recrossing the Atlantic with ourselves in the midst of
them until they waved goodbye to us as we rounded the Cape
of Good Hope and anchored at the Cape and at Durban at ports
where the lights were bright and there were good things to
be had for the asking by the soldiers who had been quartered
for five weeks and more below decks on ships that had not
been converted to troopers.

We gave a sigh of relief mingled with apprehension as
we boarded the Oronsay for the long and dangerous convoy to
the Middle East, around Africa to Suez, a voyage of some
eight weeks' duration.   Some thought we were being shipped
so that we could bring disaster to Alexandria.

We of the anti-aircraft artillery that was engaged in
the air defence of Great Britain had become objects of dislike, derision, and worse among the bombed civilians.   They
were bombed despite our efforts to shoot the bombers down
or to deflect them from their mission.   There were some
civilians, firewardens, air raid policemen and the like, who
thought that we made matters worse, that the flashes of our
ineffectual gun fire made a target of their factories and homes.

The Germans had begun to switch their night bombing
away from London, and to attack the less protected cities to

the north. These cities were vital to the war effort, because of shipping, factories, and population centres. These targets for bombing were chosen by the Luftwaffe it seemed, at random. Liverpool, Hull, Crewe, and Manchester, even Cardiff.

As night was falling on these unsuspecting cities we would roll and rumble into the environs of a town that was to be a Luftwaffe target for that night. It seemed that no sooner than we were ready for action and full night had fallen that a bombing raid would begin.

The raids were disasters for the cities, and there was little that we could do about it. The Germans were far ahead of us in bombing techniques, but we did what we could, and that was not nearly enough to deter them.

The trouble was that by a combination of radar and the breaking of the German Luftwaffe code the high brass at the H. Q. of Air Defence of Great Britain were able to forecast where the raids were going to be. We were the pawns in the chess game and were far behind the Germans in technique and equipment, but we were all we had and we fired unavailingly until the gun barrels grew red-hot.

So closely guarded was this breakthrough of the German code that it was not until the 1970's that books and articles began to appear and cleared our name. But it was too late by then and when we were encamped in Sidi-Bish not a bomb fell on Alexandria. Tobruk for some reason had quiet nights when we were there, and our advent brought peaceful nights to Benghazi. Haifa, of all places, was the only place that was bombed when we were there. The enemy intended to thrust home and explode the oil tanks, but the raid was hurried and hapless. The Italian planes fled when we waved our guns at them. There were smiles not scowls when we sought the cafes and bars on Herzl Street and people greeted us as protectors and friends along the beaches of Nathanya. Officers and N. C. O. 's were made honorary members of the Sodom and Gomorrah Golf Club and enjoyed marina rights at the Dead Sea Yacht Club.

In the meantime in 1940, the Army had issued us with a flash that was to be worn with pride upon our battle dress. It was a small square cloth patch that showed our guns bringing down a bomber in flames. We were ashamed to wear it. The gunners so decorated dare not walk into a pub save in their shirt sleeves on their home leave unless there was a gang of them, and they had to drink their tepid beer alone, served by a surly landlord, amid a silent and hostile crowd of regulars who would wrinkle their noses, swallow their tipple down, and leave the bar to us, as if we were a bad smell. There was a brisk market in unflashed battle blouses. I remember seeing Joey Donnell, five feet two if he was an inch, going off on leave in an unmarked jacket made for a six-footer. His feet were nearly tangling in the belt of it, and I did not have the heart or voice to stop him. Neither did the guard at the gate. Joey was wearing his steel helmet. That saved his skull from being split by some tankards that crashed down on him. Despite his unmarked battle dress he was suspected of being one of us. Joey was not very bright at dissembling, nor was he very bright: he had been an altar boy, like me, for years. He became a regular latrine orderly and he was good at it too. He was sufficiently recovered by the end of the Tunisian Campaign to be promoted to Chaplain's Assistant and at the end of the war he became a dungaree lay brother at Bodmin.

There are many references to the P & O and its satellites in English writing. One of Somerset Maugham's best stories Mr. Knowit All uses the P & O as a base. Evelyn Waugh's fine and self-revealing novel The Ordeal of Gilbert Pinfold takes place on such a ship. The very English word Posh comes from the liner traffic, for it was more highly regarded and more expensive to be cabinned on the port side out and the starboard side home: that was the Posh thing to do, and it was reflected in the rank and wealth of the passengers.

There are very few good soldier songs. Most songs about soldiers are of the Sweetheart of the Forces variety and have little or no bearing upon the reality of the soldiers' situation. The only time soldiers could be heard singing them was in some drunken or maudlin state. One of their own true songs, that became popular, when it was cleared of its service obscenity and cynical reflection upon their state, was "The Troopship was Leaving Bombay." The Army troopships were a far cry from the P & O liners and this song reflects that, among many other things.

The Oronsay had not been converted into a trooper. There had not been time, so that the officers occupied the first-class accommodation and the rest of the ship was crowded with men. They occupied the holds that usually held cargo. Their sleeping accommodation was hammocks and there they lived and were fed, in a semi-darkness, being allowed to take air in relays on the deck during the early morning and late afternoon. The ship's company accomplished marvels in running the ship under the sudden and changed circumstances.

The holds were strictly compartmentalised, to guard against fire and flood. Guards were mounted at all the dividing doors and it needed real organisation to keep the thousand or so soldiers fed, aired, and free from dangers of mutiny.

An old admiral was in command of the entire convoy. He commanded from the bridge of the Oronsay, with very limited communication with the rest of the ships. He never left the bridge where he ate, slept now and then, and changed his clothes, well-nigh inaccessible to all: there was nobody to share his terrible responsibility.

Somehow as we were boarding at Gourock in the Firth of Clyde he heard my voice cajoling and ordering the bewildered and reluctant troops aboard. He sent down a message that I was to be the ship's sergeant-major, responsible and answerable only to his bridge command. As a result I was set up in a cabin of my own, port or starboard I have no idea, and the adjacent cabin became my office where my staff reported to me. I was largely responsible for the well-being of the troops, the setting of responsibilities between the various units and having a daily conference with those N.C.O.'s detailed to carry out my orders. The commissioned officers had little or nothing to do, save occupy the first-class quarters that were still organised on the old Posh lines.

The patience of the men under these most trying and nerve-wracking circumstances was extraordinary. The sergeants, as is the British Army custom, had a mess of their own where they could lounge and relax, and that was a help.

I was in a position of great responsibility. There were innumerable details that I had to cover, and three or four times every 24 hours I would make the round of the ship, checking the guards at the hatchways, at night pushing my way through the swinging hammocks, hold after hold of them. I used to enjoy talking to the hammockers who were members of my battery. Many of the first young group of draftees were now among the N.C.O.'s and were sort of a praetorian guard to me, doing all of the work, or most of it that I was responsible for. I needed to send notes by the score and since the public address was properly reserved for

56

emergencies and general ship's orders that affected every one I relied more and more on foot notes and personal visits. Above all I relied on going around and meeting people long before any message need be started.

I had no sensible reason to be aboard the Oronsay at all. Just before we were ordered off our guns and sent to Southend, a town that had almost been evacuated and taken over by the Army for embarkation procedures, I had been interviewed at Chester by the Army Education Corps and assured of a commission on the staff of the Army Education Corps. When orders for embarkation reached the battery we were invited to opt out, all the original remaining members of the Officer Producing Unit, and proceed to Shrivenham for a course in anti-aircraft gunnery that would lead to a commission.

I did not care for either prospect. Not even the Army in 1941 was likely to greet me with enthusiasm as an officer of anti-aircraft gunnery. Guns were things that I would circle around and pat. I never went near the things if I could help it. The Liverpool and Glasgow intake, that we called our early draftees, loved machinery almost to a man. Every gun has a limber gunner, an oil-stained soldier who spent his entire time around the gun, maintaining it in good condition whether it was firing or not, on the road or settled in a gun park. He slept among the cases of ammunition, ate and hunkered under the barrel. Whatever needed to be done to the gun he told the bombardier or the gun sergeant who was responsible for every two guns--there were four to a troop, and my substantive rank was Troop Sergeant Major. If necessary the limber gunner would leave his perch and come seeking me, with the gun sergeant and bombardier. Between us we would settle the matter by word of mouth, or by my taking some piece of the gun to our Artificer Sergeant, an old regular who had been on the guns since he had been a boy soldier. He was a member of the Royal Army Ordnance Corps and had his own mobile workshop and assistants. If the flaw, crack or worn-out part could not be fixed on the site he would take it in to the nearest Ordnance Workshop that could fix it. All the fixers, it seemed, had been boy soldiers with him. They stopped whatever they were doing and helped Ben to get back to the gun park with a new or mended part. Sometimes they would even make a part for him, forging and casting then and there.

Ben was as much a part of the Army as any other

part of the regular institution. So were nearly all his companions in Ordnance. They had known no other kind of life, some of them proceeding straight to Ordnance from orphanages, as boy soldiers.

I often went in to Ordnance with Ben, and many a night at the gun park I used to listen to him over beer as he told me long tales of his life that otherwise I could not have believed. They would never be in print, for every sentence was laced with obscenities, as was my talk also. How else could I communicate?

I had never lived among the poor, the really poor, until my time in the Army. When the Officer Producing Unit went off to camp in July 1939 I met in the Naafi's, as they called the refreshment and recreation centres of the Army, the really poor. They were men who had been raised in the slums, in a casual, godless fashion, by parents who had been raised like them. They generally worked as casual labourers or did menial tasks as generations of their like had done in the past. Their education was minimal and, such as it was, barely affected their standard of living. Their conversation was limited and obscene. Gradually improving, with better health and unemployment care, better housing, some opportunities for their families in a new society, they were essentially the same types as Bruce Bairnsfather had captured in his World War I cartoons. I found them to be the salt of the earth, and they took me in.

The one common characteristic that permeated all ranks was their insularity. They remain an island folk. Since that time I have visited many islands great and small. The Greek islands of the Aegean remain the most beautiful and entrancing, because of their location perhaps, but most of all because of their people. I have heard and read the same about Crete and I was steeped in school of the glory that was Greece. Later I lived on Prince Edward Island in the Gulf of St. Lawrence. There my growing family built a shanty cabin on some land that I bought there and still own. The Prince Edward Islanders are a very insular folk, regarding the North American mainland as something apart, to visit or to settle in for lasting employment. Fortunately for us, our family name is common there. In the small communities the name strikes a bell. There must be twelve or more different families of Readys there: the first Lieutenant-Governor was a Ready, and Patrick Ready was a name known to all over the island. One day we were in a church that was in process of becoming a historic monument. The Roll of Honour contained names of the men of the rural neighborhood that had served in all armed branches of the Military during World War II. There were Readys representing the Army, the Navy and the Air Force. I was kin to none of them yet all of them.

When I decided on my future, if there was to be one, I realised that it must be with people. They give me more pleasure, I learn more from them than from any other way of living. They are a constant source of surprise. The years and their experiences have changed many well-nigh out of recognition. Frequently I meet new people of every standard, nation, and degree.

By the time our trooper ship, the Oronsay reached the Cape I was beginning to be sure that my future, if any, lay in the area of librarianship.

It was books that got me into the game in the first place, but it was people who confirmed me in my intention to stay and progress, if I was spared, among the books. That is what a library meant to me then and still does at the end of my career: Books and the necessary corollary of People.

Durban had welcomed our arrival with relief mingled with delight. A lady with a most powerful contralto stood at the Pier Head and welcomed ship after ship of us with loyal songs, stirring even the bunting and the flags. She sang both loud and clear, was a Durban institution.

Her voice did not begin to quaver until she sang us on our way, three days later. Small wonder. We were enough to have brought a squeak into the voice of Chaliapin, the greatest of the basso profundos, and all that Caruso could have done was to wave at us flaccidly as our ships pulled out.

Her farewell voice echoed the unease of all the folk we left behind us on the shore. Durban was the very heart of British South Africa. We must have brought bitter smiles of satisfaction to the bulk of the Afrikaners, and Cecil Rhodes must have spun in his grave, Sir Bindon Blood's bones must have clattered, and the reports of our parade conveyed by secret agents to Mussolini must have broken him into a martial dance of an anticipated victory. His troops already had Abyssinia in thrall, and his army vastly outnumbered the few British troops in the Western Desert. The Union Defence forces, pledged not only to defend South Africa, were fine-looking husky men. They were by far the finest looking troops we had ever seen. They lined the docks and were clad in safari-type uniforms that were well cut and scrubbed and pressed to an attractive bleached neatness.

We had never worn khaki drill uniforms before, and when the bales of them were broken open they left much to be desired from a sartorial standpoint. They had been stored in the bottom hold of the ship, and were so wrinkled that no efforts at steaming or ironing could possibly smooth them out. The wrinkles gave the clothes a crawling and live look, that along with the smell of brine, of the deep hold, and of the years of storage in some warehouse, imparted a look and a smell to the clothing that made it different from any clothing any of us had ever seen, let alone donned.

The crates were broken open and the uniforms issued early in the morning of the first day in port. Some of the officers were near hysteria, frantic at the sight of the issue, and they had their batmen steaming and ironing them in the all too inadequate laundries before breakfast had been announced. Along with the call for breakfast line-up it was announced that there would be a parade through the streets of Durban at noon, of the many units and regiments in the convoy.

The intention was to reassure the Durbans of British armed might and men, to alleviate their fear of an Italian invasion from the north, maybe with a stiffening of German troops. South Africa was a great prize for any enemy, and there was no doubt that the Italo-German war effort would benefit greatly from its occupation of South Africa.

During the morning then, along with the steam that mounted from the laundry, there could be heard the marching band of fife and drums of the Essex Regiment, the squeal of the pipes from the Scots contingents, and the brass bands from all the ships blowing, drumming, and practising for the parade as if they were the only troops in the world.

All the soldiers were busy dressing in their khaki drills. There was more than a feeling of silence about them as they did so.

The uniforms must have been rejects from Allenby's 1916 campaign in the Middle East. The trousers were shorts,

with deep and abundant roll ups, so that nightly they could
be let down into slacks and secured around the ankles with
tapes. In the morning the trousers were intended to be rolled up into shorts. There were buttons securing the roll-up.
The buttons were metal, and in most cases had cut or worn
through the cotton that stitched them. Some resourceful soldiers found pins or twisted metal from bottle tops to hold
them up, but in most cases the trousers dragged or drooped
to the ankles from the knees. They were a dreadful sight,
the thousands of men in their droopy slack-shorts. The
shirts were so wrinkled that they were crawling with a life
of their own, like lava around a volcanic mountain top. To
crown the whole dreadful outfit were solar topees, of a cut
and style that would have been rejected by free-booters in
Turkestan nearly a century earlier. Perhaps that is where
they originated. The large button at the very top of these
topees had parted from the helmet, so that the topees spun
around during a breeze and salutes fell back defeated as the
hand as often as not hit the peak that swung to the side.

I felt sorry, in the midst of my own personal and administrative woes, for the library attendant. The Oronsay
was still filled with P & O abracadabra and among them was
the reading room and library in the first class quarters.
The old man who looked after the library had come to the
Army with the ship. Dressed in battle dress that somehow
looked on him like semi-clerical wear, or the uniform of a
retired lay reader, he was a bewildered duster of a man
who kept the books neat on the shelves without ever reading
one and sorting out the copies of Field and Stream, the Tat-
ler, the Illustrated London News, The Countryman, The
Salesman and the Otter-hunting Journal so that they were
neat and available on the low tables by the lounge chairs.

Man and boy he had spent his entire life in the service of the P & O and this billet was his reward. Rarely
had Pengelly set foot on shore. He preferred puttering about
the library. The books were of the hunting, shooting, and
fishing sort, with a large dollop of Dernford Yates, Jeffery
Farnol, Stanley Weyman, Harrison Ainsworth, Georgette
Heyer and Kipling. It had become a conference and classroom on the long voyage to Durban. There was much play
of blackboard technique and a pointer, and Pengelly cleared
up after the daily meetings. The lectures, classes, and con-
ferences were of little or no use, but they kept Pengelly busy
and, following a brisk walk around the deck, gave the officers
a taste for a chota-peg before lunch.

Pengelly deserved better than being a part of the parade. Besides, he would have worsened the condition. He actually doddered. When he was garbed, his khaki drill hung on him, I sent him off to the sand dunes that we could see from the deck, with a butterfly net to refresh the collection that was mounted in a frame on the library wall.

That was all that I could do to better the situation.

While Pengelly wandered with his net through the sand dunes the rest of us marched or rather hobbled in a parade through a silent main thoroughfare--on parade to show the Army might that the population could depend upon. It was the worst parade that I have ever seen or shared in. There were thousands, tens of thousands of us, nearly all with the pallor of six weeks below decks seeping into the very bones, the usual pasty pallor of British faces. The bare knees were even worse to view, for they had never seen the light of day since the men had gone into the long trousers of puberty from the shorts of childhood when they were nine- or ten-year-olds. Just when the silent and hopeful-until-then pro-British South Africans thought that they had seen the worst, there was a groan arising from the silence as Sammy Crook, one of my favourites, a well-nigh midget Liverpudlian with a remarkable left eye that was both cast and swivelled, fell over his shorts that were like slacks to him. As he did so the shorts unrolled and in his efforts to contain them and roll them up he somehow got them wrapped up around his throat and arms. His left eye swivelled wildly. He could not call for aid but only emit a strangled grunt. As the spectators remained on the sidewalks silent and still four fellow gunners picked up Sammy and carried him along between them. The grunts from his tangle of trousers and shirt that was far too big for him made it appear that his bearers were toting between them an angry and trussed little porker. At the same time they were clawing with their spare hands at the rolling-down of their own shorts. No band could keep in cadence with the parade. The South Africans regarded us as another hazard to be faced, worse even than pro-Axis Afrikaners and the Duce driving down from the North. Rather than the clenched and mailed fist that would send the Duce and his myrmidions reeling back and get the Afrikaners on the track, they saw us as a hobble in a wrinkled crumple, with fingers not fists trying at best to roll their trousers up. The South Africans were all so well-fed and clothed, bronzed if bovine, and we were so pale, small and skinny. During our time at Durban the men, very

62

rarely, got into fights, generally with the Merchant Navy men who had crewed the ships that brought us, but there was no fracas that the shore and ship patrols could not handle, especially since I dressed the ship patrols in their British battle dress when they kept the peace through Durban of an evening.

The people were very kind to us. Kinder perhaps than they would have been if we had seemed more military. The guilds of ladies put on tea and parties and fed the soldiers well on dainties "to put the roses back in your cheeks. " Some mothers even cried into their handkerchiefs over us, thinking of what would happen to us when we faced the bellicose bronzed and battle-tried enemy.

The lady whose voice had been raised in song at the Pier Head to welcome our arrival was there to sing farewell to us when we sailed away up North on the third day. Her songs were still of the patriotic and British Loyalist variety but this time when she sang "There'll always be an England" there was a quaver in her voice that had not been there before. Cecil must have spun his grave on Table Mountain and the bones of Sir Bindon Blood must have rattled as we passed them on our way to battle.

6

We sailed out of Durban north on the Indian Ocean. Passing Madagascar on our starboard we made for Aden and the Red Sea. The short time we stayed at that rocky promontory while we took on water made it clear to me why one of the pipers of a Scots regiment who had been stationed there, wrote the sad squealing lament "The Barren Rock of Aden." All that I saw there were some waterworks of ancient times, several miles out of the garrison town, that the guide attributed to King Solomon. My doubts on their construction have remained. To verify the time and nature of their construction might mean a return on my part to Aden and I would much prefer a trip to Dubuque, Racine, or Memphis.

The Red Sea lapped against the sheikhdoms on one side and Ethiopia, Nubia, and the Sudan on the other. As we approached Port Suez where we were to disembark we passed the burnt-out hulk of the Georgic, beached and bare, stranded with only its struts remaining, baking in the blaze of the sun. It has always been a wonder to me that when we again could sail in the Mediterranean this wreck was towed back to Britain and rebuilt again as a troopship. I sailed in it later in the war.

We were met at Port Suez by all kinds of movement officers, clerks of all kinds. The R. A. F. personnel that we were carrying, and whom I had used as waiters, steward and pantry hands, had R. A. F. staff waiting to receive them. In charge of a parcel of clerks was an R. A. F. sergeant who had married the girl next door, in Splott, Phyllis Probert. I was glad to see him.

Len had been an insurance clerk in civilian life. He must have been worth his weight in gold as a chief clerk in a unit so young that all those good and healthy enough were still jostling to get into action.

He stuttered, like me, when he was at ease and at home, so we grimaced and spluttered together while the tens of thousands of men from the convoy were disembarked.

He told me that the R. A. F. files in Cairo were ready for burning and the whole British set-up was getting ready to evacuate. "If Stalingrad falls to Von Paulus" he said, "and if Mussolini keeps on going we'll all have to hole up around Haifa. That's in Palestine you know. Very near the plain of Armageddon." He gave me a knowing look that cheered me up. When he looked portentous or pontifical he looked funny, as clerks often do.

We had a good half-hour shouting and gesticulating against the crazy noise, colour, and apparent shambles of the debarkation until the manic screams of the sergeants, the silly expostulations of the officers, and the efficiency of the Movements staff got some sort of order about. Units were assembled and marched off. I handed over the marching orders to my Scots and Liverpudlian N. C. O. 's and went off to find six of the old-time soldiers who had come to us as sergeants, to make soldiers out of us. I had busted them down to gunners while we were still whiz-banging in England, but I could never get any unit to take them. One of them, Pilton, was extraordinary. He could take a Lewis gun, a Bren gun, or a rifle to pieces by passing his hands over it as if it were a well-cooked chicken. He was a real wrong-'un.

I did not feel anything like a good shepherd as I flagged my way back to Suez looking for the absent six gunners who had not shown up with our collection from Suez. Six absent out of two hundred and forty gunners, after a convoy trip of nearly ten weeks, barring the three days at Durban and the few hours ashore for some of them at Aden, was better than expected: I could hear some other units positively baying as they sought their absent ones.

The driver of the 15 cwt. Movement Control truck nodded to the left as we passed one of the lanes that led to the off-limit alleys of the suq.

"That's where they'll have holed up, sir. All the missing convoys end up down there--the real hard cases, the old sweats, the regulars. They spent most of their time in jankers when they were serving in pre-war days. It always was the suq, either here in Ismailia or Alex. that they made for. The Military Police and Shore Patrols will be down there already before they get to the tunnels, a regular rat's nest of them there are."

He slowed up and stopped for me. I stepped out into the crowd of merchants, gawkers, and Egyptians who had gathered to watch the action, as the MP's were frog-marching and hauling some of the runaways to the paddy wagons that had pulled up on the sides of the main drag, adjacent to the suq alleyway. There was a feeling of deep latent hostility to me and all of us among the crowd. They had nothing to thank us for. We'd been occupying the place on and off since Gordon, fifty years ago and more. The Italians might well be better military masters. They had promised to be, anyway.... Just as I got to the nearest backed-up paddy wagon four of my missing six were being flung into the back of it. They were naked save for women's blouses and straw hats, beflowered and wax-fruited in a mid-20's Harrogate or Chelthenham style. They had flagged all their webbing equipment, boots, rifle, even their crinkled khaki drill for whores and arrack of a rot-gut sort, all within the hour.

"You'll not be seeing them again and you'll not be sorry--eh?"

It was a Military Police sergeant who was talking to me.

"They'll be trucked down to the Port Authority jail and be charged from there. They'll be in jankers long before you reach the Desert--if we ever reach the Desert. The Western Desert, I mean, not the Sinai."

I nodded. "There are two more of this mob"--I nodded to Purden, Cockburn, Leydell and Devins--"They must have got away. There were two more, of the same kidney as these four."

"Aye, they got out the back way when they saw us coming. They were still wearing boots and them awful long draswers." He glanced down with half a grin to my pinned-up slacks. "They'll be back with your unit before you. They must have done some time in jankers here before." The Sergeant shook his head.

"It's a rough one. It's run by the Gyppos. They don't like us anyway, small blame to them. Those two who

67

got away are aiming for the Cairo glasshouse. That's run by the Army and the jailers are the likes of them, only they got away with it."

I nodded farewell to the sergeant and flagged a lift back to the entrainment area with a feeling of relief. The six of them had spent time in the locker on the convoy voyage. They had been the last of the shower that other units had unloaded on us to make up our numbers just before we sailed. They were old sweats, the six of them, with records of larceny going back as long as their service, which dated back to the late '20's.

The Orderly Officer had already handed them over to the M.P. squad that had a mobile jail in a caboose on the train. They dismounted near Cairo, still wearing their flowered blouses and decorated straw hats. I never saw them again, but I learned a lesson from them. I had failed to make anything of them, but I kept moving. Keep moving, leave the debris pile up behind. Keep moving. Hope only lies ahead, never behind, never static.

On the next day, still in the chuffing train, I saw my first camel. We had passed hundreds of peasant Egyptians who seemed in high spirits. Always they returned our waves out of the train windows with a gesture that we thought was welcome and affectionate. Only later did we realise that it was an obscene gesture of derision and contempt that in their eyes we deserved.

Later that day we disentrained within sight of the Pyramids. We lurched through deep sand to where harassed permanent staff had put up some tents. Somehow I got the battery sorted out and had the men fed and bedded down before I realised that night had fallen; it was full dark. Then, when I was ready to fall down and sleep myself the officers sent for me. In their lounge tent they offered me a drink and some shook hands with me, in their own dumb way wiping out their faint sense of failure and the trouble they had given me. They behaved like mock gentry. For some reason these minor characters had adopted at commissioned graduation a country squire type of jargon. They never said "Good morning" or "sit down" but instead hailed us and each other with "Good morning to you," and "sit down" became "sit you down" and so on, as if they were talking to ostlers, stablemen, or fellow huntsmen and horsemen.

I'm all for hierarchy. My first published article was

on Plato. There is anarchy where there is not hierarchy.
But while hierarchy is set by defined circles of professional
or other rigid structures there must be room between the
rungs of the ladder, the interstices towards the seats of office. I have always been unable to appreciate to the full the
great importance that we yield to professional decor. To
me it always had been both enviable and a blanket of security
but a mix of good and bad. How else had it been that so
many of the great librarians have been so professionally un-
qualified?

My trouble had been that I have never been able to
step off into a parade on the correct beat or with the right
foot and it may have something to do with my stammer, but
I am never quite sure where lies left or right; they both
seem the same to me. I love to march, for instance, but
it has to be on my own, where I will not confuse a rank.
A military tattoo gives me inordinate pleasure and to see
the Marine band, the bugling quick-stepping Ghurkha Rifles,
the majestic military-band of the Papuan Army, the measured
tread of the British Coldstream Guards, moves me well-nigh
to tears.

John Philip Sousa composed marches that I can listen
to for hours when the rest of the family are away, and I
march up and down around the hassock in the living room
with my walking stick on my shoulder like a rifle.

During my Army years and despite all my professional
qualifications the men called me The Snake, particularly in
the desert, because my small round head was cropped to the
bone and my long neck was scrawny. That, I think, was the
reason for the nickname. My superiors called me The Penguin because of my rotund gait and waddle of a walk. Prod-
nose has always been my nickname in more academic or
library circumstances and I can understand them all, and
even sympathise with those who called me or saw me thus.
Although I have spent most of my spare time writing, when
I wasn't reading, I was never much to write home about.
But I have always been more like The Good Soldier Schweik
than I should have desired.

Introspection is not good for the soul, not for my soul
anyway. I always remember Joyce Cary, one of the best of
novelists, saying to me once that for vanity or other reasons
we neglect the power of luck upon our fortunes, and, reflecting, it does seem that luck plays a greater part in our lives
than perhaps we realise or ignore. Why else was Willi

Gotaas killed at El Alamein and I was not? Bombardier
Wellaway in the wagon lines by shell fire where I had been
talking to him just a minute before? Coming out of the fox-
holes at Anzio down to where the trucks were waiting on the
other side of the hill--there is a military term for the off-
side that I cannot recall--I was within an inch or so of a
fragment of a mortar shell passing through my neck. It
cut into the shoulder of my leather jerkin and went right
through it leaving a large hole in the jerkin without my feeling even a breath of it. Now that was another kind of luck,
and most welcome it was and has remained.

When I recall that bit of luck with the mortar near-
miss I remember that the gunners broke into a sort of cheers
as we passed them. I was in the Infantry by that time.
Commissioned after the Desert Campaign of '42-'43 that had
cleared the Axis out of Africa I had decided that since experience was what I was after I should enlist in the Infantry,
The Queen of Battles. After an incredible two months on
the square, where they tried to teach me how to drill with
a swagger stick and I failed them, I went to Infantry School
at Sarafand where I was happy for three months, graduating
second in my class, all of whom bar myself were Australian
or New Zealand sergeants being commissioned, like me, now
that the North African wars were over and nearly all the
Afrika Korps prisoners and Italian forces were in compounds
in Egypt or being sent to sweat, shiver or bask the war out
in North America.

7

The world's a stage, we are the players. Shakespeare was
right when he gave that soliloquy about our seven ages to
Jacques in As You Like It, one of my favourites of all the
plays. So popular is the speech, and the crowd is waiting
for it, that often the actor who plays the part is called on
again and again for an encore. This may be very flattering
but rather tiresome, especially if the play is enjoying a long
run. I remember that Herbert Marshall, a good actor who
served in World War I and lost a leg at it, delivered the
speech so well in later days that he was regularly applauded
when he played Jacques. Once he had to deliver the speech
six times to satisfy the encores of the audience.

This has never happened to me when I have told the
tale of my fourth age or act when I was a soldier. Actually
I have never appeared formally in a play, although I have
written them. I played the lead in a Shaw play once, the
title role. I was the Lion in Androcles and the Lion. I
was neither full of strange oaths nor was I bearded like the
pard. I was however whiskered like a beetroot for a while,
just after we landed in Egypt.

Gradually the men got their wrinkled K. D. 's into
shape, pressed, washed, and starched even by the flying
dhobis, free lance itinerants who were to be found near
every camp around Cairo and smartened up the uniforms for
less than a song and more than a piastre.

The men, pasty and generally meanly built, the product of the industrial cities, nearly all of them, took to the
desert like lizards or the desert rats who became their cog-
nomen. They were bronzed and agile in no time at all.
But I could not join them in their thriving under the sun.
My skin couldn't take it.

While they were stripped to their shorts, now pressed, bleached, and fitting them, and went about under my direction getting the camp in order, I was directing with my arms, neck and wherever my skin was visible, swathed in bandages as layer after layer of my skin frizzed.

It was Wee Mac who saved what was left of my bacon. Wee Mac was born in Pasadena. In his early youth his parents had returned to their native England--they were in the film distribution game--and Wee Mac, as the Glaswegians first called him, spoke like a native of Southampton. There he went to school and was commissioned straight from the school's Officer Training Corps into the Artillery. He was assigned to us and was married just before we sailed. Wee Mac was concerned about my scrofulous condition. When Brigade Orders noted the condition of decrepit artillery pieces in an Australian battery near the Syrian border where a Vichy French force was opposing us, Wee Mac arranged for a task force of our fitters, artificers, and gunners to be sent up there to aid them, under my direction. Somehow Wee Mac had learned that the climate was cooler up there. North of Nazareth where the Australian battery was encamped the sun which had been my undoing in Egypt smiled on me. My skin grew another layer that took well to the sun. In a week or so I was free of bandages and my head, arms, and knees could take the sun. I was never troubled again, as long as I did not take my shirt off. My solar topic I stamped on and worse and donned the side cap of the gunners.

The Australians were tall bronzed men who looked as if they had been bred in the open. They regarded the puny size, the difficult jargon of my task force--there were about a dozen of them, mainly from Glasgow and Liverpool--with a sort of affectionate disdain until they saw them swarming like ants around the guns, ammunition, fuses, and motor vehicles.

I can still see Gunner Haines looking with pain at a gun breech that they were greasing and saying sadly and with real emotion to the Australians gathered around him, "Sergeant, gunners, you've been very unkind to this breech."

My draft and their Australian companions became like one team of limber gunners. When the news came that the Australians were being issued with new artillery equipment our time with them was extended to months. We trained together. When they became as gun-wise as Gunner Haines and his muckos we returned to our encampment to find it testing out at full strength wholly new equipment under all sorts of trying conditions. Then they issued it to a newly arrived or battle-weary troop and stayed with them until they had mastered it. Bombardiers Wellaway and Chapman would then go back to the Artillery Depot at Aswan with a team and draw another complete issue. Now and then the Battery would try out the guns in battle but things had slowed to a stalemate west of El Alamein and under Auchinleck the British 8th Army was building a redoubt beset with mines, foxholes, camouflage where they drilled and built up their strength for the coming showdown with the Afrika Korps.

This was a pleasant time, more than a year of it. The Battery had become the best of its kind. I was detached for weeks at a time to serve with the Australians at their request. We would trundle past Tyre and Sidon on manoeuvres, turn left at Damascus to make a rendez-vous with an infantry group near Baalbek. Beirut became my favourite town in the Middle East. I got to know Jerusalem well, followed Gordon's Folly to the place of the Crucifix, heard Basutos chant a Gregorian Mass in the Church of the Holy Sepulchre with a glory in the voices that rivalled that of the 50,000 Welshmen who sang "Cwm Rhondda" at Cardiff Arms Park in 1981 when at their centenary Cardiff Rugby Club played a team composed from the best of the rest of the world and beat them.

The rest of the war years has nothing to do with my tale of Me. There have been some good books written about it, especially by Douglas Moorehead, the Australian writer. He has also written so well books about the White Nile and the Great Barrier Reef. Denis Johnston the playwright who wrote The Moon on the Yellow River in the 30's, a play that should be often revived, wrote my favourite book about the Desert War, Seven Rivers to Jordan, but it is hard to come by.

The war ushered in a new phase for me. Of all the days in it the first time I really saw the sun steady within me, beaming as if it was come to stay for a while, certainly for the duration of the war, was in December '41 when the Japanese bombed Pearl Harbour. Then I knew we could not lose. As I climbed out of the gun emplacement--we were retreating from Rommel at the time--I hummed to myself one of my favourite songs of George M. Cohan "The Yanks are Coming."

73

I am a great singer and talker, but nearly always when I am alone. My secretaries and colleagues always knew that I was at it when my door was closed. Suppliants, complainers, and other visitors used to get puzzled when after a knock at my door, a murmur from me and my secretary, her composed reappearance to tell them that I would see them now, and when on entering my office to see me standing alone by my desk in a sound of silence that almost was reverberating.

I have written and published elsewhere some of the incidents in my war. The time I saw the Pope with some Polish generals and U.S. admirals, of my sailing through the Aegean Islands in a caïque, a story about Sorrento that became a favourite of mine, and is well illustrated in colour in its version in the Saturday Evening Post, but it was "Venus Arising from the Sea" in the Palazzo Venezio and my year as Staff Officer Education that I spent at Perugia that were the life of me forever after.

All my life I had seen reproductions of Botticelli's "Venus" and of Michelangelo's "Pieta": the copies had become banal and worse, as they have done to most. Then, in Rome on my way to Perugia, that is among the hills of Umbria, near Todi and Assisi, I saw "Venus."

The Italians had placed on display in The Palazzo in gratitude for their being saved from the power of the Dog, about eighteen of their best paintings, almost one to a room. I wandered alone one morning early, just as the art show was opening, into the Palazzo and there, facing me was "Venus Arising from the Sea." It has an impact on me still. Whenever people complain, faculty, students, administration, readers of all kinds, that I have spent too much time and energy and money as a librarian on originals and first editions "Venus" comes like life to my mind. I wrote an article about it once, "The Shadow and the Substance." It has remained a main tenet of my creed. If I am to be remembered it should be for that: as one who always preferred the real, the primary source, to the copy. There was a great Henry VIII, the Tudor savage, by Holbein on show also. That was more frightening than any copy could be. I did not have this spiritual experience again until years later when the Chicago Museum of Art mounted a great display of the real Gauguin. His paintings were so sad and near despair that they revealed the awful condition of mankind in the Satanic grip of hedonism. A far cry, a cry for help, are the

paintings of Gauguin far from the ukeleles and swaying grass
skirts of the copies. The real alone is the truth. A letter
from Ezra Pound spluttering with mad indignation, written
from Rapallo in 1937, to Bertrand Russell and T. S. Eliot,
berating them for their anti-fascist attitude is altogether different from any copy or printed version of the text. Many
great libraries in the U.S. and Canada have spent thousands
of dollars on beautiful books, carefully prepared, printed in
Switzerland that are copies of The Book of Kells. They have
brought comfort and joy to thousands of readers. Then one
sees the original book at Trinity College, Dublin. When I
see it, every third year or so, I feel like destroying all the
fair copies and making pilgrimage mandatory for all who
would see the book. All copies of primary sources should
have stamped across them COPY like the signs that once
the lepers used to wear.

Russell and Whitehead corresponded almost daily over
Russell's concept and eventual publication of Principia Mathe-
matica. These letters have been published and studied and
all to some good by scholars and students: there is no doubt
of it. Yet the reading, the handling of the original in whatever form, adds a new dimension. There is no doubt of it,
yet it is difficult to explain or even to understand.

I was lucky to get to Perugia from Caserta. Before
I left the hospital, where I had ended up after some trouble
with a mortar on the Anzio Bridge Head, for good and all, I
had a medical board under the chairmanship of a colonel of
the old fire-eating brand. He had lost an arm, an eye, and
an ear in combat. For all I know he had lost a leg also.
I stood at attention before the Board. The medicos shuffled
their papers. The colonel screwed in his monocle and read
their report of my condition. He looked up at me, cleared
his throat.

"Ready, I have bad news for you." Oh Christ, I said
miserably to myself and swallowed. Back to the fox-holes
for Willie. The delousing, the foot inspection, the mortar
bombs, the patrols.

"Ready, " the colonel said again commiseratingly,
"you'll never fight again. "

Somehow I kept my face impassive, stamped, saluted
and marched out. I swear I stamped on a cloud. I never
felt the ground. I marched out it seemed, but I was wafted

out on a cloud of relief and a long slow smile came over me
with happiness and relief.

The next day I had to appear before a board that al-
located non-combat officers.   Most of the jobs were in
charge of Army dumps, of trains taking prisoners to Naples
for shipment, office work in administration around transit
camps, in Movement Control.   All or nearly all the alloca-
tions were of a drear order.   I had applied for military at-
taché employment in the most desirable places.   Washington
came first, then Canberra, Madrid, and Dublin.   Even Zagreb
sounded as if it could be interesting, although perhaps rather
hazardous.

I was offered none of these, not even charge of an
Army dump near Avellino.   They wanted to give me command
of a burial company.   This company, Italian diggers with
British N. C. O. 's went out into recent battlefields and bagged
or packed the dead soldiers for burial in an official War
cemetery.   Each body had to be identified whenever possible.
The ground was littered with live mines and was as dirty
and torn as any patch of earth could be.   I expostulated, near
to tears.

The chairman said weakly "But Will, we thought you'd
like it.   You have your own jeep."   I persuaded them to give
me some time and I went and told my tale of woe and for
help went to an Inniskilling who had gone the same route as
I had but, because of family clout and connections had got a
job in the palace at Caserta as secretary to a secretary who
was secretary to the Military Secretary for the British.   We
had been more than nodding acquaintances; he owed me about
£10, and, like most of the battalion thought that I was a connection of Sir Felix Ready, who was Quarter Master General
of the Forces.   He got me out of the grave digging and assigned me to Perugia, where the British Army School was to
open.

When I got to Perugia, having stayed off along the
way in the Abruzzi, I found myself getting more and more
in love with the Italian landscape and even more with the
people.   Before I left Rome I had visited various archives
and libraries.   In nearly every case I found an Irishman, a
neutral in the war, more than happy to welcome me, to bend
the rules a bit to get me into the stacks.   I was awestruck
at the untapped wealth and extent of the collections, well-
nigh unused for years, and with no apparent intention of ever

throwing them open, ever. That condition still remains.
There is so much early Americana still in the archives of
the Church, and in Europe generally, that negotiations on a
high national level should be in progress, should have been
for years, to bring them to a well-housed and safely guarded
and funded depository over here. Preferably, I believe that
depositories should be underground in the vast caves that are
available, with ample reading space and rooms for scholars
of all kinds. This should be the task of a national academy,
U. S. and Canadian.

Perugia housed an institute that was established under
the Duce as Universita par gli Stranieri. A mural of Mussolini, in a most belligerant pose, covered the back of the
Auditorium Hall. Perugia had been known to me only as a
town where they made chocolates and had a soccer team.
The road wound uphill to the peak, the crown of the town.
There I spent the last year of my life in the Army. It was
a Brigade H. Q. town and the Army had taken over the municipal offices. There was a steady flow of men and materials
to the front, where the Germans under Vesselring were bat-
tling brilliantly and well, making the Allies pay dearly for
every advance through Northern Italy.

The Universita par Stranieri was taken over by the
British for postwar planning, for giving the squaddies a ba-
sinful of what to hope for after the war.

Britain was far less generous than were the Canadians
or Americans on postwar education for the troops. Universities in Britain were still very restricted, and not properly
funded or prepared to offer anything like G. I. education
grants. Only those in the Military whose university education had been interrupted by the war were awarded grants to
continue. There was no provision for the thousands who
would have benefitted from the chance of going to University
on a grant similar to the G. I. University instructors who
could not avoid it were pressed into uniforms and flown out
to further the higher education of those who had started in
universities before they had joined up or been drafted. This
was a grave and mean mistake, thoroughly old English in its
philosophy.

The British Army School was under the direction of a
"schoolie, " an old-time regular school teacher. He had
taught the children of regular soldier families abroad for
years. The great bulk of the School's intake was from the

77

ranks, with special emphasis on what they could expect when they returned to civil life. It was all well-intentioned, but turned out to be far from the reality, as planning generally is. However, it gave the soldiers a break, something of a rest as the war ground down. It was a wonderful time for me as it brought me to a library again and into Adult Education for the first time in my life. I loved it.

To begin with there was already a collection of some tens of thousands of British books in the School Library. These had been collected as a come-on for the university's tourists and students during the 1930's. They were good reading books generally, and by the time the Army School opened for business in the late fall of '44 boxes of new books were arriving from Britain.

Anthony Burgess was opening the same sort of boxes sent to Gibraltar where he was stationed at about the same time as I was uncrating them in Perugia. We have talked about it now and then and in his novel A Vision of Battlements he makes reference to them. They were delightful books, selected mainly by flâneurs, art books, books on costume, large expensive coffee-table books that had survived the war in some warehouse or other, and the book selectors must have cooed with delight at the quality and style of them. I added them to the library collection that was being denuded of foreign language books, very properly, by those other units and armies that had need of them, save for the Italian books. Those I kept.

I used to lecture to the whole assembled classes of the aspirants after knowledge of what it seemed they could expect to encounter in Britain when the war was over. The Association of British Current Affairs published a spate of pamphlets on the matter that received great circulation. Often I would go to an infantry unit that had been pulled out of action for a rest, for some kind of cultural break. I enjoyed these visits too. I found these units, being infantry, extremely cynical of the How it is going to be pamphlets. One outfit, that I recall with pleasure, was commanded by a very civil Commanding Officer who was mainly occupied with his Quarter Master. They were dealing with a rascal of a black marketeer who was anxious to obtain a load of used boots. They had two truckloads of these old infantry boots. The unit had been issued with new boots by a supply officer who still remembered the legend that was truth, that General Montgomery, who loved the infantry, had demanded new boots

for them all before El Alamein. When the high-ranking officer in charge of supplies had expostulated, he sent him
packing, out on to the road that led to Burg-el-Arab and ordered him to report to his base in disgrace as best he could.
The base was in Britain, and the successor to the expostu-
lator had new boots for all the infantry within 72 hours, as
Monty had ordered.

So it presented no real difficulty, the getting of new
boots, nor did the traffic in the discarded footwear.

The deal with the black marketeer was concluded
while I was still with the unit and with the proceeds the
colonel had a banquet, Arab style, under the trees, where
all the battalion stretched and lounged around huge glowing
red-and-grey spits where whole oxen were roasted along
with every other form of living thing, and there were grapes
to swallow, oranges to eat, good bread that was baked on
the spot. There was wine and beer for all. The villagers
who were hired to prepare and serve the barbecue wandered
around with their families. It was like a scene from Robin
Hood. Two days later I gave my lecture in the open, where
the barbecue had been. The news I brought them, culled
from the ABCA sheets, was received languidly and pleasantly,
but this I learned, and it has affected my teaching ever since:
the fact that it was an infantryman talking to them made
them realise that there might be something in it. I was one
of them. The next day I gave a talk on America, mainly
based on my history work for a degree, from all the books
American that I had read, and from the Americans whom I
had met in the Desert around Tunis and an air force unit
that was stationed near the Syrian border. They were new
and strange to me, but since I had met them while I was a
serving soldier, and since then had been Infantry among the
Greek Islands, Monte Cassino, and Anzio, they listened to
me tell the truth as I knew it, and respected me.

8

A teacher needs respect and it is only come by when there is evidence of fellowship with the student. I have been able to introduce this into my teaching, in library schools particularly, and in more academic courses in Bibliography and Library Management. I could not teach without it.

By the beginning of 1945 I was teaching therefore in Adult Education, persuading a transient population of the School to read and use the library and organised groups of student soldiers to make field studies of Perugia, other hill towns, such as Todi and, most of all, of Assisi. With them I had discovered a pottery works still in production, metal workers, and the manager of the famed chocolate factory that was gearing up for postwar production. The "Venus," the Holbein, the "Pieta," the drawings of Leonardo had convinced me of the essential need for primary sources in any research project such as a cadaver for anatomical drawings, an original Botticelli and not a slide for Art History, statues and not classroom casts. All this experience should be transferable for credit, for professional recognition. While this did not affect me, since I was professionally qualified already, it enhanced my work life enormously, and, more importantly and still in abeyance, it should be recognized as qualifications by the governing bodies of library, education, social service and other organisations.

Another feature of my life there that has sustained me came when I had become an impresario--but more of that later.

The Army School had a fine auditorium that under the Schoolie Colonel was used for audio-visual lectures, commendatory and warning addresses. There was great concern that the students have highly polished boots, webb equipment especially belt, blancoed, bleached, and blanched. This would have had a dreadful effect should the soldiers have to face combat duty following their course of instruction. People like that colonel got a glow in their eyes whenever they were able to promote the use of blanco. There must have been a drug in it for old soldier sahibs.

During my stay in hospital at Caserta, where I was punctured every few hours with needle injections of the new drug penicillin, a hem-stitching job had been done on my arm and sinews. While I was recovering I picked up the lingo of the ward maids and other workers around the Army complex of Caserta, which at the time held both an Army HQ and hospital area. It had been the palace and grounds of the Bourbon kings of Naples. There were hundreds of local people working out and around there for the Allies; cooks, ward maids, gardeners, road menders, translators, doctors.... I was shuffling around the yards and gardens before I could walk properly. My left leg was in a cast and my left arm, the one I use the most, hence my stutter, was strapped somehow above my head, with wires coming out of the fingers and attached to a rubber band around my shoulder. It gave that part of me the look of an Aeolian harp. It was a great conversation piece. I went to Confession there once and all the priest could talk about--he spoke English--was the wires. He gave me absolution without my confessing anything, which is as it should be anyhow.

Because of my walks and talks with the locals, and with my final healing at Sorrento, I spoke the lingo fluently. When I got to Perugia I engaged the Peruginis in conversation and greetings.

To cap it all I was wearing a caubeen. Caubeen was a hat word I had not heard before. Alfie Burton brought me one as a present just before I was discharged as whole, fit for anything but combat. Caubeen was a hat that Alfie had devised out of some captured Axis grey-green overcoats. He had made twenty caps of them, enough for the officers and some of the band. I never saw Alfie in a caubeen. He always looked as if he was selling something, dressed as nattily as any salesman, with his well shaved hatchet face that broke into a smile when he wished it, a piano opening, with great white keys of teeth. He wore a service hat that he had acquired somehow from a Quarter Master in the Brigade of Guards. Alfie was our Quarter Master, a real old sweat. He never took his hat off and wore his socks to bed.

The caubeen had the shape, style, and dimension of
a Basque or Breton bonnet, but about twice as roomy as a
beret. The right side drooped to the shoulder. The left
was elevated by a motif of the Inniskilling badge, a castle
and a flag. This motif was about the size of a man's hand.
It was cast out of smelted metal cookware that gave it a
dull sheen. Dramatically--I did not know the couturier,
the haberdasher, or the culprit designer--the badge nested
in a plumage of pigeon feathers dyed a pale blue, with a
beak.

If the caubeen was new to me, and looking anything
but Irish, it was a positive apparition to the people of Perugia. Il Capitano Irlandese was their name for me. As my
lingo lessened and the gentle Umbrian sky and space made
one even of the caubeen and myself, generally my time in
the storied city became one of peace and excitement. A
time of beginning again it was for me as I learned of the
prospects in the future of running a library. Until then I
never really though I'd last the war.

Anybody who has run a Library of whatever size and
condition, and I have run them all, from school libraries,
commercial branch offices, law offices, archival libraries,
the collection at the Stratford Shakespeare Festival Theatre
in Canada, as well as my usual beat in the academic libraries, knows that there is more to the job than saying
"shush!" and often along with the job came other positions
that seem far removed from books yet are an essential part
of the library economy.

Actually the Library is the circle centre, like the
inner of the rings on a curling rink. We tend to think of
a library as shelves, stacks of books, a building full of
them, all giving employment to a library staff that becomes
increasingly concerned with their own status and security,
their place in the hierarchy, technology ... about everything
that keeps them away from books and people. Just as a fiddle is a piece of wood and gut, a picture just a daub, so is
a library just a pile of print in varying condition of decay,
until it is wed to the reader. It is the fiddler and his listeners, his listeners, not just only other members of the
band, who bring the instrument to life. The painter brushes
thumbs and spatulates for him or her, he knows not who.
No library worker can know the union that occurs between
the book and the reader. All a librarian can do, and that
is plenty, a life's work, is to bring the books, shelve them

in an order on the shelves, let the reading world know about them, and go riding off like Shane to save the books from a dusty death some place else and bring them back to safety. It's nice work, if you can get it.

The union of books and readers, readers of all ages, sizes and conditions, is a private affair, but every librarian is involved also in administrative affairs that on the surface have little or nothing to do with his essential job. Teaching, either collectively as a staff, or as an individual, is an essential part of the game. I often wish that libraries were able to devise something like the confessionals on wheels that are used in Italy, and in the Brompton Oratory, a church in London.

In Italy during the war Italian priests, who believed that they had a knowledge of English, would advertise discreetly with an English Spoken Here sign on the outside of their boxes. They would push their curtained cabinet around the chairless church to where there was a possible group of likely penitents, and beckon for custom or just wait in the box with the curtains pulled back, seemingly reading their Office but watching the traffic with one good eye. It was in one of these that the priest got so fascinated with the wires from my fingers that he gave me unconditional absolution without my confessing any thought, word, or deed that may have given Heaven some concern.

So delighted was I with the wheeled convenience, and the idea of these mobile penitential boxes that I wrote a story on one of them after the war, called "The Sin of Cement." It still so fascinates and amuses me, I often use it as the mainstream of a talk, provided I think the audience is right.

All this is a prelude to an idea that has only recently come to me that we should have them in the libraries, with a librarian on the seat on one side and an inquiring reader in a comfortable seat, not kneeling but relaxing at ease on the other side, with no grill in the middle. There any reader seeking advice and book news, not just the way to the washrooms, could come for counsel and advice.

All through Library life we get embarrassed and muttered enquiries about books that seem not quite proper to the would-be reader. Books can furnish the knowledge for a crime, infuse a revolution with reasons false or true, like Das Kapital, Mein Kampf, or the writings of the Webbs or of Towney. In Dubious Battle by John Steinbeck or his Grapes of Wrath, Waiting for Lefty by Clifford Odets, hundreds more that can start a fire in the belly and readers can look askance or do more at their leaders because of book reading. That is why Hitler burned them, why the English kept their subject people illiterate as long as possible. They were wrong, both Hitler and the Raj. Illiteracy is a dangerous thing to foster, showing a burning concern with the nature of the book is equally foolish. It is better to foster alliteracy--a word that I have coined--which teaches people to read badly and never books, save for information.

So there is a fertile field for librarians. To foster the Commonweal encourage the readers to read only what is relevant for information. Make spaniels out of the books, to be used for Information Retrieval Only, or for titillation or scares, or manuals of how-to-do-it.

The mobile counselling cabinet that I would call a mobilaire is a thing of the future that has arisen from the past. There will be more and more need of them as the libraries become places where only the books that are needed are in constant use and demand. They share the prime, extravagantly shelved and housed, space in the Main Library with all the other books. This is a cause of great and unnecessary expense and severely curtails the readers from free access to their books. The popular reading is smothered by a plethora of books that are essential to any library, but need and should receive more austere, cool basement space. They make up about 80 percent of the holdings.

The whole of the library economy, if it is to succeed at all, as it has not yet, must make full use of its resources. We hear, read, and accept the revolution that the new technology has planted in the old scheme of things yet we neglect the most powerful revolution of the lot that is in the life style and thinking of the people.

We have entered into a world that never was before, dragging our canoe behind us when we should be hang gliding at the very least for people to see us and to begin to understand the benefit of books. Books in the popular conceit went out with the buggy. Librarians, teachers, scholars, readers of all kinds are likely to contain, entertain, and promote this fallacy.

There is many a professional academic, anxious to

85

obtain a slice of the budget pie to rear a new building in
his or her image and likeness, or a newly equipped listening
room, or a theatre or studio workshop, who will nod towards
the general direction of the library in the course of his presentation and say:

"After all, there is money to be salvaged from the
library budget. Now anything we need in the way of information can be got by pressing a button, or getting a reprint
for a dime. We can get a cassette of Dante's Inferno in
the Lurgan translation, lie down and read it on the ceiling,
with the Dali illustrations." This is but the tip of the iceberg. The technologists are out to do the library in, and
not with malice aforethought but because they are romantics
at heart. Romanticism is and always has been the harbinger
of great troubles to come. It is the very devil.

We are experiencing, not necessarily enjoying, a
standard of living better than people, save for the very
privileged few, have ever known before in our society. We
are concerned with our health, our comfort, our longevity
as never before. Thorstein Veblen, the great economist, at
the turn of the century said that people, once they have benefitted from a more prosperous and easier way of life, are
loath to give up any of it. We have become consumers who
prefer to press a button than to handle a spade. It costs
more, but we can afford it, at a terrible cost to the have-
not people of the world who experience a misery around them
that is the more galling as they see on television the hedonism that we have embraced and that they want to share.
The Foreign Minister for Canada said recently that we have
more to fear from the wrath of the have-nots, who are the
greater part of the population of the world, than we have
from our own preoccupation with technology and the new order that we have not only accepted but delight in.

The family, the neighborhood are vanishing and we
pay for their extinction greedily.

The small schools have vanished into the maw of
large administrative units. The teachers are becoming specialists. "I know nothing about Physics," says one. "I'm
a Sociology person myself," says another.

The small local stores have been replaced by large
well-packed malls. Why learn to read when the press of a
button will bring the information. Why learn at all, when

86

learning is so hard and is becoming the preserve of research specialists. It is in finding the relation between Physics and Sociology that real progress towards what we inchoately seek --that the real breakthroughs in our ignorance--lie.

Librarians like most professionals spent too much time together in a world that they have made. It is becoming more and more esoteric and technological. They talk a jargon full of acronyms and in-jokes. Worse, they even bring it home with them and at parties seek out one another to exchange the gossip of their trade while their families look on and wonder what they can do about it. Gossip can be a curse.

That is one blessing about being an impresario. There is nothing more different from usual library practice.

At Perugia, with the help of Epiphano, the funeral director, I set up the Sunday concerts. The great thing about them was contributed by Colonel Schoolie. He insisted that for every Italian artiste there should be a British one. Italy at the time was teeming with artistes, forlorn, without a stage to present their talent, and they were hungry and well-nigh ragged to boot. Epiphano could find them all. We had surplus food, flogged boots and blankets to pay them with, and a light truck that I could send almost anywhere to pick them up, their entourage, and instruments, and back-up bands. The Army had established a Women's Army Centre at Perugia--I remember Pamela Frankan and others of her ilk who held high rank coming around on tours of inspectation. Everyone of them who were stationed at Perugia, as officer clerks, cooks, typists, drivers and a few teachers at the British Army School, all of them were a great help and enjoyed the forays and the hospitality they could afford the women artistes, making them members of their barracks, turning it into a household.

Those Sunday concerts became famous through Perugia, all over Umbria. The artistes left on Tuesday or Wednesday after a week's stay that included rehearsals and the dance I held for them on Friday nights. Peruginis were invited, the nurses from the nearby Canadian and British hospitals--altogether it was a ball.

Besides the Army School whose attendance at first was obligatory and perfunctory, the nurses and the Women's Army, more than two-thirds of the seats in the Auditorium went to the Peruginis. The tickets were all free; it was the getting of them was the problem.

The hall was full long before the hour of concert. The artistes were being nervous and artistic around the green room, the Italian artistes I mean, the British contingent was well-nigh a steady one and took it all with more of a bovine good nature than any show of emotion. There was Sergeant Gormley who was for openers every week, straight after the National Anthem. He sang "Old Father Thames" one week, bowed and marched off. It was a rare occasion when he yielded to the demands for an encore from the bewildered Italian audience and then, taking a deep breath, he would recite "The Road to Mandalay." It stunned the Peruginis, confirmed them in their deep-held view that the British were a subtle people whose art was beyond the comprehension of their most erudite commentators.

Sergeant Gormley was a regular, every week. Students of all kinds could come and go, sing "In Summertime on Bredon" or "Sweet Lass of Richmond Hill." Now and then a piano player would tinkle the ivories with such well known favourites as "One of The Ruins that Cromwell Knocked Abaht a Bit" or with a song accompanying his piano-playing from "In a Monastery Garden."

But Sergeant Gormley was a regular. He was in charge of our motor transport pool. I could always depend on him, and he did have a good bar-room baritone. My other two standbys who performed every week were Ianto Taliesin and Claude Wickham. Ianto was a little gnome from Blanau Festiniog where they split the slates and my regular runner for all the time I was at Perugia. He didn't speak English, only a broken form of Welsh, but was a great performer with the spoons that he would play while dancing a strange Druidic jig. Claude was our barracks man, in charge of the cleaning staff. He had a light operatic tenor and could be depended on for a solo, accompanied by Epiphano on the piano, from The Desert Song, The Pirates of Penzance or Floradora.

The Italians on the other hand, were twanging with nerves, invariably, as they prepared to go on. I remember a little piano player, in formal evening dress that was still deeply creased since its folding during the war years. He wore white cotton gloves. Taking them off, adjusting the piano stool were great entertainment that Victor Borge would

88

have envied. He was surrounded by his entourage. They called him Maestro, nearly carried him on and off the stage, crowded the wings and gave him barley water to sip between numbers.

At the interval, when I could get away from Colonel Schoolie and the Army Staff, the Italians would be surrounded by Army trying hard to make contact, to relate, for one reason or another. I was the centre of it all, Il Impresario, Capitano Irlandese.

They were happy days and we were one with the people. They came to visit me for books about Britain and Americana. The books I had uncrated from the flâneurs in London, the coffee-table books were a great help to both me and the would-be readers since they were all picture books. I learned more about the Italians than I had ever dreamed of. While they learned something about us we remained a mystery to them. They all had relatives in Britain or North America. They intended to join them as soon as they could and these concerts were a help that way.

This relationship I see more and more important, even vital, and it all leads back to books in the end. There was plenty of room and help for me in the future that I found in Perugia.

The general and well used books should be shelved at eye level. It is folly to shelve browsing books on bottom shelves where the only way to read them is by squatting and crawling. The high level shelves should also go, to be replaced by space for pictures.

All these ideas came to me as a result of my years in Cardiff Public Library. I had time to try out the most minor of them in the British Army School at Perugia where the shelves, denuded of all save British and Italian books, gave an opportunity for such eye to book relation.

Most of all it was as an impresario at Perugia that I learned a presentation skill, that my experience in that Italian hill town library was to stand me in good stead. More and more librarians are adopting it so that, outside the academic libraries, it is a rare one that does not offer some kind of non-book performance.

When I went into a public library today I saw that

there was showing a film of Krishnamurti in Room 201, a talk on mimes and puppets in another room. Coffee would be available and readers were encouraged to bring their own bag lunches. These shows were an example of the kind of non-book activity offered daily, Monday through Friday. They were obviously scheduled for office workers and the early evening shows provided on the same day were on consumer reports, legal aid, social security with on Wednesday evening a showing of a silent film comic of Ben Blue or Charlie Chase, one of my favourites. The University Libraries need only advertise, and they should, the many lectures, debates, plays and films going on all around the campus. I noticed last week that there were two federal cabinet ministers, one talking to a Foreign Affairs Group and the other to Amnesty International. An anti-Nuke physicist from Pittsburgh was talking to the Disarmament Group. A poet was reciting her wares, on a Government grant that was financing her trip across the continent, giving readings to groups everywhere, in small towns that had never even seen a poet before and to university writers' clubs that hung on every word that they could hear. The trouble is that writers generally are not very good with the spoken word. I would go miles on a snowy night or through a blizzard to hear Eudora Welty or John Betjeman, but William Yeats above all, and most others, were appalling readers and continue to be so on the tapes and records.

Most of the larger libraries, public and academic, have good collections of this material that can be borrowed, and following, but not emulating, the listening room at the Lamont Library in Harvard there are listening rooms with their own non-circulating collections of tapes, videos, and records and, most important, set in a book room with books that relate to the audio-visual collection and a librarian in charge who is a buff on this area of library endeavour.

I was never a buff in the audio-visual, but I actually quickened my pace for it when I got near the Lamont, where Jack Sweeney ran the poetry reading room, the audio-visual, that was part of it and participated in the Browsing Room, so that students and others, like me, went there not to doze but to crop at the pasture of the books that were collected there to read just for the pleasure of it.

The keeper there was a grand New England type. There are Yankee influences to be found strong as far west as Michigan's Ann Arbor, but Boston is the wellspring of it.

A sprawling sleeping student is an ugly sight but there was never one to be seen in the Morison Room. Should a student even be found nodding over the book selected for reading Miss Pruitt came floating along with some celerity in her gait and fire smouldering in her eyes. She would shake or something the dozy student and curtly, or as curtly as she could, for she was basically kindly--

"Read! Damn you, read! You are to browse in here, not doze. You'll be sleeping next. This is the Morison Browsing Room. See--on the door? So browse, damn you, browse. Or get out and--what's the word? Ah yes, Kip. Go and kip in the basement. Or, walk over to M. I. T. You'll find lots the likes of you over there. Now, Enright." Her voice dropped and she nodded Enright up to her desk.

"You're right, Enright. There are few lawyer writers, not like the doctors. Like the fellow Crichton who wrote The Andromeda Strain here in the middle of his final medicals. And that Jonathan Miller is a doctor, a medical doctor, I mean. So was Treves, who wrote the Elephant Man. We've an edition of it here, 1920's I think, that's a joy to handle. And one of that Monty Python crowd...." She made a moue of distaste "a reformed alcoholic--he talks about it-- he's a script-writer, and so it goes. He's like a character in those awful Doctor TV series. But there are good lawyer writers, or writers about the Law. Poor old Galsworthy was just a nag of a writer, but J. G. Cozzens has written two good novels about the Law, as good as his book on the Military, Guard of Honour. But best of all is a local boy. I think nobody here pretends to know him, because he went to Boston College. George V. Higgins. I wonder where he got that George from? It's like that McCarthy girl in the Catalog Department whose front name is Rowena.

"Here, I've got the last novel of Higgins here. The Digger's Game. It's very good, his best. He's too full of locker-room dirty talk that you'd hear from B. C. College men, but it's a better novel than we've turned out here in years. They made a good movie out of Eddie Coyle and his friends, about the low-life southies, but his Kennedy book has caught the heart of the matter about those folk: it's very melancholy, with the gallows humour you find among the Jews and the Irish. Higgins got above himself and wrote a couple of books like Ivy Compton Burnett: he's nearly all dialogue. He's good, very good. I'd put him up there with the younger Walker Percy, The Moviegoer." She nodded briefly to Enright and passed him the Higgins book.

91

"Here. You can charge it out at the Main Desk. It's from the general collection, not the Browsing Room."

That is the way to run a Browsing Room. There are few if any others like it. Keyes Metcalf built the Lamont to clear the student crowds from the Widener, big, vast, ugly, and awkward, with ten million books on the shelves and a catalog that filled rooms with its cabinets. The Lamont was very popular, and remains so, but filled so many students with a desire for more, and an ability to use libraries with far less help save what the catalog would give them, and the bibliographies, that the congestion in the Widener became thicker than ever.

The Widener was enlivened now and then by one of the curators of the catalog. It could be a boring and meticulous job and the questions of the myopic readers often matched it. There can be no more arrogant and self-centered a person than a scholar hot on some research scent or other. The curator was peering over a catalog tray that was still in the catalog with this crusty old scholar who hated Oxford.

"I wouldn't send a cat to Oxford." He almost spat these words out, or similar ones, frequently.

The curator's father had not been to Oxford but had friends there at one time. This Harvard scholar was a Wittgenstein disciple and very anti-Bertrand Russell; in fact he was researching an attack on Russell and his circle. He had been pestering her about some bibliographic data in the catalog. He was critical, rude, and wrong. The curator could stand no more of it. Russell had been a companion of her Dad.

"Here" she said, pulling the tray of loose cards out of the cabinet--it was loose because she had been interpolating in it--"Here. Look it up for your self." And she crowned the crusty head that was still bent down with the upended tray so that cards nearly smothered him, and the vehemence with which she had slammed the tray on his head left him dazed and bewildered as the cards slipped off his head, most of them, and gathered around his feet. The curator walked away with a sigh of relief. Other colleagues set the tray to rights; it took hours of work, while two others led the curmudgeon scholar out on to the steps of the Widener and sat him in the sun. Gradually he got over the shock of being the bitten biter and was never so unpleasant again.

9

Although I did not know it then the tap tap tap of the donkeys as they trotted down the cobbled streets of Perugia, delivering the milk and the kindling for the fires during the coming winter, were the first I really heard of the clop of the horses through Harvard Yard some years later.

I got back to Cardiff on an acronym leave before the war was over, in April 1945. It was but a brief leave of less than a month, and it was called LIAP: Leave in Advance of PYTHON. PYTHON was a leave based on a serpent with his tail in his mouth. It was intended to show that no soldier would be allowed home until he had been replaced by another. Then, with the war in Europe slowing down, the brass decided that the names and numbers of the lucky few who had been overseas for about five years, had been in combat, and had a few more qualifications, would be drawn by lottery and a small number allowed a brief leave before PYTHON. They were the lucky LIAP men, and I was one of them. For all intents and purposes the war had passed me by. During the month of April I was home. I visited Cardiff Public Library, saw many of the same old faces doing the same old things and decided to give in my notice. My job until then had been secure because I was in the Services.

Somebody stole my caubeen on the afternoon of my wedding day. We visited Truro, Newport, and London before the time of my return was up, and during the voyage back from Italy the war came to an end. This is a tale, my LIAP leave, that deserves relation as a separate by others than myself; I am too close to it still. But at Naples I stayed at a Transit Camp full of LILOPS. These were soldiers who were granted Leaves in Lieu of PYTHON meaning that they had lost their PYTHON privileges if ever they had had them.

93

Then, on an Air Force Base near Caserta I met the
LOLLIPOPS. These were men who flew home on the daily
Mosquito flights and were flown back in a week or so and
they were enjoying or accepting Lots of Little Leaves in Lieu
of PYTHON. I became a lucky Lollipop in September '45. By
this time big bombers were flying home with soldiers instead
of bombs in the belly of the planes. My plane caught a fire
in its engines and had to land again at Bari, delaying my return by over a week. Then, on a gusty airport in East An-
glia I was told to report to my regimental depot which was
at Omagh in the North of Ireland. This, by ground and sea
transportation, would have delayed my return home by at
least another week. It revealed also how muddled were my
records. I had never been to Omagh, to the North of Ireland for that matter. I was commissioned into the regiment
in Sarafand, in Palestine as it was then. Since that date,
the Royal Irish Fusiliers tried to claim me since I was the
only officer attached to that battalion who got away from the
Aegean damp squib of the campaign that only Churchill and
Hitler recognised as a potential threat that their generals
denied. But the Irish Fusiliers found a real officer of their
own somewhere in the Middle East, and my papers were on
the move again. This time the Army Education Corps claimed
me as a staff officer. I persuaded the Movements Officer
that my papers were at Beverley, in Yorkshire, at Army
Education HQ and, sure enough, they had a record of me
when I reported there late that night.

They gave me an indefinite leave the next morning,
and I rejoined my wife at her hospital near Aldershot. We
took off for Cardiff right away. The Welsh Regiment greeted
me like a brother at their Cardiff depot, and gave me a pass
and travel orders so that we could proceed to Dublin on vacation.

I remember clearly visiting the National Library.
There the noble foyer was piled shoulder high with bound
volumes of newspaper. Hayes, the National Librarian, and
I got on well together for he had written a book on the history
of rugby football. Through his candid friendship I was made
free of the library which even then was run in the 19th Century style. Even the catalog of some of its best holdings
were hand-written in a ledger. I visited Trinity College Library and found it very much the same. The riches to be
handled in books and manuscripts were beyond any concept
of collections that I had ever dreamed of. Imagine having
The Book of Kells in the Trinity College Library, surrounded

by master works of the same order, dating back to the 7th
and 8th century. Samuel Beckett used the Trinity Library. He
was a student there until the war, when he was an instructor
in France and became a hero of the Resistance. The National University that was founded in the 1900's, to counter-
balance the Establishment influence of Trinity, had no real
library of its own, so James Joyce and the others used the
National Library where James Stephens, a great little man,
poet and teller of tales, was on the staff. So was Thomas
McGreevy whose poem on the burial of Red Hugh O'Donnell
in Spain is one that I recall nearly daily.

There was a good tight Library School being run by
Miss Power at the National. Reading Frank O'Connor's account of his years in the county Library System gives great
joy to the reader, but must bring wide-eyed apprehension
about the system in the '30's even to the likes of me, who
regards O'Connor as being up there with Tchekhov, one of
the masters of the world when the short story is regarded
as among the great forms of art.

Digression is an essential part of any writing such as
this. It is not easy, for the writer, above all, is writing
for an audience, and once the reader is at a loss, wonders
what the writer is at or up to, he is likely to put the book
back on the shelf and try another one that is not so demanding of his memory and time. All the editors tell me this,
that a story must keep rolling. They are right, but thinking
of Beckett, Joyce, and O'Connor I am bound to take a chance
and tell of the strange bond that exists between all sorts of
university people. The Public Relations and the Fund Raising Departments, save for Harvard and a few others, are unable to understand this somehow mysterious bond or ring that
binds university people together. University people, that is,
who are of the often undeserving kind, that are full time students in their youth, generally centred in quarters altogether
too grand, where they can survive indifferent courses, planned
and compulsory curricula that are generally planned by
enthusiastic visionaries and muddied up by calculating faculty.
Students can survive all that, even flourish on it, as long as
they get together and talk, talk about anything, and use the
library services, however ignorantly and reluctantly.

This is the main path through a university education.
It imparts an air of kinship that is a puzzle. Somehow it
reminds me of military boot camp, or a campaign that you
have shared with others. Somehow this cannot be communi-

cated, even by writers of genius, to those who did not share, however meanly or otherwise, in the actual campaign.

Serious and better students who missed out in their youth at a university experience, often in their later years regret it, or suffer for it, they think, because they lost out, remain outside this ring.

This is something that librarians must realise, yet generally fail to do. They can supply the earnest who come, yet the life line, the only one that will save us, it seems to me, lies drooping in their hands or they coil it up to stop tripping over it.

We have confused information with learning. We lessen and diminish the value of the Book as the great, perhaps the only way to learning, by depending more and more on intercommunication.

The great ploy of my life has been union catalogs. When I began writing and talking about this in 1952, to groups of librarians in California, in Illinois, in Wisconsin, the reluctance to accept my arguments was based not so much, hardly at all, on philosophy as on the hard fact that it would make redundant the librarians who had catalogued in hundreds of institutions the very same book.

The union catalog is now established in the U.S. If there was an onlie begetter it was John Cronin of the Library of Congress, but scores of us have been wounded on the road that runs through the slough of particularity that had to be banked, drained, sodded, and stoned before it was used, more and more generally. We owe a great deal to the Ohio centre. The British National Bibliography is swinging alongside and Canada is in a process of delivery.

The short-title catalog is to me the basis of bibliography. It leads the reader to the books. There is no unanimity of purpose or principles between the librarians, the archivists and the scholars as yet, and the book and the readers suffer. We are brawling in groups against one another, and nothing that I have been able to do had led to an agreement that fulfills our needs.

Here, at this stage of the game of my life, now Emeritus, in calm of mind, all passion spent, I look back on the field of library economy and management and see behind me a litter of failure.

The sunken library, the economy and values of going underground, remain fully or partly realised in very few places. The great underground malls that are developing in metropolitan centres show some of the economic advantages that could accrue. In several of them I have seen the Noonday Theatre: the best version of Shaw's O'Flaherty VC I saw in such a place, and from these little, brief theatres there have extended groups of players who, funded by boards of education, now tour the schools, improving the wretched lot of actors and bringing drama to children who before had never seen a play save on the screen. The great difference between a live show and a screened version of the very best shows how much better is substance than shadow.

My mobilaire remains to most a comic puff on my part. Actually it is designed to remove the librarian from behind the desk, the office. It is a desk and an office, the bane of my life and the dream of most others, that are the guerdons that young graduate librarians crave.

My reshelving reform, whereby the books are being stacked or shelved where they will do the most good, is catching on among the better academic libraries that were already doing it before I realised the full value of it. I have seen it working in the underground library at Yale, across the road from Sterling, at Illinois where the new books in demand are also housed underground below the holy ground of the campus mall. They also have a good browsing library there in the Union Building. Part of the library at the University of British Columbia is built into the side of a hill, with a tree growing through it. The University of Minnesota has a vast reading room near the books on demand and the bare austerity and economy of the building is improved enormously by trees planted in and around the tables. I wish I had an opportunity to write more on this. Robert Downs, who was both the dean of the Graduate Library School at the University of Illinois and the University Librarian was one of the great librarians. His constant book writing of valuable and much needed quality in library literature is unique. As I grew more and more into the Library system of the U.S. he became more and more a friend of mine. I taught a term at his request in the Library School. It was he and Larry Powell, another great librarian of a different kind, who were responsible, I feel sure, for the award and honor of the Clarence Day Award coming to me when I was librarianating at Marquette University in Milwaukee, one of my most favored and favourite library positions.

Helen Waddell, who wrote so well on Héloise and
Abelard, on Mediaeval Latin lyrics, also wrote a fine book
The Wandering Scholars. In those days with Latin the lingua
franca of Academe a student could wander around Europe,
with one year in Padua, another in Bologna, a third in Paris
and a fourth in Oxford, listening to the great teachers in his
field performing from a stage to many hungry, many turbulent, many ragged and hungry who came to hear. There was
less, if any, registration or university administration in those
days. The fellows of the College ran the place. They gave
short shrift to trouble-makers and there were violent deaths,
beatings and jail following some of the lectures, or due to
the outraged citizens of the town who regard most students
as rogues and vagabonds anyhow, as they certainly were, unless they were clerks in good standing within a religious order or under the wing of a lay patron.

These turbulent ne'er do wells, as they were in their
lively youth, heaved the teetering stone of Europe upside
down. They were the scouts and more of the Revolution,
the revolution that is still going on and will continue as long
as the earth turns.

They began to grope for a harmony that they had
abandoned and achieved a cacophony instead. This must always accompany a revolution, an intellectual turnover that
had to come about as a result of their learning and condition.
That revolution was often bloody and always stumbling, and
learning was the cause of it all. A learned man is not necessarily a wise man and, save for the saints, is as voracious as any other.

Ignorance is the state of mind that the Devil and all
tyrants prefer to see flourish. Ignorance of certain kinds
is fostered by nearly all, for there is no balm in the truth,
especially not in learning. Learning improves the mind, and
there is no solace in that save that now and then there is a
shaft of joy that breaks through. It comes from the books
besides the entertainment and revelations that have been waiting for us if only we know where to look.

I began to spend most of my time in libraries following my doffing of my soldier's uniform. Luckily there was
at Balliol College in Oxford one of my teachers at University
College in Wales, and I was admitted to Balliol in 1945,
rather late in the year but with no red tape whatever, and
I began to read History with Christopher Hill. He later be-

came Master of Balliol and is one of the best of the 17th-century scholars. We opposed one another vigorously when I read my essays to him but it was more of an intellectual exercise that we both enjoyed rather than an attempt to persuade or reason one another into what each of us thought was right. We were as apart as could be. He was a Marxist, but no bigot, I was a Catholic with a bias so strong that it would have ruined any game of bowls. By the end of the year my bias had dissolved and Christopher Hill saw more hopes in pre-Reformation Europe than he had ever thought to see, along with much wrestling and brawling in his rooms on matters of great moment. He was a great scholar. His first book was published just after World War II began. It arrived on a gun site for me just about at the same time that Churchill was making his "We shall never surrender" speech. Somehow it survived the war in my knapsack, along with a book of poems by Louis MacNeice and a small missal. They were queer companions but made good reading now and then for me when I was never expecting to work in a library again, either as a reader, a writer, or a librarian. Least of all did I imagine that I would get the time ahead when I would become a constant reader at the Bodleian.

The Bodleian was a great library, if by library one thinks of just a collection of books and papers. That is just about all it was. The classification system had grown with the years, to locate the most recent collections. It was an essential component of the scholarly researcher, but otherwise it was a failure as we who work in libraries began to realise. Barring some of the Scots University Libraries there were none to match its usefulness. The books never left the library under any circumstances, and they could only be found, if they were at all old and obscure, as most of them were, by their keepers. Below the ground the Bodleian must have writhed in all directions. There were old old men, I have been told, who lived among the books, seeing the light of day but rarely. They were happy in their subterranean quarters. Man and boy they had never left the books. For more than fifty years the knowledge of book whereabouts was their sole delight. Younger and more harassed members of the Library staff would descend looking for them, to help in locating a book, or a collection of old books. The glimmer of a candle would direct them, and the rheumy-eyed old shelver, dusting the crackers from his front and swallowing the last of his tea, would peer at the list of books, his mind wandering over the miles of shelves, hover and circle, and he would totter off returning in an hour or

more with the desiderata. It was no wonder that books often
took days to reach the reader. The colleges all had adequate,
more than adequate, libraries of their own. There the young
students could easily find plenty to read and pleasant, often
even trained, assistants. A fellow of the College, and the
fellows own and manage the colleges, was often the Librarian.
Every book stack in my college was dedicated to a Balliol
man who was killed in World War I, and bore the inscription
Ave, frater, atque Vale. There were about 180 Balliol men
on the College roll of honour, and that number, larger by
far than a year's intake of students, was by no means excep-
tional for Oxford, or, probably, for Cambridge. The fallen
generally contained those who, had they lived, might have
changed Britain. Recent books, however, have shown that
perhaps they wanted to die, as they realized the state and
the reasons for what was to come to them if they had lived.
Their deaths however did knock the stuffing out of the old
order but left nothing to fill the new.

     This is what a librarian must be able to cope with.
On the one hand there is the tardiness and the reluctance of
the traditional keeper of the books to rock the boat of Privilege and to upset the course of centuries, and on the other
hand there were the papers, diaries, and journals which it
was his duty to collect and to conserve. These private papers of the privileged few, meant only for communication
among themselves, can effect such changes in the accepted
idea of how things were and why that they can totally change
the general impression of history. A librarian has to conserve the originals, get at the bedrock of fact out of which
the imaginative work of Proust, O'Neill, and of Anthony
Powell grew. Powell's twelve volume book A Dance to the
Music of Time is, for us, better than Proust, better than
Tolstoy. It is comic, deeply so, yet the school days of the
hero-narrator reveal far more of the function and cold purpose of the British public school system than any serious and
earnest attempt to explain their proliferation and enduring
position in the fabric of government. The position of the
two older universities in the scheme of the British system
of government is far better realised in the relation of Sebas-
tian Flyte by Evelyn Waugh, in Brideshead Revisited. This
was the beginning, reluctantly, to let loose his genius that
finally flowered in his great trilogy, Sword of Honour, a
Samson Agonistes of a book, wherein, reluctantly, for he
cherished what he brought crashing down, he exposes the
whole riddled and rotten system of privilege that has hobbled
and spancelled the people of England since they emerged as

100

a nation state, to the benefit of their masters, the regicide landlords. These landlords could not only pay a bounty for the head of a native, as they did in Ireland, drive them from the only good part of the land to Hell or Connacht, depopulate the Highlands for grouse moors ... there is far more of this than Marx ever knew, for all of his years of time studying and reading at the British Museum.

It is only now that some suspicion has begun to show as, reluctantly, the government in Britain has begun to allow access to the papers that it has kept locked away, locked away but intact in many cases because of the care and conscience of some librarian or other. The same development is burgeoning here in America, where, for instance, the Harvard Law School, the Wharton School of Business Administration are beginning to be revealed as bastions of a society whose standards are those of wealth, privilege, and an interlocking net of condominion, whose function far transcends those normal and popular standards that they have created for general consumption and belief.

There is much to be done here on the high level of academic librarianship. The functions of a university or research institute librarian are almost totally different from those of the public librarian, yet they are all birds of a feather and must fly together. Yet they rarely relate to one another. Some have their noses in the air, others their ears to the ground. They are beset by self-interest, tradition, archivists and those more radical members of the faculty and other readers who suspect them, and with some reason, as being obedient servants of the University Establishment. There are faculty clubs in some places that will only permit partial membership to librarians because they are not quite academic or scholarly enough: there is one such situation where only partial membership was offered to the University Library staff, of whom about 80% were women, by the first woman president of the faculty association, because they were not quite good enough. That caused a bubble and hiss on the whole stove, set the tea pot boiling and the tea cups rattling in Sexomania.

Then there are other rejections of equal club privileges to librarians because they were not faculty but the servants thereof.

Here and there radical faculty, or those who said they were, and maybe believed it for their own materials gains and means, refused to accept them as their fellows, generally with good reason.

Sometimes, to add muscle to their hardnosed and brazen demands for better pay and even more privileges, the faculty has accepted librarians as equals, to get union action on their side. The faculty has invariably denied the final rights of equal pay and privileges. Carefully pocketing their own ill-gotten gains they have agreed that the librarians be treated equally, only less so.

Altogether this is a fascinating and important matter that deserves a book and more of its own. Some of the good medical librarians are or have been practising physicians: they have been models to envy and admire. They have outdistanced us in the care, collection, and maintenance, often without having attended graduate library schools. Law librarians are generally lawyers, and this works well. The same is true in other special libraries and collections. Another was Archie MacLeish, a great Librarian of Congress, so was Luther Evans, and the present one promises by his performance and record to equal them. They have generally been appointed despite protests bitter and shrill from professional librarians who have sometimes descended to base tactics to further their own graduate library school candidates, and have dirtied themselves in the process.

A book, a Cantata, set along Longfellow lines,

Who is a proper librarian?
Who is the person that we
All should wish to be?
A He? or a She?

set to music by our Music Librarians, could be our Red Mass, sung by massed chorales of us, banked by flowers, at the opening of our Annual Convention. It could rival the liturgy if not the mystery of the very Mass.

This is a break in the narrative, something to be avoided by writers who seek an audience, especially an audience among their own folk. I am encouraged to do so since this is a matter that holds this book together. I was told, by experts and editors alike, that a writer must address his audience in words that they can understand and to talk of a subject that they have experienced, or could have, or dreamed of. So I called my first story "Barring the Weight" and it was about a rugby football game in Wales. I wrote it in Winnipeg and it was rejected for these cogent reasons in all the sports, local, and other magazines until by an inspired fluke it was accepted more by luck than judgment by the Atlantic Monthly. It became the most popular story I ever wrote, has won me prizes, has been anthologised, translated into other languages, and published in a Sunday supplement in Australia. Yet the title "Barring the Weight" bewilders readers, and the ploys of the game of rugby are beyond them. Yet I told the truth of the matter. This autobiography is only of use if it does the same thing: engages the mind of the audience. The reader does not have to be a daft knight with a rueful countenance to embrace Don Quixote, nor does he have to tilt with windmills or be defeated by his own image, as I have been, in order to get some relation out of this.

Here am I, sitting in the sun in April, on an All Fools Day, in the retirement haven of Victoria on Vancouver Island when perhaps I would have been happier nibbling cheese in the basement of the Bodley, trying to sort out the tangles in the California library systems, raising my family in Wanwatosa, that place of the fireflies contagious to Milwaukee, instead of traipsing them around North America so that they were born in places thousands of miles apart. One was born in Winnipeg, one in Victoria, one in Albany, two in Palo Alto, and one in Milwaukee. I have lived longer and in far more places in North America than I ever did in Europe. For the twenty-five years that I spent in Britain I have so far spent thirty-six over here. Through fair and foul we have lived in places as different and as remote from one another as Connecticut and California.

Sometimes the wolf was howling at the door; there was no money to buy Christmas presents for the children, when something has turned up. It was payment for an article on Dylan Thomas that came late in December 1948 that saved us having strongly spiced Wolf Stew for Christmas dinner in our Quonset hut, in a veterans' village in St. Paul, Minnesota. Out of the proceeds from that same article we bought a pedal motor car, brightly painted red, at the Goodwill store in Minneapolis. It weighed about two hundred pounds. Since we did not have a car we had to tote it on cable cars and buses, making three changes, to our village home, where Bill Flood, the college cheer leader, was babysitting for us. It was on the same route, returning from a visit ballet show at Northrop Auditorium at the University of Minnesota that we, along with a professor of chemistry and a visiting instructor

103

in English from Notre Dame, became involved in the solution
of a murder mystery. Our testimony was rejected and the
killer freed, only to confess many years later as he lay dying. But that is another story, and the only advice that perhaps you will get from this is that travel not only broadens
the mind but is a great experience. You may meet Murder
on the way, but also Maria Tallchief and Robert Frost. When
there is a growing family travel presents difficulties. Most
of my library experience and my teaching and my writing
have been around Stanford, California, Milwaukee, Wisconsin
and last and most of all at McMaster University in Hamilton,
Ontario. Wherever I have been I have found the library to
be the only place outside of home that I really care about.
There are art galleries, like the Frick in New York, the
Beaverbrook in Fredericton that draw me to them. There
is the Exploratorium in San Francisco, the best science museum in the world; the Chicago Art Institute, the Prado, and
London's National Portrait Gallery. All these and more,
along with theatre, countryside, people, archives, books and
papers have come only with travel, but travel for a growing
family is not easy. Often I have had to travel alone, like a
hunter, avoiding the rings of booksellers who have heard of
a coming kill, in order to gather in a collection that otherwise would be divided and disposed of among them. Perhaps
I am better known for the books and papers, the collections
that I have gathered in, than for my general administration
of a library. Yet it is as an administrator that I should be
judged, for it is on the successful management of the library
that all else falls into place.

Above all the Library is a service area. That has a
poor sound, as if it were a hatchway to a cafeteria, but service must come first. Of all the aspects of library economy
this is the one that has enthralled me the most. In many of
my presentations before the budget committees of the universities where I have been responsible for the library submission I have used a phrase taller and stronger than I, a
phrase that I use with reluctance for it means that I cannot,
from the length and depth of my experience, give the budget
committee any gleam of hope that this submission of mine
will be lighter, less difficult to bear, in the years ahead.
"The night will grow darker yet, the seas rise higher. I
have naught for your comfort save to say that these are the
words of a vision, conjured or what you will by King Alfred
reading a book. " That, along with some ribaldry, some hu-
mility mingled with a share in their pride in the quality of
library service, and offering to sacrifice my arm if they

104

thought it would help. During the years, certainly since 1966 until 1979 when I handed over the reins to my successor, I had to present this budget, millions of dollars every year as the inflation spiral spun more and more. My histrionics were based on realism, and my business manager and associate sitting behind me had them to present, were they called for, the dollars and cents.

I rather enjoyed the budget presentation and as long as Arthur Lawrence, my old companion who had been around and about the guns of Navarone the same as I, briefed me with the figures and the facts over coffee in my office every morning for a while before a meeting of the budget committee, I was well set for the encounter and far less nervous than when I had to mark Jack Bassett, the Welsh international rugby player, at Arms Park when I was younger.

10

I really got into the research library world in earnest in 1948, never to leave it again, hardly ever even for a day, when I began to write a dissertation on a famous Canadian political issue ... The Manitoba School Question.

We had left Oxford to come to Winnipeg where I got a job teaching and librarianating in a Boys' School, and teaching part time the Canadian equivalent to the G. I. 's in the Anglican College of the University of Manitoba.

There, at the University I met W. L. Morton at the beginning of his career as a major Canadian historian. It was he who opened up for me the glowing scenes of Canadian Western History, the flag of the republic of the Assinaboia, shamrocks and a flag, the plight of the Métis, their leader Louis Riel, whose name had been O'Reilly.... There were literally hundreds more facets that were new and strange to me, raised on the history of the Plantagenets, Tudors, and Stewarts and, even worse, the Hanoverians.

The Hudsons Bay Company ceased to be a comfit box, a toy in the hands of Prince Rupert of the Rhine. Norway House at the northern tip of Lake Winnipeg, I discovered, was not called so because of the abundance of Norway Pine that surrounded it, but because there was a company of prisoners leased from Norway and then sent back to jail in their homeland. The factors, the chief hands of the Company, were at first Scots almost to a man. They married au façon du nord, and sent their Métis sons, who succeeded them, back to School in Scotland and brought them back as their successors without their having seen any town in Europe south of Stornaway, or Inversary, if they were lucky.

Scratch many a Canadian you'll find anti-Americanism.

107

The Earl of Selkirk who suffered a virulence of it, established the Selkirk Settlement near what now is Winnipeg and hired a mercenary Swiss company of soldiers to protect it, lest Rupertsland fall, and the Americans move in. He moved the hapless settlers from Scotland and hired the de Meuniere Swiss regiment to protect them from the incursions of the American Nor-West Company and the Indians.

Selkirk's preoccupation or worse came from the time when as a boy he had seen his lordly home at St. Mary's Island in the Firth of Clyde ransacked, looted, pillaged and torn by terrifying American sailors, one in particular, the captain of them all, who was looking for his father with a naked sword. John Paul Jones was born of a servant girl of the Selkirks upon whom the Earl had abused by his droit du seigneur, and cast out when she was pregnant. The child she bore therefore was the bastard brother of the cowering son and heir. He was one of the great sailors of his or any time. He looked like a Selkirk and would have strung his father up on the yardarm of his sloop The Wanderer since he had failed to burn what there was of the British fleet in Whitehaven.

This and many other facts of the Canadian West are not even in the textbooks yet. Louis Riel whom the Anglos hanged after the Métis Rebellion of 1885 was sheltered in the Dakotas when he failed to establish his Republic of the Assinaboia, and the Prime Minister of Canada secretly paid his keep, so that he would not return and lead the Métis who were shamefully treated by Anglos, to fight for justice again along the banks of the Saskatchewan. The treatment in history books and in politics of Riel and his Fenian Lieutenant O'Donaghue shows through the desire, the need even, of the Americans to move north. Lincoln and Seward during the Civil War were inclined to let the South founder, cut them from the Union and spread into the vast tracts, so like America, that lay northward and unpeopled. This has been played down, and the times of Riel have been murky ever since, troubling and obscure, underground but by no means dead.

All this history was new, startling, and infinitely strange to me. It has not yet been written. I read the primary sources of it all in the Provincial Library of Manitoba, in Winnipeg. There I spent my summer vacation months preparing my dissertation for a Master's degree in Canadian history, and spilling into print from the well of archives. Myself and Jackson, who later wrote a fine history of the province began a column on early Rupertsland history. So startling,

108

unknown, and exciting it was until then that it was published regularly in the Winnipeg Daily Tribune. Just as my first article appeared in Education, an essay that I had written on Plato's ideas of education while I was in Oxford, I was appearing also in The Beaver, the very good journal of the Hudson's Bay Company, to be followed a while later by an article on the convicts of Norway House. It seemed as if a dam had been broken. My mind was opening after years away from the books and for the first time to research in primary sources and their implications to scholarship, politics, and more.

Soon I was the secretary of the Manitoba Historical Society. The Earl of Selkirk, I recall, looking parboiled in a tuxedo, came across from the Lieutenant-Governor's residence to address us and a group of descendants of the original Selkirk settlers who had been bussed in to meet their Laird. It was 35° F below zero, typical winter weather for Winnipeg. All that the earl could find to say, so snapped was he by the weather, was to ask us urgently whether we were mad, penal, or incurables, that we lived in such a climate. We had great times turning over the archives, so startling, fascinating, and exciting were they, but carefully controlled because of the revelations they contained, many times to the detriment, real or imagined, of the present establishment.

Johnson, the provincial archivist, was a jewel. He had worked all his life in provincial affairs before being rewarded with the plum of archives. He and his staff did all they could for me. By good fortune I had become related by marriage to a senior civil servant, one of the mandarins of Manitoba. While I did not get to know him well, and his untimely death came as a shock to me, he introduced me all around the provincial offices as his cousin. That opened many doors, many catalogue trays to me.

W. L. Morton was a research scholar who was to win renown that is well deserved. I reckon him in the first flight of Canadian historians. He was my tutor for my dissertation. I would have failed if it had not been for him. The exhilaration of research had so possessed me that I forgot--this was in 1948--that I had to pass a written test in Philosophy in order to qualify for the degree. Somehow or other Bill Morton persuaded the Philosophy Department to accept my submission that was very far removed from the questions they had set: I rather believe it was on Plato and the Essential Education, whereas I should have written on Hume and the Common Sense Philosophers.

109

As a result of my two years under the tutelage of Bill Morton I received an offer of a teaching fellowship at the University of Minnesota. There we hied, not without some difficulty. A second son had been born to us in Victoria where we had summered in a family cottage, and I had begun my research--that was to be lifelong--on Thomas D'Arcy McGee. His murder in Sparks Street, Ottawa in 1868 was the only political assassination in Canadian history, and the more I studied him, with great help from the provincial library of British Columbia, the more I began to identify his background with my own. Eventually my dissertation turned into a novel, The Poor Hater, that did receive a considerable degree of review and other praise in the U. S. , where it was published, and no reviews or mention in Canada, save among my friends and some others, who tended to deplore it because the fiction either puzzled or offended them. The book had been out of print for some time and, like my book of short stories, The Great Disciple, commands prices that keep rising in the booksellers' catalogues. Were it not for The Mortmain of Libraries, the title of an article I wrote just after I began librarianating and teaching at Stanford, they would be out of reach of the general reader: there are moves, however, to reissue them both in cheap editions, and I would welcome inquiries, in order to persuade a publisher.

Living in the States was a new experience to both of us, and we loved it. We continue to do so, and return there whenever we can. We have a family and a grandchild in Minnesota. The only two things that I have ever made with my hands until recently, when I have taken up carpentry, are two rocking horses. Zach Goldstein rides one in Little Rock, and Nora Ready bestrides hers in St. Charles, Minnesota.

I had got to writing other than articles, essays and theses while we were still in Winnipeg. It was the North American climate, the new world to me, that set flowing the vials of my pen. Often the stories were so strange and comic even to me who had experienced them that they flowed easily, especially after I had told them to myself and others. Many critics, including the most benevolent, and they outnumber the others, tell me that in reading me they are learning me, although they have never heard my voice. One of my stories, Angharad, is based upon the Welsh lore sound of it, and it is the favourite of many because of this, although they cannot even pronounce Angharad.

One of the strange and unfortunate symptoms that affect

librarians is their reluctance to write other than reports, professional experiences, or statistical data. I remember some years ago anticipating with pleasure an article in a professional journal on undergraduate reading at the University of Illinois. To my dismay that I feel even more now as I am writing this the article did not refer to a single book or author but was compiled and presented as statistical data culled from computer printouts.

There are many librarians who read books other than those that are the tools of their profession. There are many physicians who write fiction, poems, and plays.

Lawyers, like that fellow Higgins whom I referred to earlier, number more good novelists and short story writers than I would have believed. The same probably also applies to accountants, teachers, architects, and soldiers, yet there is never any evidence of this, quite the contrary, in their professional journals. There was one happy case of a doctor in St. Louis, a laryngologist who became editor of the medical journal dedicated to the Ear, Nose, and Throat syndrome. He was a devotee of the poet John Keats, and every article that appeared in the journal while it was under his editorial control had a reference to John Keats, who had happened, as had been also Noll Goldsmith, to have been something of a medico.

Literature of the critical literary kind should not be confined to book review journals or supplements. They deserve a place, a prime one, in all journals of a professional kind, especially in the periodicals of the library profession. I have urged, coaxed, and encouraged colleagues to follow my example in this matter, with little or no success. Indeed, among those who have been most successful in implementing the technological processes that have been innovated or espoused it is only by making them collaborate with me, often against their will, that I have got them into print at all.

It is with mixed feelings that an appointments board, generally all non-librarians, regard the curriculum vitae of any candidate for a position of some importance and find a complete blank under the heading of Publications. And when they do find entries they are almost invariably of the technological or managerial kind, and therefore gobble dy gook to the general reader.

The energy and drive, criticism and rejection of the

111

young members of any profession are essential if that profession is not to atrophy.

As I wrote this autobiography, recall comes flooding in and ebbing like a tide. This is no Pippa's passing. Some of the more uncomfortable and unpleasant parts of my life are recalled with difficulty. It is the easy, pleasant and less turbulent times that skirt the rocks, barbed wire, and other barriers to a pleasant landing on the further shore. Good times remain in the memory fresher and clearer than the bad times that have been, come and gone. The French have a phrase-- they have several phrases that I often recall--the one that I recall the most is tout passe: everything passes. Another one dear to me is partir: c'est mourir un peu. To say goodbye is to die a little. And the so typical Spanish proverb: "God says: Take what you want. But pay for it. "

I was on the tip of my toes with the ball at my feet when I came to Minnesota. Canada, where I was happy, was still Protestant and Anglo to me. Among the French Canadians I found a deep down resentment of the likes of me, not as a person, far from it, but because I was one of the English Speaking Breed, the Irish Catholics, who had been elevated to the increasing bishoprics and influence of the Church in the West and were totally out of sympathy, even the most Sulpician-trained among them, with their dreams and aspirations. England had established and financed the seminary for the Irish clergy in Maynooth. It was staffed to begin with by emigré French Sulpician clergy, whose near Jansenistic "purity" and devotion to the old order were to have such a deleterious effect upon Anglo-Irish relations in the future.

But when I came to Minnesota I did not feel at all a stranger or a poor relation, although immigrant and penniless I was. I tapped away at my typewriter every night in St. Rita, the name of our Quonset hut on the campus of the college of St. Thomas in St. Paul where Vincent Flynn, the president, had befriended me because he had read and enjoyed my Atlantic Monthly prize story "Barring the Weight. "

Every morning I stepped off the campus twenty minutes before my classes were to start at the University of Minnesota about 12 miles away, and there was never a morning that a car did not pull out of the ruck of the traffic in response to my flagging. I would generally catch the cable car and bus back to St. Paul in the late afternoon. Maybe I would bathe the two babies in the sink--we have a good photograph of that--

112

have dinner and visit or be visited around the Village. All
of us were ex-G. I. 's, early teaching or late learning vintage.
We were completely at home, and snug, all of us, in our
Quonset huts that had been divided into two apartments.
There were children everywhere, common experiences to
share and to remember. They were happy days. One of our
friends from those days was Eugene McCarthy, later the Senator. His state manager, Joe Gabler, taught with me and his
family were among our closest friends. J. F. Powers was
just coming into his strength as a writer in The New Yorker.
His two books of stories Prince of Darkness and The Presence
of Grace have captured the best part of his work, and the selection of his comic novel Morte d'Urban for the National Book
Award was one of the best choices ever made. Jim had served
a term in jail as a conscientious objector. He was one of the
best raconteurs I have ever known. We used to meet in Ryan's
bar, a solid oak and stalled room then that never closed during Prohibition. Jerry, the bartender, had a great respect
for booklearning. He had seen our names on the magazines
in the lobby and whenever a patron--the bar was a discreet
caravanserai of politicians and others--ordered a side order
of sandwiches or hors d'oeuvres to be served in a curtained
booth where business was being discussed he would double the
order to make sure that we had enough to eat, on the same
charge.

There was never a breath of scandal or of carryings-
on in the Ryan bar. It was more respectable than a temper-
ance hotel, and should some inquiring reporter inadvertently
allow a coarse word to pass his lips Jerry would immediately
order him out.

These memories come flooding back of times when I
was so fully occupied with study, reading and librarianating,
besides getting used to being a father, husband and provider
that I wonder now what we do really remember of the times
that are good.

Three times a week I would lecture to a whole freshman class of about 250 on English history. Then three times
a week I would meet with quiz sections, making a total of
twelve hours teaching. I was a good teacher and one of the
professors other than my tutor asked me to do the same for
him, on European history. I was glad to do it, enjoyed it and
felt no strain. Unwittingly I was become a pawn in faculty
internecine intrigue and later, at my oral comprehensive examination I was given a hard time and given a referral on

English mediaevel and 17th Century constitutional history, but this was unknown to me then. When I did learn about it my dissertation topic of D'Arcy McGee, the Irish-American-Canadian statesman, had grown so important to me that these intrigues that were intended to do me in to spite my tutor who, I believed, deserved it, were of no moment to me then nor ever have been.

I spent hours and hours every day in the University Library. It was the first great library that I could wander through at will. Never a day passed that I was not among the books there. I was so much at home there that readers thought that I was one of the staff and would ask me to help them, especially amid the indexes and bibliographies.

This is one area that we have been unable to face and so to conquer. The guides and references to book information and further study remain closed, locked books to most readers and there is little that we have done about it. I may look, walk, and seem like a penguin until I get among the bibliographies and then I appear and feel at home and as easy and graceful as a penguin does when freed from the shore and swimming in deep water. Sometimes I even get the exhilaration of a killer shark on the trail of a school of herring. I feel a different man, I look a different distant person to the smiling public man who ambles elsewhere in the library, just enjoying the pleasure of it.

The hardest thing in the world to get librarians and readers to realise is the labyrinthine ways that are the path to real knowledge and learning. This is what Bibliography is all about. We oversimplify often, to persuade the reader, and make a freeway where there is needed really a winding and encumbered path. We make a clockwork fox or electric hare to replace the real hunt while fields of Bibliography are waiting to be the prime arenas for librarians to hunt and readers to hunt alike.

Few readers, and not nearly enough librarians, know the bibliography that is so much the lifeline to learning. It is a dangerous subject, as are most worthwhile matters; otherwise the bittersweet taste of the hunt becomes the bland pablum of diluted twaddle.

I began to learn a hard fact at Minnesota; I am glad that I realised it then, when I was able to duck and weave and even seem capable of counter-blows, and that fact is that if any person, being, or thing has acted with malice towards you, or done you an injustice out of ignorance, fear, or folly that agent of wrong-doing will never be able to like you, ever again, no matter how they try.   There are some who attempt to make amends, even out of self-interest, some who try to change their dislike into liking, their envy into admiration, but it never works.

These gobbets of information, hardly acquired, are cast into the book for the reader's benefit, bits of armour, hard to realise and to acquire, and even harder to put on for defence.   But it gives this autobiography some heft, some ballast that otherwise would be lacking, thereby presenting too false and too much a tale of tra-la-la.

I have been lucky, lucky to have survived.   Only physicians have saved me from the power of the Dog on several occasions.   That I am alive at all gives me a singular pleasure.   To be gifted, as I have been, with challenges that I could face and mount, has always been a source of wonder to me.   For all my enemies there have been more friends. Fact has passed fiction when I come to recount how good people have been to me.   I never believed that I would see the day when I could look back in good health for over thirty years of marriage and family, years that they have both endured and often enjoyed, leaving me free to librarianate, to teach, and to write.

After two years at Minnesota, my fellowship was running out and I was looking for a job.   Poor Vincent Flynn, the president of the College of St. Thomas that had hired me, was having a rough time making ends meet.   The large sums of money that had come to the colleges with the arrival of the G.I. 's was running out, as more and more of them graduated and sent out into the world or furthered their studies in the graduate schools of universities.   The small independent colleges that had so benefitted from the early postwar years were up against it with dwindling enrollment and the costs of a plant that had been constructed to hold them who were no longer there.

For two years I had taught a writing course on Thursday afternoons at St. Thomas.   That paid for our Quonset hut rental and, along with the money from my writing and the $100 a month from my fellowship, allowed us to live a good life.   But all that was coming to an end.   Besides, a 25 per cent disability pension that I received from the British Army ceased. A letter from the British Ministry of Pensions explained that I was still entitled to it, but because of the tough currency crisis in England they had to cut off all payments to the U.S., or to all countries on the dollar economy. I knew that the money market in Britain was difficult for my family in Cardiff, knowing that I would be hard put to it, had tried to send me some money. Nora, my sister, the most generous, most suffering and by far the most afflicted of us all, wrote me near to tears to say that she had money she wanted to give me but the currency laws prohibited it.

There are few, if any, faculty book departments in University. The Peabody Bibliographer, a position held by Phil McNiff at Harvard before he became the Librarian of Boston Public Library, is a position unique of its kind. There is not a chair of Bibliography or a consequent academic department anywhere that I know of save, to some degree, in graduate library schools, where Bibliography is generally treated as a part of the course on Reference Services.

The University Librarian at Minnesota at this time, the beginning of the '50's, was Errett W. McDiarmid. He later went on to the hard diaconal world where he was befouled by the insurgent students. I hardly knew him in his palmy and peaceful days when I was passing through but one day a student assistant who helped pay her way through college by helping at the Circulation Desk called me over.

"One of my girlfriends who is a typist in the Librarian's Office has been writing letters about you."

"She's wrong then, tell her. All that fuss about my having overdue books has...."

She shook her head.

"It's nothing to do with overdue books. By the way," she ruffled through her papers on the desk. "There is a book here for you on Inter-Library Loan. It's in French, from Laval University. That's in Canada, isn't it? I thought you spoke English in Canada."

"Some do. More think they do. Others can and don't. What's the book?" She mouthed the title off the card, "Le Métis Canadien."

"Oh, aye. I've been waiting for that one. I'll go and pick it up. But what's this about writing letters about me?"

116

She looked at me and grinned. She was a perky little thing, married to a graduate student in agronomy at the St. Paul campus. That was over thirty years ago and her face, grin, and tone of her voice just passed across the view of my mind as I write this as clearly as if it was but yesterday. "You're a bit of a genius, Dr. McDiarmid says. He's answering letters from Michigan and Berkeley asking him if he can recommend anyone to teach Bibliography. He says that you can, that you are the only one that he can recommend. Say, what is Bibliography? It sounds like a course in that Billy Graham Bible College."

"No, it's about books, all sorts. The Bible's a book. Biblio means book. There's a journal called Biblio about books. Surely you've seen it?"

"What would I do with a biblio? I still don't know what you're talking about anyhow, with that funny accent of yours. Move on now. There's a line-up behind you of people wanting to get their books stamped to get out. Don't tell anyone I told you about those letters about you to Michigan and Berkeley."

I nodded and went back to my notes I was making for the quiz section I was preparing for on the Tolpuddle March and protest, and the Manchester Martyrs.

When I got home that late afternoon, with dreams that maybe what Mary Ellen Hansen had told me at the Circulation Desk that morning might have some promise of a job, my wife was at the door with Vincent in her arms and Park at her skirt waving two air letters at me. She had opened them and from her whole look I knew that they contained good news.

"Where's Ann Arbor, in Michigan. That's just south of us, isn't it? And Berkeley is on San Francisco Bay. I know that because they've got a cyclotron there or something, and a famous scientist from Sweden."

"Here," pushing the letters at me and pulling my booksack off me, "Where are we going then, to Michigan or California? They are both offering you a job as an instructor, at $5000 a year plus benefits."

We were both so relieved as we sat down on the couch together, with Park crawling up on my knee, that somehow even the babies shared in our relief.

Michigan or Berkeley. Which was it to be? I tended to favour Michigan because it was nearer--there was a bibliographic desert it seemed to me between Berkeley on the Pacific Coast, and Chicago.

Nearly all my friends at St. Thomas and the University favoured Berkeley, because of the climate and the growing prestige of the university. Most of the teaching fellows and assistants in the department were having a hard time getting placed. Some of them went back into the obscurity of small church-affiliated colleges, one got a job in a state institution in Colorado, and Ben Rogers, my friend among them, landed a job teaching in Florida at the State University in Tallahassee. Others left academe for jobs in business and government while one, whose father was a beer baron, went back into the business of brewing. They all should have got jobs before me: they deserved to, but they all were extremely reluctant to write, either because they could not or were afraid to become a part of a controversy wherein their publication could be quoted, denied, derided, or used to bolster up an argument that they had never heard of.

Along with this reluctance to commit opinions to print, there is also the unfortunate fact that most historians along with most other academics are unable to write well enough for even their colleagues to understand them. Sometimes I have been called in as an external examiner on a Ph.D. dissertation and generally it is only pity on my part, and a feeling that it does not matter anyhow, that have made me refrain from a thumbs down verdict. Journalists often turn out to be the good writers. That was true of Hemingway, Alan Moorehead and Churchill and Dickens.

My whole world and concept of writing about matters of great concern, matters that have needed years of learning even for the writer to understand, has been turned topsy turvy in these later years by scientists, not the popularisers, not those, like Jonathan Miller and George V. Higgins who have taken for relief to release their talents to fiction, drama or poetry, but those who have written about their own science gravely, lucidly and with flashes of insight that reveal to the reader what they have been missing by reading the literary scholars like Leavis, Bradley, Saintsbury, dozens of authors, so remote and ineffectual that they have long failed to be of any concern to me. There is not a critical work on Jane Austen, Dickens, Kipling, Melville, Joyce, Beckett, O'Casey, Thurber, Faulkner or O'Hara that has come near to helping

118

me save in sending me back to the original writing to form
my own opinions. This is such a topic with me that I shall
return to it. And I hope you will still be with me.

It was Mike Curry, a professor of Chemistry from
Brooklyn, with his graduate work from the University of Wisconsin, who finally persuaded me that Berkeley would be the
better place for us. He was a constant visitor to our Quonset hut that, since it was on the campus, was an easy place
to visit. There were forty apartments such as our own.
Each had a saint's name instead of a number. We were
Saint Rita. She was the saint, among other things, of hope-
less causes, she and St. Jude, I believe, but while I have
never heard a girl called Jude even by Thomas Hardy, who
was a bit of a Jude himself, Rita was a popular girl's name.
I remember an early musical movie, featuring Bebe Daniels,
one of the Mack Sennett girls who graduated from the gyra-
tions and the chase in the early days of the cinema, who
came to fame in a film called Rio Rita. It was the beginning of her subsequent star career. She and her husband
Ben Lyon played in Britain where they made their home, and
they played to crowded houses through the years of bombing.
They were a lesson for us all. What they lacked in talent
they made up for in tenacity, and there is plenty of room for
librarians of all kinds in Alaska, the Aleutians and the Yukon,
for those of us who want both to blaze a trail and save the
libraries from overmuch technological zeal.

It was the years in Minnesota that finally cemented
my career. Towards the end of that two years I was beginning to be known as a writer who had a future that would be
affluent enough, if I devoted my time to it, forsaking my professional career. The Saturday Evening Post was in its heyday and was offering me more than $3,000 for a story. My
first fifteen published stories were collected in a book, The
Great Disciple, and brought me further praise from the re-
viewers and readers. The New Yorker invited me to submit
stories and the Canadian Broadcasting Company came down
to visit me regarding the reading of some of my stories that
had a Canadian content on the radio. They decided, however,
that as I was born and raised in Wales, and now was resi-
dent in Minnesota I was not Canadian enough for them.

I never could see writing as a career nor have I ever
been able to. Writing to me has always been a reflection of
life, and all that it has meant to me ever has been the chance
to communicate my ideas and experiences, not from any place

119

apart but from a temporary shelter in the midst of my life. I have relished writing; I am writing all the time, but for refreshment and enjoyment and glad I always have been to put the pen down after some hours, generally in the early morning and seek grist and fuel for my mill with the family, with people, friends, and others, and above all with my work.

I have been dismayed by the sense of loss I feel at not being able to work again. A sense of leisure, like a magic bouncing ball, kept running and bouncing ahead of me through the miles of stacks. There were times when I nearly caught it in my hands as it lay among the papers and the drones on committee tables. Fondly I thought that I had mastered the skill of being able to sit through committees and meetings of the senate in a comatose rest and near sleep with the eyes open, my head upright as if I were really there. Years passed before I realised that it was Fred Johnson, a physician, and Lynn Urquhart, an economist, who invariably sat one on each side of me, not for the pleasure of my company but to anticipate my head dropping and my snores trumpeting.

Berkeley it was to be, following all advice. The family went ahead of me, to await on the farm of St. Benedict's College, near St. Cloud, my arrival in Berkeley where I could find housing for us.

There was a small mini-Austin for sale around the campus. Mike Curry had been teaching me the rules of the American road--I had not driven, and then reluctantly, since I passed my driver's test when I was commissioned as an officer in Sarafand, years before. Mike was to drive the car and I was to observe him. Somehow my presence beside him in the Austin, even when I was not driving, thinking he was, so unnerved him that he found it politic and more to discover that he was badly needed in New York so that I drove myself out from Minneapolis to Berkeley by myself without incident but by some subterfuge whenever I was questioned by highway patrols.

I found a house that was all too expensive but available in El Cerrito, an area that lay adjacent to Berkeley. There our family was reunited and our third son, Liam, was born in the hospital at Albany. He was born on September 16 and my hospital coverage from the University of Minnesota expired on September 15. I engaged in some spirited correspondence with the health administration offices at Minneapolis and even-

tually received from them, with some reluctance, the sum
of $48 towards the delivery, as if the birth had resulted
from spontaneous combustion as soon as my health insurance
expired, like a fuse that set off a bomb.

The Graduate Library School at Berkeley was a new
experience to me. The class was a mixture of candidates
for the degree in librarianship that would make them professionals in all kinds of book endeavour. They were my first
class within a library school. Memories of it remain fresh
in my mind although it happened thirty years ago. I rather
startled some of the students and they startled me. They
presented a real mix, from backgrounds of many kinds.
Some I still meet at conventions and often fail to recognise
them until they make themselves known but there are others
who have become a part of my life, surfacing and sinking in
my years of hauling at the oar of my life boat, or letting
the waves break over me bearing the tiller up against my
breast as I wait and veer with shock awaiting for the storm
to pass, as it will, Tout Passe, as long as you keep going
through it.

The dean of the School was J. P. Danton. Edith
Coulter, near retirement, was a good librarian and teacher
of the old school. She had become friend and mentor to
many of the California librarians. The original dean, a
Canadian, was retired and had become world-famous as a
horticulturist. Donald Coney was the University Librarian
who sometimes lectured in the School. Coney was a man
of great administrative skills; he was often the vice-president
of the University to some degree or other. He cultivated a
cold exterior, rather a forbidding cast. I was not by any
means his cup of tea, the sort of librarian that he did not
wish to be. However, despite his antipathy for my kind he
was a great reader of books. We enjoyed more than an
armed truce. There were hours talking books together. I
remember once as we were going in together to a meeting in
San Francisco he was asking me my opinion of Lawrence
Durrell's Alexandria Quartet. I knew Alexandria well. The
Chief and Petty Officers Club there was my favourite club in
the Middle East and we had been stationed around the harbour
and Aboukir Bay when the daring Italian submariners had been
blowing up some of our better ships in their one-man craft.
"Fecund" I told Coney. "A word to be pronounced and pon-
dered over with care. A word that needs to be used with
care."

It was an instant review, and one that I still stand by.

121

The four-decker novel is as ripe and as rotten as Alexandria itself: Fecund. A sharp tart book that he wrote on Cyprus during the Makarios-Turkish troubles, Bitter Lemons, is a better book, by far.

Altogether during my time in Berkeley at the Graduate Library School I realised that nearly everything that I had done in the past had been leading up to it. My early days in Cardiff Public Library had conditioned me, prepared me for all sorts of library endeavour from culling, sorting, selecting, ordering, and processing books for the school libraries, and then delivering them on a truck to my last working period there when I was the librarian in Special Collections and Research. I had spent a year at the University of Wales learning palaeography, archives, and archaeology, and I had passed the Library Association examinations that made me a professional, a dues-paying member of NALGO, the National Association of Local Government Officers. There was a sharp division, far too sharp, with the ranks of library workers, as there is today between librarians, technologists, and archivists, each group claiming to be superior, different, and apart from the others.

In my day very few librarians were university graduates and they had little in common with the university and college people who held the good positions, generally with no knowledge or interest even in a library economy.

University graduates were a rare breed in the '30's. There were fewer university graduates in Britain per 10,000 of the population than anywhere else in Europe, save Turkey.

We are going through the same caper here and systems analysts, public librarians, commercial librarians, archivists, commercial information retrieval experts, school librarians often double as teachers. Firms like General Motors and the great banks have the equivalent of a vice-president in charge of records control. It is so easy to steal a manuscript, diary, or typescript from some archival cache or other that it is only when some inquiring detective journalist gets on the trail of some government skullduggery or other that a sliver of the existing chaos comes to light. The primary source of our history is often lost, stolen, or rotting in bags or folders in a basement.

I did not see eye to eye with the dean of the Berkeley Library School at all. Some of the other faculty found me a puzzle as did some of the students also, but I met many California librarians and found them to be better, more receptive, and more fun to be with than I could have hoped. Sure, there were some rascals among them, political appointees to some of the library plums, but out of Berkeley Library School when Mitchell was dean had come some of the best trained and most lively people in the business. Librarians like Larry Powell, one of the great ones, and many others. A reading of the <u>California Librarian</u> of those days and the times preceding it are among the best of library literature.

The office next door to my own was Ray Sontag's study. He was a first class historian, a man of impressive mien, and he and his wife, John Agar's sister, became good friends of ours. There was another first-rate historian along the corridor, Carl Bridenbaugh. Many other friends I made there. I grew hot under the collar when I saw the proliferation, the spilling of public funds to make the library resources overly convenient and the casual multiplicity of libraries all over the campus, all doing their own thing. This, I was to find, was one of the features of our society. The casual expenditure of public funds to put jam and butter on the bread, and the increasing use of them to establish a bureaucracy. The general answer to anything that improved the position, comfort, or power of any group or individual meets not so much with gratitude, with humble thanks, however publicly expressed, but with a clamant, even if otherwise expressed, for <u>More</u>. Our present society is not a just one. It is based entirely on the oppression and dereliction of the "developing" peoples who outnumber us by far and who are biding their time, unconsciously or not, for their share of the comforts of the world that we control and consume. This has always been the way of it. The increasing methods of communication, the availability of information, often stored within the library orbit, makes the day of the break-up of the present order that rules the world approach more rapidly than ever realized before. The aliterate approach to the growing crisis makes the learned readers ever more likely to become the arbiters of our future. Learning rarely goes along with goodness. Wisdom generally leads to repression.

Few of my friends, if any, in my early days of librarianating, realised this. We are approaching a revolution whose extent and implications are still beyond our understanding.

The last twenty-five years have seen microforms,

123

permaprint, rays of sound, light, and heat bring information into the very home, without benefit or need of print. The eyes of the young are glazed with vision, of sights, scenes and lessons almost entirely in the control of the great business conglomerates that own or control the prime TV circuits and radio, and all other information media.

TV was in its infancy when I began to work and teach librarianship at Berkeley.

The faculty club in those days was a kind of Frank Lloyd Wright timbered building. Lunch there was lively and abundant.

It was at Berkeley that I met Reuben Peiss, among the most favoured and intelligent beings of the West. He joined the faculty of the Library School at the same time as I did. We became fast friends, one of the best friends that we ever made. He was a constant drop-in visitor to our house, and he and his mother, although so far apart from us in background and culture, became closer than most nextdoor neighbours, although they lived miles away. He knew he was dying even then. Some mornings I would drive up beside him on a hill overlooking the campus. He would be slumped over the steering wheel, his hands gripping it tight, his face sweating, waiting for the cancer pain to let up so that, calm and insouciant, he could begin his day. He would after a while look up, greet me with a smile of absolute sweetness, a dry remark or a joke and we would drive down the hill together.

Reuben's library life had already made his name well-nigh a magic one. Had he lived he would have been one of the great librarians and more. He had already written his translation of A History of Libraries by Alfred Hessel that the Scarecrow Press published in 1950. He was a graduate of Hartford, Michigan, and Harvard. Early in his career, he had become a mover and a leader-to-be, bringing some sense to the Harvard List of Serials for a start, and incorporating them in a proper form in the great second edition of the Union List of Serials. This was a bibliographical task that I would never have even attempted, yet Reuben took it in his stride. His work in Europe during and after World War II would make a great thriller; it serves as abundant testimony to this great American librarian. From his State Department office in Lisbon he organized, handled and controlled a major library reorganization that redounds to the benefit of the United States and the free world. His postwar

124

office was established in Bern, Switzerland and he was a
frequent and official visitor of England, France, and Spain.
Some of the tales of his encounters were masterpieces of
comedy. During all this time he was pursuing his translation of Hessel. When it was early out of print, and his
early death had eased his pain-racked body, there was a
Memorial Edition published in 1955. A preface was written
by Verner Clapp of the Library of Congress, by David Clift
of the American Library Association, Fred Kilgour of Yale,
Harry Lydenburg of New York Public, Keyes Metcalf, Andrew
Osborn, and myself. A reading of this preface is well worthwhile for anyone in libraries who needs or hopes to see the
art and craft of it being practised by a master, and chroni-
cled by his colleagues who knew him. We cherished him and
all knew him in different degrees, in different places, but it
was his humour, learning, kindliness, and courage that showed
through in every case, masking his great qualities of leadership.

I lack a visual imagination. I do not see my loved
ones even in my dreams, nor can I recall clearly the features of my father, my mother, my sister Nora, who have
gone before me. Yet I can still see Reuben's face grinning
up at me as I delivered my first talk in California to the
state library association gathered in San Diego. It was called
Transatlantica or Common British Ephemera.

I find it never an easy task to deliver a talk. As the
time comes nearer when I have to stand up and deliver I get
more and more worried about it. Luckily for me Reuben had
come down to San Diego with me, and his sparkling good humour, his many stories, easily resolved any sense of apprehension I may have had. After all, I had never confronted
such a group before. Without him there would have been no
me. All this was done to set my feet firmly on the road.
Reuben was both my friend and believer, my very first.

Many think it was the best talk that I ever gave. One
feature of all my talks is that although I write them out I
never read them, but address myself to the audience and re-
spond to their reaction, using the script as a baseboard or
a trampoline. My speech is far from the written text. On
one occasion, in Boston, I actually threw my text away as I
could see the pleasure and maybe learning that I was giving
by my extemporising.

I have always been bewildered by those who stand at

125

the dais and read a written text, without any departure from the printed word. Generally they diminish the worth of it, for they are not good readers anyway and I often feel, with good reason many times, that they are poor speakers also. This is true about most of the speeches, hundreds of them, that I have endured through the years.

There is a dramatic or theatrical quality about a good speech. Good speakers are rare, rarer than good actors. Most often they rise to an occasion, and fall back into mediocrity or worse when the occasion passes. One of the best speeches that I can remember was the speech that Eugene McCarthy made nominating Adlai Stevenson for the Presidency. Another was Churchill's No Surrender speech after the debacle of Dunkirk. William Faulkner made a fine speech when he accepted the Nobel Prize. In a minor key, very much minor and lighter, did I make my mark at that speech I gave to the librarians at San Diego.

I did not know it then but it was to be a momentous occasion to me, one that was to mark me for good. I remember the first formal speech that I ever made. I spoke in opposition to a Welsh Nationalist proposal in College, and I was a failure. My nervousness about the debate worsened my stutter, and that made it worse and it was bad enough anyhow. The stutter was a fairly usual speech defect when I was growing up. Two of my friends, Duncan Brown and Bernard Guise, both now retired school teachers, stuttered also. The stutter was more common, much more common in those days, for it was thought that to be left-handed was to be both rude and wrong. In school they tried to cane us out of it, for our own good. It was considered to be bad table manners to eat and drink favouring the left hand. The tables and cutlery were always set for right-handed people. Brown, Guise and I, when they were in teachers college and I was in University, used to walk out of a Wednesday evening to Rumney Village and drop in for three half-pints at the Rompney Arms Inn. The brother of Ernie Bevin was the landlord and Ernie, taking a break from his union office world (he was the panjandrum of the Transport and General Workers Union), spent some days off there. I saw him, who was to become the best Minister of Foreign Affairs that Britain ever had, pulling the pump behind the bar for the tankards and glasses of beer.

Wednesday night was rather a quiet night at the Rompney Arms, and we were not customers, regulars who were

126

Will and his mother.

with Brother Jack.

At the Christian Brothers School in Cardiff.

Opening the Gabriel Fielding Archives which he acquired for
McMaster University (1966)

Reviewing the
Russell Archives
(with packing
trunks in
background)

McMaster University
(1968)

In the stacks of
the Eighteenth-
century Collection
McMaster University
(1975)

Photo courtesy of
The Spectator,
Hamilton, Ontario

Will at his retirement party, McMaster University, June 27, 1979, with Bess behind him and flanked by Dr. A. A. Lee, Academic Vice President (left) and McMaster President A. N. Bourns (right).

Will, wife Bess, and three of his six children, Liam, Nora, and Patrick (1979)

Will's only
granddaughter,
Nora Elizabeth,
with Daddy
(Vincent).
(1980)

On a wooded path near McMaster (1979)

known. The barmaid would look oddly at Guise, the Bastard of Burgundy we sometimes called him, as he would order three halves of bitter, stuttering as he did so. Then when Brown would repeat the order for a second round, also with a stutter, she would look even oddlier, and when I would order the last three halves with an even more pronounced "Three halves of B-B-Bitter, M-M-Miss" she was near to calling the landlord.

Imperceptibly by the war's end my stammer had nearly disappeared. I was even beginning to use the telephone without severe misgiving, and could order a dozen eggs without asking for eleven and then one more. Jonathan Miller also spoke of his stammer which has persisted longer than mine.

There is one good thing about a stammer, for one who wants to communicate, as I did: it makes one cast around for alternative words that can be delivered without gagging, and even be an improvement, like "hark" for "hear".... There are hundreds more. Ask Jonathan Miller about them. He is more clever at it than I.

Before I get back to my library speech in San Diego I must recall, for my sake as well as your own, a talk on writing that I gave in San Francisco for Mark Schorer, a professor of English at Berkeley. Elizabeth Bowen was on the same programme. She spoke with very much stammer, so much so that my sympathy and admiration were stirred by her courage, so much so that my fear of my talk was dispelled. My speech was clear of stutter in relief that she had finished without catastrophe. My talk was so well received that I went bravura and often had the audience laughing almost in unison. Schorer wrote to me after the show, for show it did become, with questions like bouquets coming to the stage to be fielded haltingly and gracefully returned by Elizabeth Bowen or by myself who answered them almost in comic relief.

Mark told me that I should have trod the boards as an actor. Rarely if ever before, he said, had he seen such a sense of timing by a lecturer. His compliments pleased me so much that I have rarely forgotten them. Timing is well-nigh all, that and talking as if riding a horse, slowly enough to be able to take the jumps and hurdles as they appear amid the listeners.

Reuben's presence put me in the right mood for my

talk at San Diego so that I started with humour, showed from my familiarity with references that I was talking about a topic that I liked and was familiar with.

Librarians, there were hundreds of them, crowded around me after the speech was over. Reuben was grinning like a Cheshire cat.

Although I was new in their game to all of them they saw my future as a rosy one, for all of us. One of them and his wife, both librarians, were of Irish stock. He pulled me aside and out of some Celtic wisdom told me that I would end up at the Library of Congress. He was sure of it. I only had to want it, and I did, there and then.

Robert Downs happened to be there. He was touring the country, preparing for his inauguration as the president of the American Library Association that was to be held at Los Angeles. He had chosen as the theme of that convention "The Books of the West" and was in the process of getting good speakers to present the theme. Western writers like Ambrose Bierce, Bret Harte, Frank Norris, the writers of the cowboy and thriller stories like Zane Grey, Edgar Rice Burroughs, Ray Chandler, Erle Stanley Gardner were either all too little known or quite ignored by the Brahmin Literary set that dominated the field of letters. He had assembled a fine panel of speakers of national renown but was seeking a keynote speaker for the entire convention theme.

He had hoped to obtain Wallace Stegner, from Stanford, but Stegner would be out of the country and he was at a loss to find a speaker good enough, well known enough to replace him.

Until his visit West I had only known of Robert Downs as one of the best of librarians. With the help and cooperation of his faculty friend James Gray he had made the University Library of Illinois at Champaign-Urbana among the best in America. The research collections approached the marvellous to me, the Library School of which Downs was dean as well as being the University Librarian was probably the best in the U.S. He showed a daring and enterprise in his writing and in his library administration which were at a peak at that time and the peak was going to stretch out into broad sunlit pastures such as have never been seen before.

Bob Downs was fortunate in his family life and above

128

all had a commanding presence, a schooled straight face
that was no mirror to his daring. He was a model to me,
even then, and he showed more than his daring when, after
hearing me deliver at San Diego and maybe having read some
of my stories and articles he asked me, a fledgling, to give
the keynote address at Los Angeles.

More of this later, but it has been a continual surprise to me that Bob Downs, and many others, relate me to
that speech in San Diego rather than to anything that I have
accomplished since, in any field of library endeavour. I
owe this to Reuben Peiss, and convinces me of the validity
of the belief that there is life after death.

Reuben realised that the Library School at Berkeley
was not for me, nor was I what they were looking for. My
time at Berkeley opened up the world of librarianship to me.
At that time the University supplied the cars that were used
for official purposes, and I got around the State quite a lot,
visiting librarians, talking at regional meetings and generally
meeting people. I remember in particular taking my class
to San Quentin, the famous gaol with the writer-warden
Duffy. This was by way of being a model gaol, and Herman
Specter was the devoted librarian there. I have never seen
anybody so devoted to his job. He was not particularly good
at it, being rather more concerned at being a prison librarian than anything else, and, after all, it was rather a con-
fining job. He and his trusties did a fine job, I am sure,
of getting the legal works of reference for those prisoners
who were working on their appeals, but there was more of
that than of anything else. Specter, to occupy some prisoners with useful work, gave them his suits to mend, his
shoes to cobble. He lived in the prison himself. I have
never seen, before or after, a suit so neatly patched and
darned as the one he wore. It was nearly all patch and
darn, and his shoes were the same. He would be an ideal
subject for a novel. Better that, than the prisoner who
years later copies by hand a rather obscure novel, and very
nearly had it accepted as his own work by Random House or
an equally prestigious firm.

129

11

The students, men and women, were wide-eyed at the prison experience. During the years I had visited several prisoners in prisons. After all, it is a cardinal work of mercy, but the prisoners I visited were in temporary jails for military misbehaviour and the like. San Quentin was a regular, well-known prison. The smell of it alone was like hell. There were nights after that class visit when I could not sleep because of what a prison came to mean to me. I would close the lot of them. I would burn the gallows, defuse the electric chairs, twist the rifles into shapes or melt down the metal parts and save the good wood for carving. Some incurables I would put to sleep, and find work or something to do with the rest of them in the open.

I drove back a carload of students over the San Quentin ferry leaving a student gourmandizer off somewhere near his home and refusing his offer of a soufflé. It was a quiet carload of us who returned to Berkeley.

Reuben had met Ray Swank and Elmer Grieder from Stanford and persuaded them that they needed an order librarian. Before the year's end I was installed in Stanford as the Assistant Librarian in charge of Acquisitions. Stanford was a good place to be in. The weather was the most perfect in the world to us, and we were lucky to get a large campus house on the Alta Vista estate for $45 a month, with a more than willing Buildings and Ground Staff who came and fixed dripping taps, leaking windows, did all the household tasks as part of their campus program. The estate had been built by a Lathrop, the brother of Mrs. Stanford. He was in charge of the building of the University in the 1890's. Leland Stanford was one of the great landlords, a railroad robber baron. When their only child, Leland Junior, died in his mid-teens, it was a terrible blow to both of them. They

131

went to Harvard, offering to enrich the university if the enrichment would bear the name of Leland Stanford Junior. They were rebuffed as being rather roughneck and Western, so they built a university of their own, called Leland Stanford Junior University. They bought the best faculty available, built a magnificent plant on 10,000 acres of rolling land in the Santa Clara Valley and endowed it more richly than any other university in America. The eminent David Starr Jordan was the first president, and within fifty years it was as solid an institution of higher learning and more as any university in America. There was a fine medical school and hospital established in its name in San Francisco and the great engineer and humanitarian, later the unfortunate U.S. President Hoover, was a graduate who deposited there in the Hoover Institution his collection on the rehabilitation of Europe. The collections housed there are still breathtaking to me. It flanked the University Library or vice versa, and the processing of their material was undertaken under some sort of Hoover aegis along with the library's own. Somehow by dint of my position, because I was third in the hierarchical library line, all the processing areas fell in a sort of way under me, and so did the Special Collections. Nobody could make a real stab at me for while I was preparing the library budget--the first time I did it was a nightmare--I was also a member of the distinguished English faculty. I taught with Wallace Stegner, who liked my writing, and with Richard Scowcroft, most of the courses at the Creating Writing Center that became well enough endowed to become centred in the University Library. Yehudi Menuhin grew up just around the corner in Los Gatos, the hillsides and tops had all sorts of lovely homes scattered among them, including Wally Stegner's, and the Jesuits had a winery and vineyard between us and their Santa Clara university that was as pleasant a place as Stanford on a small scale.

I started a Library Weekly News, fully of comment about books and authors and library news. Once, I recall, as I write, I replied to a sour remark that Donald Coney had made in his library weekly about how a writer thanked his staff for their help and commented that they would inherit the earth, that the writer did not necessarily mean thereby that all librarians were meek. There was no need to be Uriah Heepish about being a librarian, I replied. It was the fault of the Protestant Authorised Version that translated the Bible for the English: "Blessed are the meek" indeed! The French Little translation from the Aramaic is far better. In their version of the Bible the phrase reads "Benis

soient les debonaires" and if librarians would only become
less meek, less of Uriahs, and become instead more debonair, how much better would be the libraries and themselves.
"Consider, Coney, " I said. "How many debonair librarians
do you know, including yourself?"

The trouble with words is that they change their meaning often, with the times. "Naughty," "villain," many others,
mean not what they used to mean. I don't know whether
"debonair" was ever used in its proper connotation in English.
Somehow there is a jaunty, jingle, Psmithlike, quality about
it, but to be truly debonair is to be of good heart; to whistle
passing a graveyard in the dark is debonair to me, and that
shows a quality that all librarians should strive for, to be
cool cats on the hot tin roof of their world.

Every Tuesday afternoon I put a show on at the fine
roomy theatre next door to the library in the Cubberley
building. It always attracted hundreds and they were remarkably well behaved. One week it would be a film like Of
Mice and Men written by John Steinbeck, a Stanford graduate,
and featuring Burgess Meredith in his prime, long long before he became Mr. Penguin in the TV show Batman. Another week it was an advance agent talking about Kabuki:
the troupe was to tour the Bay Area before crossing the desert and the Rockies to New York. Sometimes we had lemons,
but there were not enough of them to sour the apple cart.

There was a constant stream of writers to the campus,
to the library, and to my home. Joyce Cary was the one I
remember the most clearly. He read a part of one of his
novels for me on tape, in the company of students. I wanted
him to read from Mister Johnson, one of the best novels in
English ever to come out of Africa, or the scene from The
Horse's Mouth where Gulley Jimson goes into an elegant art
shoppe to buy a canvas, but he made no bones about saying
No. He read a piece from his Northern Ireland novel Castle
Corner.

Later he gave a talk to a crowded audience in the University Theatre. There he stressed the importance of luck
in life. A truculent seminarian from a nearby Jesuit institution challenged him on this, in the question period after, and
Cary was nonplussed, saying that he had talked this over
many times with his dear friend Ronnie Knox, then the current Newman of Oxford (Cary did not say this about Ronnie--
I did, and do, many times) and found that they were in com-

133

plete accord. The seminarian sat down muttering. The Irish never liked Knox, and with good reason, any more than they had liked Newman. I feel sorry for both of them, but being redneck Irish myself, I feel the same way about them, for all their goodness.

Later that night, in our house, Joyce Cary talked, just to me and my wife, for an hour or so while waiting for the sleeper train to Los Angeles. We grew to be friends out of it and wrote to one another fairly regularly. Towards the end he grew more and more crippled with a painful disease, and he was confined to a chair that had a fixture that allowed him to guide his hand up to the end in slow and painful writing.

When his family opened his papers at his end there was a last letter to me, commending me for my care of books and reading. I set about making sure that his manuscripts and letters would be well taken care of. I anticipated no difficulty in paying the family for them and getting them transferred to Stanford, but Cary had good friends at Oxford. After a score of years of neglect his worth had become recognised. The American Friends of the Bodleian bought the papers and Bodley accorded them a rare honour, setting them in a special room, even including the chair wherein he spent his last painful years.

In his letters to me he was tranquil and more right to the very end. I was especially grieved at the painful way of his passing because he was a small, elegant, high-nosed patrician of a man who walked so well and in so befitting a manner to his appearance that it was a pleasure to watch.

I wrote an article about him. Enid Starkie, his friend, professor of French at Oxford, said that of all the obituary articles mine was the best, and I agree.

One of my best friends at Stanford was Rab Minto, the chaplain. Another was a colleague of his in the department of Religion, Alexander Miller. Every year Lex Miller and his wife Jean would have a get-together with the students in the Union and I would read them A Child's Christmas in Wales by Dylan Thomas, and as an encore some of my own stuff. Lex worked far too hard, spreading the good word across America, writing books about it, and counselling the students. It was he who brought Dorothy Day to the campus, a demanding saint of a woman, the fire behind the Catholic

134

Worker Movement. The New Yorker ran a three-part piece
on her. She was the darling of Eugene O'Neill when he was
coming into his power as a dramatist. Dorothy was of un-
compromising quality, with her pacifism, her anti-Franco
writing and actions. Her House of Hospitality on Mott Street
that was always open to the destitute, the rejected and the
dying, became a centre of young Liberal Catholic Action,
and a burr under the saddle of Cardinal Spellman, the fat
little real estate expert and Chaplain General to the U.S.
forces. When she came to Stanford, at the invitation of Lex
and Jean Miller, the Catholic chaplain made himself scarce.
She made a disciple of me, and the more I saw her as the
years went by the more I became sure that I was in the
company of a saint. It was Eugene O'Neill's drunken recita-
tion night after night as they were sitting over their drinks
in some shebeen or other that brought about her conversion
to Catholicism, that so sorely embarrassed and worse the
Establishment of that august institution in the U.S. but saved
the Church for the rising crop of those young idealists who
had benefitted from the rising flood of education that, even
with its faults, was to save the Church and topple the old
order therein. Nobody has caught this to rights so well as
J. F. Powers in his books of short stories, The Presence
of Grace, the Prince of Darkness and his novel Morte D'Urban.
They were dead to rights.

Frank O'Connor spent a time with us there at the
Writing Centre. He and his young wife came into my circle
and I learned a lot from him. He had been a librarian in
his early Irish days and often questioned me closely, colleague to colleague, about circulation systems that were a
thing of the past. They must have been, even in rural Ireland. He was a genius on occasion, and I use that word
sparingly. His reminiscences and tales of his early days
are heart-rending, beautiful, and funny. It was always a
sorrow to me, and always will be, how good writers have
to teach, lecture, become involved with the demands and
worse of writing students so that they can make a living.
Their own work suffers from it. They are the prey while
they are on the campus circuit of the well paid and better
fed and dressed faculty who insist on giving parties for the
literary lions and feed on the results that accrue for years
and years.

"I remember Robert Frost telling me...."

"But as I was saying to Dame Edith...."

135

"Jessamyn West was wearing red shoes the last time I was speaking to her...."

"Evelyn Waugh was telling me about the shocking quarters in the hotel. When he called the manager he was full of apologies and ushered them into the proper suite that had been arranged for them. The room clerk had made a mistake. There was a convention of deodorant salespersons, and the clerk thought that Waugh was the representative for Mum. He was still fuming as he told me about it."

"As I was telling Sir Basil...."

"Lady Langford is charming, quite charming and, my dear, such a writer, and such a talented family."

There were some writers on the lecture circuit who liked it, were tough or had enough guile to benefit from it. Carl Sandburg was the prime example, but Robert Frost was good at it too. One evening, after his talk to a crowded theatre at Stanford, a tailored talk, one of the several that he carried about with him, he was seated in a party surrounded by crowds who would be saying after and for years to come "As I was telling Robert Frost...."

He was ignoring them all quite rudely, not even answering them, but enjoying the comfort of his chair after his hours of standing up and around the lectern. He was waiting for the student who was to drive him back to his hotel. This was in Wallace Stegner's home in the foothills near Los Gatos.

I was talking rapidly and with some humour, I don't know about what, to Dick Scowcroft, Bill Irvine, John Loftis or someone when Robert Frost caught my eye and beckoned me over. He talked as if there was nobody else around, about Edward Thomas, a poet, and friend of his from his days in the Cotswolds where he had written A Boy's Will, his first success, just before World War I. Edward Thomas was killed in that war, but Robert Frost, and this was more than forty years later, remembered him with love. My intonation had caught his ear in that crowded party room and the Welsh cadence of my voice was like that of his dead friend. We talked together as if there was nobody else there, for him, anyway, of Edward Thomas, Wilfred Owen, Francis Ledwidge, Edmund Blunden ... all the poets of those days that we held so dear.

136

The next day he came to call on me in the library.
I got a few students together and we sat around a table in
the Special Collections Room and talked. He offered to read
some poetry for us and I got John Priddle to set up a tape
machine. The making of audio-visual material was in its
infancy in those days, and John Priddle who ran the building
maintenance of the library, was the engineer. Unluckily
John taped the talking but cut off the machine whenever Frost
got to reciting. I have always distrusted audio since, and
with good reason.

Stanford had a good book budget in those days. Already I was restive about the number of librarians and clerks
it took to process the books, and the length of time. Through
no good management on my part, Edith Falconer ran a sharp
and very efficient order department. The bookseller's bills
were cleared after vetting on the very day that they arrived,
and this gave me an enormous advantage in dealing with collections if I had to buy them through booksellers. The sure
fact that they would get their money quickly made me a favoured customer.

Bertram Rota visited us from London fairly frequently.
I had been dealing with him man and boy for years. He got
nearly all the British and some of the European trade.
There were good booksellers along the West Coast and about
two or three times a month I would spend a day in San Francisco around the bookstores. David Magee became a good
friend of mine. When he negotiated the sale of a Thomas
More Collection to the University of San Francisco, he tidied
up the sale to everybody's satisfaction by selling me the
peripheral material. When I write that it was to everybody's
satisfaction I remember now that it rather startled some librarians at the University of California at Berkeley. They
had started a rather stately pavane to acquire these books
for themselves, and were surprised to find out that I had
quietly purchased them. I did this without any knowledge
that they were in the market for them too, and Coney, for
the first and only time, was quietly courteous and urgent to
me, asking me that if I came across any collection that I
thought did not fit into my scheme of collections for Stanford
would I please consider referring news of the collections to
the library at Berkeley.

I still went across the bridge to Berkeley fairly often.
The editor of The Magazine of Fantasy and Science Fiction
lived over there and he had become a fan of mine. He pub-

lished in the Magazine, in the form of a novella, my Cuchu-
lain stories, my Coo-Cullen cycle. "Devlin," one of my best
stories, and "Weerawannas," a Stanford story that related
exactly to Alta Vista, where we lived, to Park, one of my
children, and the academic life. For some reason that still
eludes me the Magazine paid me quite highly for a critical
article on Bridie Murphy, a cause célèbre in the 50's,
about a woman in Colorado who went back in dream or trance
to Ireland of a century before. Anthony Boucher, the editor
of the M.F.S.F., I remember, when he received "Devlin"
wrote to me and said that while he would be happy to print
it it would be better by far if he published it as a reprint,
that it deserved a far better first appearance than his magazine could afford. Sadly I replied that I agreed with him,
but none of the few quality magazines that still featured
stories wanted it, so it was M.F.S.F. or bust.

By this time I was enjoying the Bay area part of my
work very much. San Francisco was a great town to visit
and I got to know the booksellers, got to know Joseph Henry
Jackson, the literary editor of the San Francisco Chronicle,
and could help myself to books in his office that I would consider for review.

David Magee and Warren Howell had bookshops on Post
Street almost one above the other. It seemed strange to me
then, and it still does, that librarians tend to sit at their
desks and wait for the booksellers to court them, rather than
get around the bookstores themselves, meet the booksellers
in their own habitat. It can be a great economy to both sides
if the librarians can pay out of their hip pocket, or very
nearly, for some collection and clinch the deal. This saves
the bookseller the cost of cataloguing, of apologising to the
librarians who write in for a book in the catalogue that has
already been sold, and, most of all, the money comes to the
bookseller right away without having to pass through bureaucracy channels that are both very expensive to the institution
and delay an authorised payment to the bookseller often nearly
a year. This is something that no business should have to
afford.

During the past thirty years I have been responsible
for spending about thirty million dollars on books. Every
year a small part of the book budget has been left to the
Librarian's discretion, while by far the larger part, more
than 90 per cent, has been divided among the departments
for their book buying. Should an extraordinary situation

arise, requiring speedy action, I have always been able to obtain it either from University reserves or from the book fiends of laggardly departments who have neglected to spend their book allotments. This has often required quick thinking, talking, and footwork on my part, but it has been well worth it, and the more successful my efforts have been, the easier it became to loosen purse strings, private as well as public, and give others a feeling of sharing.

Once, in San Francisco, there was a public dinner of the University of California. There was a shy but wealthy and worthwhile alumnus at the high table sitting next or near to President Sproul. Sitting near was another California alumnus who also had graduated from Stanford. He heard the shy California alumnus, a gentle man in his later years, tell Sproul that he had been a good friend of William Somerset Maugham for many years, that he had helped Maugham escape from the South of France when the Germans moved in and took P. G. Wodehouse to Berlin where he burbled from the Adlon what jolly decent chaps were the Germans. The English put him on trial as a traitor when the war was over, but Maugham had escaped to the U.S., and this Californian friend had helped him re-establish his fortune. Sproul listened with a smile and half an ear, and as a result I went to call on the gentleman who lived in a marvellous house, with a butler-controlled staff, under the Golden Gate Bridge. It was clear that I knew and respected the cut and craft of Willie Maugham, and the Maugham Collection was transferred to Stanford for safekeeping. About the same time I called on C. S. Forester who lived in a fine house in Berkeley overlooking the Bay. He was suffering from a circulatory ailment and so was resting in a chaise longue. Although the Hornblower series, that I enjoyed, had made his fortune, I spoke to Forester about his other books, the ones I liked the most, Brown on Resolution (a fine title that), Payment Deferred, and, most of all, The General. His eyes lighted when I spoke of The General, the story of a decent donkey general in World War I who had led his men to death in infantry actions in Flanders, time and time again, when "attrition" was the buzz-word of the Imperial General Staff. Even so-near-Blimp a soldier as the General, one of the Haig's cavalry compadres, had some doubts about the waste of British and Colonial blood, but "dogged does it" and when the war was over and the golden promise of the youths stone dead, he retired with honours, and in his old age his wife pushed him in a wheel chair amid the palms potted within and without, of the resort areas of England's South Coast while his veterans were ill-housed, ill-clad, unpaid, in the homes further north that had been promised as being "fit for heroes to live in."

It is in meeting the authors, the artists that it seems that one has seen Shelley plain. What a difference it makes to school children and to all when they meet a writer who can personally communicate with them. The author W. O. Mitchell has this quality. It is encouraged and financed by the Canadian provinces to a degree, and it is one of the best peripheral means of learning and of appreciation that I know. Every library, every library board, should encourage this, with rooms and funding. I have talked to many amateur writers' groups in library rooms, in the board room of a temple, in people's basements and gardens. Although maybe they will never be good writers their enthusiasm for writing, their own above all, their criticism of self and of the others is a pleasure to join in. They have become enmeshed in the reading arts and should be cherished and encouraged. The pleasure that one of them gets on the occasion that his or her work has been accepted for publication is transcendent; it lightens up the whole room.

To a degree this sort of atmosphere has permeated my whole life; the fact that my running of a library had to do with it has lightened my days, my years, my decades.

Shortly after getting the Maugham collection we heard that the Pacific Union Club was going to replace its library with lounges and billiards rooms. Ray Swank, the University Librarian, and I went up to see the officers of the Club and transferred their book collection to Stanford. It was about that time that Swank and I drove to the Big Sur to see Robinson Jeffers. Jeffers looked more like a poet--translator of Medea--than I had hoped to see. Altogether it was a memorable experience visiting him, but his collection was already promised to another. Probably Larry Powell had gathered it in for his rapidly growing book complex at Los Angeles. The university at Los Angeles had been very much second fiddle to the sister university at Berkeley, and this showed in the library collections and service, but Larry changed all that. He was a book collector par excellence and he ran a good library to boot. These qualities rarely go together. Book collectors, like booksellers, have always eyed me rather askance, for I believe that library administration comes first, an administration that can both absorb, improve, properly care for the collections, and ga-ga bibliophiles are quaint, should work in bookshops, as sometimes I suspect they do.

140

Larry was envied and disliked by the traditional dullards of the profession. He had played in a dance band on
cruise liners, taken a doctorate in French at Dijon when the
lightning struck him. He graduated as a librarian and changed
the whole library scene on the West Coast. The younger librarians championed him. He won their support with honeyed
phrases, with his constant references to them in his books
that he wrote about writers, readers, and collections, and
he genuinely liked them, rubbed the crud off them until they
shone. Some of his bookfishing made a master trawler out
of him. He was a man to follow. I remember when the
one time cow college of U. C. L. A. achieved the goal of shelving its millionth volume. Larry let the library world know
it loud and clear. Berkeley responded with a condescending
note congratulating him on reaching the halfway mark.

When Berkeley achieved its two millionth volume there
was a considerable ceremony about it. A new book conveyor
system had been designed and installed to facilitate the rout-
ing of books to the main desk, speeding up the time of delivery. Before an invited crowd of faculty, librarians from
other institutions and others, the two millionth volume was
conveyed down the endless belt from a book level on high to
the main desk. The Chancellor, or somebody equally exalted,
was meant to lift out the landmark volume and present it to
a waiting librarian to prepare for lending to a reader. Somehow or other the gears, the intermeshing rods that turned
the corners so that the machine could function, messed up.
They totally macerated the book, so that by the time the
volume reached the main circulation it had turned to confetti.
It was a birdsong to me when Swank related it. He had been
there, representing Stanford.

These were happy days for all of us. We had an estate, jungled and overrun, for the children to play in. They
had a big black Labrador who was patient and abiding with
them. Now and again, nearly every day, he would make his
way across Lagunita and visit a women's dormitory. There
they made much of him, and then he would sedately pace to
the students' alfresco coffee shop for a drink, further petting,
and anything he cared for, chocolate, candy, anything. I
remember one Boxing Day when we were sitting in the sun
before noon, and Blackie passed us with the remains of the
Christmas turkey between his jaws. It had been set out for
our lunch. The dormitory and cafe were closed for the
Christmas holidays, and a dog has to eat.

There was also a flight of guinea hens with a real

141

chanticleer of a rooster. The birds had learned to fly high,
take off like snipe or clay pigeons, when rattlers, raccoons,
or enemies of other kinds threatened them. They would
rise above the high redwoods that encircled our house wheel-
ing like eagles yet clucking like chickens, angrily, at their
earthbound enemies. Cars would screech to a halt at the
sight of them dipping and diving in the high air, squawking
at their chanticleer, as if he was to blame for the snakes
and the raccoons.

I had a rather gloomy office in the library building,
far less impressive than the more administrative offices.
The window looked out at another wall, and when it rained
it guttered down noisily between the window and the wall.
I did not have a secretary save as a grace and favour, but
since I had never had one before this was of no consequence
to me. Then, one day, the President's Office called me up.
They had hired for academic favour a Chinese girl from Hong
Kong, and she was the receptionist over there. Norma Yu
was so graceful and lovely that she was holding up the business in the office. Callers would stay with her as long as
they could engage her attention. They were at a loss until
the President, a ci-devant Canadian, Wallace Sterling, told
them to send her over to Will Ready. There she would be
safe from the constant queries and she could do the typing--
she was an excellent typist--and other library duties for me.
A desk was found for her in the library order office just
across the corridor from me and from then on, from Norma
to Rose, for nearly thirty years I have been cared for by
secretaries who have become like family to me and often to
us. Norma had a face that would launch a thousand sampans.
I could give her the gist of a letter and she could write it
better than I. When she had completed her M.A. in English
we managed to get her a scholarship at the U.S.C. Library
School. She married, had children (I am the godfather of
the first) and took her doctorate at Columbia. Now as Dr.
Norma Yu-Eh she runs her own library. I miss her. She
had great talent and even greater prospect.

Wallace Stegner was in my office haunching against
the radiator with the rain guttering outside. His book Powell
of the Colorado, was, I felt sure, certain to win the Pulitzer
Prize that year, but the prize went instead to Paul Horgan
for his book on the Rio Grande, Great River. Horgan was
at this time librarian of the New Mexico Military Institute
and a fine writer he has been. Wally was all smiles when
he came in to see me. He brushed away my remarks about

how unlucky it was that the two books on the rivers had come out the same season of 1954.

"Never mind" he said with a grin that betokened his prize and pride. "Better than Pulitzer: I've been banned in Ireland!" This set him among the immortals, and he settled back against the streaming window to hear my beginning of Devlin. This was a story that I had written years ago. It somehow missed the hook of a beginning that would spear the reader. It was not until that morning, just before Wallace walked in, that the hook came into my hand, as if I were a longshoreman working at the docks. I read it out. Stegner was the first to hear it, a beginning that has become famous and held aloft and aloud for all writers aspirant and otherwise.

> The Devil is a man is a woman is a stretch of road is a drink or is a gun. He comes with money or with the lack of it. As a serpent he came to naked Eve, and it was as one of themselves, as Fleur Devlin, a stocky gingered man of forty summers, that he came to the parish of the Holy Redeemer and gelded it.

As the reader can believe, as I can, Stanford was a good place to be a librarian. There was a bookman, C. D. O'Malley, who used to drop in on me in my office nearly every day for the seven years that we lived there. Don O'Malley was Professor of the history of science. His wife, Frances Keddie, a Maritimer, was the specialist in dermatology at the Palo Alto Clinic that gave the University entire health and medical care: it was the best of its kind in the world, we thought.

I have always had a sort of devotion to Thomas More, the Man rather than the Saint. Tom, my fourth son, was born at Palo Alto, and was called after him. The Gannymede Press had a good copy of Holbein's portrait of Thomas More, and I always had a copy in my office to commune with. Whenever O'Malley, not a jubilant or funny sort of man, came into my office he would first of all greet the Holbein copy. "Hello, Tom" he would say or "Good morning, Tom." It might have been eerie to others, but never to me. Thomas More had that way about him even when he lived. He is the only Englishman I know who has been so universally beloved.

I picked up the habit of borrowing copies of great

143

paintings from the University of Minnesota where they were available for loan from the library. Our kitchen-living-guest room wall had a copy of Bellini's "Head of a Youth" on the wall of our Quonset hut nearly the whole time we lived there, and it did me a lot of good when I was typing at the table, the children all in bed and my wife in our room listening to my tap-tap, to look up at the Youth when I was stymied and sort of communicate with him and Bellini before resuming my typing.

It was only when I saw the original of Holbein's "More" in the Frick Gallery in New York that I realised how much a copy necessarily is less than the original.

Don O'Malley had the best private library that I have ever known. I was often over in his house near the campus looking at some book or other before our conversation closed it and we were talking of our work. He was in charge of the collection of the History of Medicine books at our medical library in San Francisco.

I am sure, although we never discussed it, he was anxious to become the Librarian of the Medical Library and he would probably have been a good one. He and his side-kick Saunders had already published their monumental book The Anatomical Drawings of Leonardo da Vinci and Don O'Malley was to reach the heights with his biography of Vesalais. I remember that the Times Literary Supplement gave it top billing. He was a member, and a strong one, of the University Library Board. He tended, without ever saying anything to me, but plenty to the Board, including Swank, the Librarian, towards regarding books as more important than anything else in the library. Since I practised this credo of his, while still running my side of the library as much as I was allowed to, he was a strong right arm to me. Ray Swank and Elmer Grieder were both in the same age bracket as I was. While Swank admired and supported me it was clear to me that I would always be a second or third fiddle at Stanford, and while we were happy there I could see that I would never captain that craft. Elmer Grieder, a Harvard-trained librarian, to his credit, made this abundantly clear to me.

There was one incident at Stanford that I always recall about this time. The chanticleer of the guinea fowl was bitten by a snake. He must have been a tough chicken for he survived, only he was lack-lustre, dragged his feet, no longer

144

had his ranks of harem who were taken over instead by his empress, a stately dame of a hen. Park, who had seen the weerawannas, took him in, but no amount of nursing revived him. He was fading fast. Frances Keddie cast her doctor's eye over him and shook her head.

"You had better bring him in to the clinic, Park. Let me put him to sleep. "

Park nodded. His feelings were too deep for words.

The next day I drove Park in to the Palo Alto Clinic. Chanticleer was shivering by then and Park carried him between his skin and his shirt. As we walked down the corridor on the main floor we passed the receptionist's desk. There were a group of doctors gathered around, shooting the breeze, checking their appointment schedules. It was a fine Monday morning. The patients were arriving, being directed by Ella the receptionist to the appropriate waiting rooms. All the doctors and the receptionist knew Park and me.

"Hullo, Park" said Joe Davies, who looked after the family. "I've not got you down here. " He checked his appointment schedule again.

"No, Doctor" Park answered slowly. "I'm to see Dr. Keddie. I've got a sick chicken. " With that Chanty poked his bird-like head out of the front of Park's shirt and gave a sad and shadowy baleful glare.

I just nodded at the group, and followed Park down the corridor to the Specialist Wing, and followed him into the Dermatology Office. Mimi was the nurse-receptionist. She was French, a lovely girl who looked as if she was bursting out of her clothes in the nicest way. The waiting room was full of patients with skin ailments of all kinds, from scabs to scrofula. And there was a plague of ringworm at the time, so many were wearing boiled white head coverings that smelled of ointment and boiled cotton.

Mimi greeted Park with a hug. Frances had told her about the state of Chanty and she led them in to the doctor's office where Frances was washing her hands and pulling on her white coat. I waited outside, found a chair next to a man who looked like a pimpernelled warthog. His hands were all covered with bandages. As Mimi and Park went into the office Chanty gave a farewell cock-a-doodle-do. It

145

sounded to me a brave and futile sound, like the horn that blew at Roncesvalles, but to the waiting patients who had not seen the rooster in Park's shirt it was such a startle that they all looked at each other with a wild surmise.

It was not very long before the door to the office opened again. There were tears in the eyes of Mimi and of Dr. Keddie. They had their hands on the shoulders of the stricken seven-year-old who was carrying a tray with a white cloth over it. Sticking out beneath the cloth, stiff and dead, were the taloned claws of Chanticleer. As we reached the door Mimi bent down and kissed Park on the cheek. She wiped her eyes and as we left we could hear her:

"Mrs. Donnell? The doctor will see you now."

We buried Chanty amid the tomato plants that the moles were pulling down. Park thought perhaps that Chanty's dead presence would keep the moles away, but the plants kept being pulled into the ground, and, a week later, when Park dug up to look, there was no sign of dead Chanty's cadaver at all. The guinea fowl took on a new lease of life following the death of the rooster. They rarely trod the ground at all but roosted in the trees and flew around high in the sky, relishing their freedom. The sun shone on their outstretched wings as they lazily glided high above the trees, and they were well-nigh silent, their chirps sounding more and more like whistles. Graham Dushane, the Chairman of the Biology Department until he became editor of Science-- he was present with Park in his lab at the birth of a sea-horse--was doing an article about it. Scientific American sent out a reporter. Tour buses from San Francisco on their way to Monterey used to stop outside our tall iron gates when the chickens were in full flight and glide pattern. Then, one morning, they were gone, the Empress and her chicken court. They were never seen again. Where they went only the God of us all knows and, as usual, there is silence from that quarter.

There were so many happenings at Stanford that as I write they crowd in on me. One day Virgil Whitaker, the chairman of the English Department, was called away to a Provost's meeting and called me to keep company with W. H. Auden who was to give a speech at the theatre that night. I went across to Virgil's house and made desultory conversation with Auden who sucked at glasses of Scotch, nodding his head, occasionally adding a muddled word. He seemed to

146

sense my antipathy to him. His face was extremely lined and haggard. That is the lot of all literary lions who are going through the hoops of a lecture tour. It's a game not worth the candle, and the candle that is the money, is burnt out before the tour is hardly over.

12

I saw more of Frank O'Connor than I had ever hoped to.
Walter Van Tilburg Clark wrote The Oxbow Incident. It is
one of the best movies ever made in Hollywood, better even
than The Informer or Duck Soup, and, like The Informer,
it kept the quality of the fine writer who created the book.
He wrote some other good books, The Track of the Cat especially. He was Writer in Residence for a while and he
got into the habit of joining us for dinner of a Monday night.
He was easy with the children, having some of his own, and
he talked as if floodgates were open. He was quiet, laconic,
taciturn in class and lecture, but as he sat in our armchairs
with us, a jug of local vino paisano as a brew, he reminisced,
commented about his life in the West. His father was a university president, and so Walter was no stranger to the academic life. It was always the small hours, often as dawn
was breaking, that he made a move towards home. My wife
and the children had been asleep upstairs for hours before
we made a move for his departure. More often than not,
another campus friend had turned up for the evening, and
when I closed the door on them and went up to bed I could
still hear them, often for hours, leaning against the car outside, talk-talk-talking, often until the rooster crowed.

Yvor Winters and his wife Janet Lewis became good
friends, each in their own way. Yvor tended to be morose.
He would sit for hours silently and alone in his office, his
hands on his knees, just thinking. But good poetry came
out of him, some of the very best, and his opinions, often
recalcitrant, were reasoned. He even began to share in my
humour, if only with a fleeting smile or a grunt, but we
were easy in one another's company. His book In Defence
of Reason remains a classic to me. There was a grant of
some thousands of dollars that came from somewhere annually to buy books for the Special Collections, and he and I

were the administrators of it. For a while we tried to choose the books together, but since he regarded most modern poets, save J. V. Cunningham, once a pupil of his, as garbage mongers, we were enjoying our selection committee (just the two of us) but we were not spending the money, since we could not agree upon an acquisition policy. So I told him to order any books he wanted through me, and I would order the rest. That way we wiped the platter clean and it all worked out to our entire satisfaction.

What with the book collecting, the acquisition, the talks and meetings with librarians up and down the Coast and as far inland as Fresno, I was learning a lot. I was learning a lot in handling people. One thing I could never abide was the security measures of renting the Pinkerton kind of uniformed guards, guides, even receptionists, at a library. It was at Stanford that I started hiring retired folk who were so anxious to keep in touch with the world that they were delighted with the opportunity to work at the circulation desk, at shelving and repair. There was a Mr. Ryan who became my prime and lasting model for the future. His son Larry and I had known one another for years, since Minnesota days, and Mr. and Mrs. Ryan moved out to Palo Alto when Larry was appointed to Stanford, where he was to make a name for himself as an English Renaissance Scholar.

I hired Mr. Ryan. When he came out with Larry and some of the children in advance of the family, they stayed with us. I can still see and hear him at the sink, helping with the washing-up, telling my wife and some of the Ryan children and our own, stories of his war career in the Military Police up around Alaska. He loved Alaska, would have gone back there to live, if his wife could share his enthusiasm. But they ended up in Palo Alto, bought a house and settled down. The University Library was a delight to Mr. Ryan; I think it was the happiest time of his life, his working there. I always called him Mr. Ryan, naturally, he was Larry's father, and by the same token he always called me Will. His granddaughter Kate and our son Patrick started school together in the campus grade school and were Joseph and Mary, I remember, in the school's Grade I Christmas Play.

We never missed a play at the University Theatre. When they put on Henry IV they came to me for the words that Shakespeare never wrote, when Glendower speaks Welsh, and his daughter, wife of Hotspur, sings a Welsh lullaby to

150

her baby. I gave Glendower a mouthful of Welsh words which, while they did not make sense, sounded fair and strong enough. They were a series of greetings, farewells and toasts that I had picked up in the common-room at college in Cardiff, along with a few patriotic slogans, so that Glendower, under my tutelage, sounded Welsh enough, but a Welsh speaker daft enough too. He was not speaking Welsh but gobbledygook which is the nearest I've ever come to talking or reading the language proper.

> Glendower: "lochi da, bo bill Ma"
> "Cymru am Byth! Gwlad, Gwlad, Harlech bachan."

And for the daughter's song to the baby I taught her to sing:

> "Arbis merion very brithan
> Arbis Wedi scrappo Jonni bach."

There was more of it like that, but the glory of the Welsh language is that when it is spoken with feeling it becomes Pentecostal, and the words don't matter. Anyhow, Henry IV was a great success, and the program read "Henry IV/by William Shakespeare/Welsh text by William Ready."

I still have a copy of the program. Handsome and impressive, large it is too, with deckle edges.

There was rarely a day that I was not in the library. There are poems and prose written galore on strolls along the winding country lanes that are bordered by the hedgerows flowering and brambled, but I have always preferred the miles and miles of stacks to wander through, stopping now and then, not to pick a flower or pluck a berry, or be stung by a nettle, but to look at some book or other, just for a minute, and find myself an hour, maybe later, squatting on a foot stool still sampling the book, like a bumble bee at a flower. Books are flowers to me. Maybe that is why Archie Wavell's anthology of poems that he used to say to himself, remembering from his reading, Other Men's Flowers, appeals to me so much.

One position I created at Stanford, that I worked out with Charles Gorham, my man in the mending and repair room, was a peripatetic book mender. This person had a stripped and shelved perambulator and used to push the pram along slowly between the shelves, stopping every now and then

151

to give a lick of paste to a book whose pages were sagging, or whose jacket was torn. It was the most elementary kind of mending that even I could handle, but this fortunate person, by giving first-aid to the book then and there, could keep the book available for circulation without having to remove it for mending and go through the tedious and often faulty job of altering the records of the books' whereabouts. Often, if I decided some books needed a change of location or had to be added to the shelves, the children would come in with me and give me a hand. A library is a wonderful place to be when it is empty of all but you and yours. None of the children ever wanted to be librarians. They thought I worked too hard, and I agreed with them: it was odd to be a librarian while the world went by unheeding, and offering glittering prizes for half my hours of work, or so I told myself. But I never believed it. Now two of my family work in a library and two more have published bibliographies. What is a man to do, who needs a plumber, a doctor, and an electrician in the family, a mechanic and a carpenter, and finishes up with a library worker?

By this time I was becoming seasoned as a librarian. The clatter of horse's hoofs in the Harvard Yard sounded loud and clear. Ed Williams and I had shared a dormitory room for weeks at the University of Chicago Graduate Library School. Phil McNiff had taught me more of library management by his example than he can realise, and Mary Stack, his wife, became a close family friend. Some of my best memories are of times I spent within their home. Mary's family had lived in Tirphil, a Welsh mining village. I believe Mary was born there. They were of the same stock as I was, and her father and mother, who lived with them in Boston, became close family friends. They had made the final leap to the States, after a generation in Wales and to go into the house on Chestnut Hill was like going into my own. Mrs. Stack, when she knew Will was coming, would prepare Welsh dishes, simple, wholesome and oh! how nostalgic. Mr. Stack was one of the best men I ever knew. He was a simple, good man, who had served in the regular British Army in the 1900's, and when he was bed-ridden--one of his legs had to be amputated --we would sit and talk for hours, enjoying one another's company, like I have never known since or before.

I was never a Harvard man, far from being one, yet my Cardiff accent, along with the others that were laid on it by University, the Army, and experience did give a Boston twang to my speech so that when I say "the Harvard Yard" my vowels sound exactly the same as when I say "Cardiff Arms Park."

Bernard de Voto was a Harvard man who was bitter about the fact that he had to pay $50 a year to use the library there. He lived in Cambridge, and I remember the last time he gave a talk at Stanford he was beefing to me about this $50 fee. He waggled his index finger at me, I remember, showing how spatulate it had become from all his writing: he was writing the Easy Chair column pages in Harper's and was a professional writer churning out books and pieces along with his good Western history. He grew up in Utah the son of a Notre Dame graduate, and there was an affinity between himself and Wallace Stegner who, while he spent his childhood on the Canadian prairie, was as briny and as Western as Salt Lake City.

We really had a flow of visitors through the Library in those days. I remember that I had bought an Aldous Huxley collection from Jake Zeitlin, and of a Saturday morning Jake was settling it to rights in the Special Collections Room when Felix Greene, who was running the Mental Health centre Palo Alto, called to ask me if I was in the Library, since Aldous Huxley, a friend of his, was staying with him, and he would like to see the Special Collections. Jake Zeitlin looked a bit odd when I told him that Huxley was coming around, but went on sorting the collection. When the rickety elevator deposited Huxley and Greene I was startled at Huxley's great height. Although stooped and peering through pebble glasses in order to see, he must have been six and a half feet tall. In fact I believe that only one of my sons, who is tall, tops him among my acquaintances. Jake had included in the sale some items that Huxley had given him, as Huxley gently reminded him as he peered at them. We spent most of the morning in a shelf bay, sitting down and talking, mainly about The Gioconda Smile, one of my favourite short stories. Huxley lived near Hollywood, was a regular customer at Jake's great barn of a bookshop on La Cienega Boulevard, and had many Hollywood tales to tell me. They had used La Gioconda in three movies. The differences in the productions, the directings could have been a part of Miss Lonelyhearts, The Slide Area, or The Loved One. Huxley's intelligence shone through, his humour, wit, and burning zeal shone through him. He became the favoured one to me of all my library visitors.

Gradually the Santa Clara Valley was dying. More

153

and more strips of subdivisions were lining the road from
San Francisco to San José. The wealthy and spacious homes
of Atherton and district were selling out to speculative build-
ers and Junipero Serra Road, that ran past the stone walls
of our Alta Vista estate and Lagunita, the Stanford lake, was
getting crowded with traffic. They were building a shopping
mall on Stanford property adjacent to the university. An engineering park was going up on the other side. Stanford men
were going in heavily for electronic industries: motors were
rearing. A new Stanford was emerging. The medical centre
was moving down from San Francisco. The university campus was as spacious as ever but was being surrounded by
buildings on its own property. This was bound to result, as
the private university had to find the funds to stay in business
with the State-supported institutions. Even I was called on
to give fund-raising talks for the university, for the funds
that Stanford received from its founders in 1900 had no meaning against the continuing procurement skills of Harvard and
Yale.

All this was lightened for us by the advent to Stanford
of André and Andrée Girard. It was because of them that I
was featured, along with Peter Ustinov, at a performance at
Lincoln Center. It was André that put me in the publishing
game. My first foray was by way of an illustrated essay by
Jacques Maritain, printed for me by the Pied Piper Press
(I called my firm in those days Chi-Rho Press). My second
publication was a silk-screen book, hand-made, coloured,
and each copy individually illustrated by André. This edition
was limited to 50 copies. It was financed by the Boegner
Foundation as an enlightened charitable and artistic contribution. Most of the copies of "Les Paroles de Jesus" were
donated to art galleries and great institutions. A publisher
was needed, so my Chi-Rho Press was selected and the book,
the few copies of it, went on the market for $500. I re-
ceived a copy as my guerdon and it is worth many times
more than the original price these twenty-odd years later.

One of the reasons that I have been able to be a book
collector for the library is because I read and write a lot
about books and the people around them. I wrote about André
in a way that I enjoyed and which pleased him. Better here
to recount Stanford's connection with André Girard, and my
growing friendship with him in words that I wrote at the time.

During the year of 1953 the French artist André
Girard came and lived among us on the Peninsula.

154

Clare Boothe Luce commissioned him to paint the
walls and windows of the Chapel of Saint Ann, the
Stanford University Newman Club chapel in Palo
Alto that she in her charity had erected to the memory of her daughter Ann.

I met him well-nigh the first day of his arrival
and he was a stranger to me. He was already well-
known in America, through the church that he had
painted at Stowe, Vermont, his serigraphs and religious paintings, his exhibitions in New York and
Dallas, but the Coast was far away from all that,
and I was far away from art, too.

It was on a sunny spring morning in the chapel
when I met him, he and his wife, two worn and
distinguished people in working clothes, mixing paint,
generally preparing for art. I genuflected, flicked
the Sign of the Cross over me, and watched them
for a while. I liked what I saw, and I told them
so. When I realized they were French, I spoke in
dumb show and in my school boy French: it is
execrable. But they saw my good will, ignorant
as it was, and I was pleased. I thought that they
were so poor, that if I had had a few dollars in
my pocket I would have slipped it to them. But I
did not, and asked them out to dinner instead: I
knew it was stew, and that that would stretch. I
came to fetch them at five o'clock and they said
that they would follow in their car. I was rather
surprised that they had a car, but when it turned
out to be a big black new Packard ... well, all's
well that ends well. We became friends anyhow,
and they became frequent visitors at our home.

As Girard's work grew on the walls and on the
windows, in the serigraphs and sketches that he
made of his projected plans, an awareness of the
art that was growing around us became an intellectual and exciting experience, especially to those
who, like myself, had never been in at the birth of
high art before.

Daily there were visitors to the chapel to watch
the artist at work, crouched low at the feet of Jesus
on the way to Calvary or high up on the scaffolding
painting in the glory of His countenance in the sun-
filled window. A woman one day said to him, as
he labored at the Crucifixion, "Mister Girard, I
don't like your Crucifixion. I find it distressing."
André looked at her, shrugged, and bowed: "Madame,
it was a distressing occasion."

155

He covered the four high windows with a complex of scenes that illustrate the life of Christ the teacher. Window One has the Parables for its theme; Window Two, the Sermon on the Mount; Window Three, the Teaching Apostolate; and Window Four, the Mass. There is exquisite detail in the window paintings, a great deal of erudition, so that the mind follows slowly the eye. Week after week, month after month I sit and watch those windows with increasing wonder and devotion.

The Way of the Cross is painted on fourteen slanting panels on the Gospel side of the church, bathed, as Maritain has it, "in a continuum of light." Maritain, a dear friend of Girard, was so moved by his work in the chapel that he wrote a brief essay entitled "A Visit at Saint Ann's Chapel," which the artist illustrated and which Chi Rho Press of Stanford has published as a booklet. The illustrations at the beginning of this article are from it.

André is a very generous man, so generous that I became cautious in my praise, for did I say that I liked a sketch, a serigraph, even a painting, it was all too often thrust upon me. The carpenter who framed the Stations of the Cross, I remember, was so impressed with the work that he tried to commission André to paint something for his children. André spent many hours painting on wood, crucifixes for each of the man's children, and he did it for the love and the enjoyment of it, not for money.

One day he was walking around with me and Father Monihan, the Librarian of the University of San Francisco, on the deck of the wonderful upper lounge of the Gleeson Library there. So lovely was the view, so full of space and air, that he gave the University for the place two of his noblest paintings on glass. Bessie, my wife, was expecting a child; He painted on glass one of the most beautiful Annunciations I have ever seen, hastily and sketchily he painted it, but it is all there, full of wonder, and he gave it to her.

When the baby was born, the fourth, yet another boy, we called him Thomas More, after the only lawyer and Englishman that everybody loves, and André was the godfather. The baby was barely home from the hospital, five days old, before André was out at the house sketching him. He

sketched Tom in about twenty or thirty poses, and
then, asking us to choose those that we liked the
most, he made serigraphs of them and printed them
on the tops of boxes of French christening candy--
drageés (I have always called it dreage after André,
I thought, but there is no such word, I see now, in
the dictionary--but what does that matter? dreage
it will remain to us.) He presented the godmother,
Pat Ryan, with a painted crucifix.

All over the Peninsula and across the Bay there
are flowing pictures of his loving kindness to his
friends, and all the time he was working on the
Way and on the windows harder than I have ever
seen anybody work. I know what work is and, barring the labor of a soldier in battle, there is nothing like the labor of an artist. It is a terrible thing
to watch, or to endure. To labor through doubt
and indecision, amid indifference, for to come down
to it, who really cares? The artist is awfully alone.

André worked through meal times and sleep
times when he had to, so that his eyes were rimmed
and his face stubbled, his hands finally deny-
ing him by shaking in fatigue. He would drive off
then into the foothills and the mounts that lie between the Santa Clara Valley and the sea, and
sketch there the landscapes and the views that so
illuminate his window paintings of the Sermon on
the Mount. (In this window there is such a splendid picture of the Lord's Prayer that it should be
printed and hung up in every school and home.)
He is a great printer, as well as a painter. Print,
the magazine of the graphic arts, devoted well-nigh
the whole of the July, 1952 issue to André Girard,
serigrapher. André prints on silk screen; his two
books, Heraclitus and Baudelaire selections are the
first books ever printed this way in the world.
They are collectors' items, only thirty of Baudelaire, thirty of Heraclitus. André designed, decorated and did the whole process himself. Each
book is an individual work of art that must be seen
to be believed. Print's illustrations give you some
idea of the quality and the article further enlightens
the reader on the artist Girard.

When his work was done, and he left us, there
was a void, which only his return can fill. Last
Spring I was in New York City and he came in from
Nyack, his American home, to pick me up and drive

me back with him. It was a lovely, sharp and
frosty day, driving along the Hudson. We visited,
in his picture and paint littered study. Since last
I had seen him the film Gigi had come to the campus wherein one of his daughters, Daniele Delorme,
gave a magnificent performance.

André was feeling rather lonely for his family,
his work on Saint Anthony's in Yonkers was coming
to an end, and in his eye and on his tongue was
France. Later, when he heard that I was to spend
that night at Princeton he insisted, with Gallic
charm that only they possess, on driving me there.
As we left his studio he impulsively picked up a
finished study in oils that he had made of a vase
of flowers and presented it with a bow: "There,"
he said, "a bunch of flowers for Bessie and for
my godson."

Later, when he left me, I was going through
the Princeton University Library with the Librarian
Bill Dix and he showed me their Print Room, and
well they may be proud of it, their collection of
the best of the Graphic Arts, and one of the first
things they showed me was one of their best, a
print by André Girard of a vase of flowers. It
was with some panache, I confess, that I flung the
newspaper covering off the original of the print and
held it up before the stricken and envious eyes of
my host.

I have not seen André since, save in his painting, but his memory will live with us, with all of
us, down to the youngest. For Patrick, only five
when André was among us, dabbled with paints himself, so to André he was "my dear colleague." He
gave him the best of artist's materials to work with,
believing that in art the best is needed. He pon-
dered, as well he might, over the painting of Saint
Patrick that was above Patrick's bed. I always had
a fancy to put a painting of their own saint over
each child's bed. After Patrick it was easy, the
Lewi print of Vincent, Cimabue's Francis for Liam
Francis, Holbein's Thomas More for Tom, and as
for Mary--well, there is God's plenty, but for Patrick, God help him, we all do know the daubs that
pass for that great grand one.

So André, after reading my story "Patrick Will
Take Over" painted a Patrick that is a better depic-
tion of the darling man than even my own story.

He talked with love and affection to us about his masters, the artists Rouault and Bonnard, so vividly, so clearly, that, three years later, coming down the stairs of the Stanford University Library with me on their way to swim, Patrick and Vincent stopped some stairway steppers cold as they said to one another, selecting truly out of an exhibition of prints, "Look, Vin, Dad, Pat, there is a Rouault, there is a Bonnard."

André gave a lecture in the Intermezzo Series at Stanford, a series that presents such notables in the arts as Robert Frost, Joyce Cary, and he was one of the most distinguished. In the midst of his painting nevertheless he had meticulously prepared his lecture and so sure was he of its quality that he steadied me, the chairman, who was nervously pacing up and down the quad before the lecture.

There is André for you, the dedicated artist. He wears the rosette of the Legion of Merit in his coat for his distinguished gallantry and aid to the American Armies during the Resistance. He is a handsome, well set up man with fine strong Gallic features and graying hair. He dresses carelessly when at work, and with a careless elegance when he visits. Unlike many artists he drives a big car fast and well. Barring the car, which is neces- sary in his work, he lives abstemiously, simply out of not caring about food or wine or other things, only for his art, his family, and his friends. He suffers as we all do, but artists most of all, from the world, but there is a gaiety, an insouciance that surrounds him on his way that makes you proud and happy that there is a man, an artist and a friend alive like André Girard.

Early one Saturday morning Wally Stegner came up the steps of our house. It was a few days before I was to leave for New Jersey to attend at Rutgers the first of the Rutgers Seminars on Advanced Librarianship that Keyes Metcalf was to present. It was to last for six weeks and this seemed to both of us too long for me to be away from home. But I was one of the few who had been both invited and had accepted this kind of fellowship, and Swank, it seemed to me, was most anxious for me to go, to be off campus for well-nigh two months. He was most helpful in supporting my attendance, and so was Grieder.

Anyhow, Wally came in. He brought a little feathered

toy bird as a present; it was something that he and Mary had picked up on a recent visit to Sweden.

"Will," he said to me, in between greeting Bess and hailing the children at their breakfast, "Benny de Voto just died. It was so sudden. I can't recall a man with Benny's vitality. And he used it, always. Do you know, he wrote over 20 books, besides his editing, journalism, essays, lectures and all? Many of his books are quite first class really. But he burned himself out like a candle. What do you think of us getting his library? It will be a good one, and we can raise enough wind to blow it here. Mr. Jones (the donor to the Writing Centre, a Texan, his brother had been a distinguished chairman of the English department, before my time) will give us $10,000 right away. What do you think?" I nodded my head. My mouth was full of tea and toast. I swallowed. "Better if you can make an offer now. I can handle it when it has been decided that we are to get it."

"Will $10,000 be enough?"

I shrugged. "Maybe. I doubt it. There'll be lots after the collection. Booksellers and all. Lots of libraries like Boston University. Those new state universities they are starting in Rhode Island, Connecticut, Massachusetts. Universities of the non-Brahmin kind. They'll be building up their libraries too and De Voto's would be just the ideal kind that they could absorb. The one great advantage is that you know Helen, his wife. If we had, say, $20,000, in cash, could pick up the collection right away, it would be a relief and a solace to her."

Wally nodded his head, agreeing with me. He picked up the telephone in the kitchen and called Wallace Sterling at the president's home. Sterling promised the other $10,000 and then Stegner called Helen, the stricken widow, at the De Voto house on Berkeley Street in Cambridge. His condolences were real. I could feel her gratitude over the telephone from where I was sitting, and when Wally said that we'd take the books off her hands, clear them out in a day or so, and pay for them then and there if the price satisfied herself and the executor, she was both grateful and relieved.

So I left early for the Rutgers seminar, going by way of Boston. Helen De Voto, the family lawyer and friend, and myself had lunch at the Palmer House in Boston the next day --Boston scrod was the dish--and we settled it there and then.

I arranged for movers to pack and deliver the books to Stanford. It is always a great relief to both the donors and others to have the books cleared away as soon as an agreement has been reached.

It was a good library. For thirty years and more Benny had been reviewing books, writing books, and as the "Easy Chair" editor of Harper's had acquired far more. I estimated that there were above 10,000 books there, a lot of real Americana, and Western often at that.

One of his little books had developed from remarks he had passed in his "Easy Chair" pages, in praise of the Martini. This attracted a great deal of attention and others who were not Martini drinkers wrote him in rebuttal or agreement, and several liquor firms sent him samples of their favourite aperitif tipple: it generally happened to be the ones they peddled. Helen asked me to take these drinks away with the collection, so I despatched them down to Rutgers, making my room a favourite gathering place for my fellow seminarians before dinner for nearly three weeks, until the bottles were dry.

Wallace Stegner edited in 1975 Letters of Bernard de Voto. All the material is from the De Voto collection that we acquired in 1956, with the additions that accrue to any collection during the years. Stegner's preface is a model: it does Benny justice, something that he never obtained in his life. He was a good historian, conservationist, and literary critic, as well as being a novelist, editor, and essayist. I was glad to have known him and to rest easy that his books would be safe in a good library because of our care. There turned out to be more than 13,500 at the final count, when they were shelved at Stanford. I always tend to underestimate the value and the number of the collections that I acquire. This, I have found, is of benefit to all concerned in the transaction and materially benefits those who need help most.

13

I was an early and eager registrant for the Rutgers Seminar.
It was the first of its kind, and for six weeks Keyes Metcalf
ran us hard. He was no teacher of the conventional kind.
He led us through libraries like the Butler at Columbia, com-
menting all the way on the lighting, seating, space, shelving,
exits, entrances, security, and staff. He had just retired
from his University Librarianship at Harvard, was in his
middle 60's. He had run successfully a library that had
hundreds of collections scattered from South Africa to around
and about the Yard. The Law Library, the Business School
Libraries breathed and lived a life of their very own, with
Keyes as a distant King, a very constitutional monarch. He
had initiated the Depository Library Scheme, he was the
drive behind the Farmington Plan, his Lamont and Houghton
Library buildings and philosophy were to affect the use of
libraries for the coming decades.

Yet, retired from Harvard in 1955 when he was 65,
Keyes kicked a second starter in him and has been active in
librarianship, heart pacer and all, ever since, only more so.
He is all Yankee, born in Ohio and educated at Oberlin. He
has been building libraries, advising on them, all over the
world ever since. He generates energy and feeds on it, a
mover, shaker, and planner. There should be a good long
videotape of the man. He is one of a kind. A videotape
interview would need an inquisitor of a sardonic and knowing
kind, to keep Metcalf's ebullience from bubbling over into
his well-nigh interminable reminiscences where he always
has the last word and the best of it. A team of interviewers
would not do. It would have to be a singleton, one who had
been in training for the task for weeks.

By the end of the six weeks' course we were bushed,
all of us save Keyes and Eleanor Metcalf. We started the

163

course at breakfast and it generally went on until after dinner, with Keyes firing shots of questions at us all the time or inviting us to give our opinion to the group on the quality of paper, the validity of microfilming journals and making space by disposing of the originals--things like that which were of immediate concern and gave him a chance in the summary to expound to his advantage.

One of the better qualities of the course was the way that Keyes succeeded in getting librarians from all over the land to come and talk to us, sharing their own experiences. I got to know a lot more of the more eminent librarians this way and found them a mixed lot.

One that I enjoyed especially was Ralph Shaw. Ralph had been a public librarian in Gary, librarian of one of the government departments in Washington, a professor of the Library School at Rutgers, and finally he finished up in Hawaii where he died all too soon. Ralph was smart and sharp enough to tangle with Reuben Peiss: they loved it. I remember once in Cleveland at a convention Reuben excusing himself early to go to bed: "I'll need all my sleep tonight. Ralph Shaw is coming in tomorrow morning."

Ralph and I, separately and without collusion, had been trying to cut down the paperwork, to speed up the process of the books. We were both well into standing ordering, so that books of quality were sent us by the booksellers without our going through the tedious process of ordering. Both of us, and many others were trying to get some sort of standard cataloguing going that would be common to all. John Cronin of the Library of Congress, who ran the cataloguing operation and card distribution there, was the drive in this. John had got over 80 per cent of the publishers to agree to publish, on the verso of the title page, along with the copyright and L.C. information, a catalogue entry for the book. This would have saved greatly both in time, money and paperwork. The 80 per cent plus publishers that were agreeable to the plan were responsible for most of the books that sold in the U.S. and beyond. The scheme was likely to succeed; most of us saw a new day breaking. But the darkness that comes before the dawn showed little signs of lifting for the sun to show through. The darkness grew darker, and put out the light that John Cronin had lit. The professional librarians killed it in committee. Cataloguing had come to them to be an end in itself, the purpose of the book. The upset of this unspoken and retrograde philosophy during the past twenty

years has been one of the most solid and encouraging features
within our professional ranks.

During my years at Stanford the Association of Research Libraries was a small informal group. Some of the
better scholarly librarians got together for a time of talk
and good feeling, somewhere around the National Convention
locale every summer, and again in winter at Chicago. Only
the directors of the libraries, who formed the group, by inviting one another, were members, and if they did not come
they sent an accredited representative. I often was the Stanford representative and the group had a considerable degree
of clout, since it spoke more or less informally to the other
university librarians.

So many of them wanted to become part of it that the
informality dissolved. A permanent secretariat came into
being. Membership was desired and often struggled for
fiercely. There are now well over a hundred institutions in
the group, with invitations to join being extended to many
more if they can meet rigid and therefore malleable statistical
data (for what are more malleable than statistics?). The
original thrust and drive that can best be delivered in a casual and offhand way by the masters has been replaced often
by the querulous demands of those who see the Association
of Research Libraries as a means of bettering their own am-
bitions.

Generally this and other things were on my mind when
I left Stanford to see about the acquisition of the Benny De
Voto library and attend the Rutgers seminar. It meant leaving the family alone for six weeks and more and this was at
a time when the eldest child was nine, and there was a baby,
and three more in between. There was an outbreak of chicken
pox while I was away. The feeling grew that I was lucky, and
preferred being away instead of nursing the family through
this more than trying time. Friends are a great help and
consolation in these sorts of times, but it is also a time
when the family should be together, instead of the father being away librarianating on the Atlantic shore while the rest
of the family needed him on the Pacific.

Before all this malaise and its ensuing consequences
Larry Ryan drove me to the airport for my trip East. It
seemed to some who were near me that I was always on the
go. Indeed I was, for that is the nature of our profession.
We should meet far more regularly nationally, regionally,

and locally. One important advance would be to meet in universities during their off-season, under canvas even, or in mobile homes, for the hotel costs are too much to bear for any institution if travel becomes, as it should, an essential part of the economy.

Larry, with one of those rare Irish looks that come when they see the future, said, as we were waiting for me to board, and he said it ruefully, for he was going to miss me.

"You know, you are leaving Stanford. You'll just be here to pack up, and you'll be off. "

And he was right. I only hope that the Irish woman who looked at me in the same way just after the war will be right in her prophecy also because, out of the blue, and I barely knew her, she told me that I was to have a long, a busy life.

At the end of the seminar, just as we were breaking up and returning to our libraries and homes, Keyes Metcalf came up to me, pressed my shoulder, and nodded for me to follow him out of the room. He had found a job for me, he said, in Baltimore: Librarian and Director of the Peabody Institute. This was an honor far out of what I had even dreamed of at this stage of the game. It represented social and public participation in a storied and redoubtable city near to the centre of things cultural and political, and in an area abounding in books and their consequences. The very Library of Congress well-nigh was near enough for constant visits. So was the Folger Library, all the other great libraries around Washington, and it looked out both over the sea and the South.

It meant such a profound change that I wavered about accepting the challenge and the opportunity that Keyes had secured for me. I would need to go home first to see about it, and, in the meanwhile, I had received an offer from the midwest that was more of a step down the ladder of my professional career, rather than leaving the ladder entirely, as I would to walk and progress in the high air of the Peabody.

Nevertheless the lesser offer, which I had received a few days before, interested me, stirred me, for it represented challenge and there was need of me to face it.

This offer, from Milwaukee, came to me out of the

166

blue from the graduate dean of Marquette University. Marquette was a large sprawling urban university in downtown Milwaukee. There were good professional schools there in engineering, law, journalism, medicine, and dentistry. The University had just built a new library, wrote John Riedl, the graduate dean, and were looking for somebody to run it and fill it. Wherever he went in search of a Librarian, and he had been all over the country, the advice that he got was to talk to me about it, for counsel and advice. The general impression was that I knew more about what he should be looking for, because of my experience and background, than anybody else. While there was no chance of my leaving the eminence of Stanford and the high regard and prospects of my career on the West Coast, I would be a good friend and adviser if John Riedl could persuade me to help him.

John Riedl did more than that. He wrote the gist of all that I have related above and then went on to offer me the job, at a salary nearly double what the position seemed to be worth. There was challenge, a good new library building that was too empty both of books and readers, and Marquette was away to go. The splendid State University was situate in Madison, the state capitol, too far away from the urban density of Wisconsin, that was in and around Milwaukee. The Marquette drama department was of international fame, and it was a good well-run city, with socialist mayors of the German socialist kind since the 1900's.

John Riedl asked me to break my journey home, at least to talk things over. It was Holy Week, the week before Easter. Both he and the Vice-President would be at conventions, but they would fly back to Milwaukee to meet and then return to the conventions if I would agree to a visit. I did so, and arrived at Milwaukee on Maundy Thursday, met with John Riedl and Vice-President Ed Drummond, S.J., on Good Friday, and decided to join them as Professor and University Librarian the next day.

John Riedl was the man who swayed me. Ed Drummond had more of the sardonic eye that matched my own. He backed John Riedl all the way. As Vice-President he was able to offer me a salary far in advance of what I was getting at Stanford, along with help in housing and a pick-up of all the moving expenses.

Together they fired me with the determination to come to the Midwest. There is no lotus land in the Middle West. The climate is as bad as the Atlantic seaboard, but there remains a feeling that after Chicago and all the way to the West, there is an intellectual desert until the Pacific Coast that has its own very different kind of action.

John Riedl became one of the finest men I have ever known. He was a philosopher by academic profession, graduating from the University of St. Louis along with Marshall McLuhan, Victor Hamm, and other movers and shakers. John taught philosophy at Marquette until the beginning of World War II when he volunteered, despite the fact that his growing family and position and his age made him a member of the "reserved" occupation who sat the war out and profited from it. For years he was officer i/c gunnery on freighters in convoy, a dangerous and uncomfortable combat area. When the war was over he became the Commissioner of Education in the American-held German partition, and returned to the U.S. to take over as graduate dean of Marquette, that under the presidency of O'Donnell and the academic planning of Ed. Drummond was becoming a university to be reckoned with.

John Riedl was no feather duster, clearing out the cobwebs, from an old and conservative establishment. He was a blow torch, even at some meetings coming near to blows with some burly conservatives or others. He never compromised. He supported all that was right and proper in a university and that is bound to make enemies among the idlers and those set in their old ways. He was of the stuff that martyrs are made of. He was unable to yield to accepting the art of the possible. He was such a Big Man, a strong man, a local man, that his actions and opinions startled and dismayed many. One of his true friends, a man more versed in prevailing villainy was Jerry O'Sullivan, the dean of the School of Journalism. Jerry had been a great newspaper man, and under him the School of Journalism had become one of the best. I met more good working stiffs of writers, editors, and commentators at Marquette than ever I had before. They all came to Milwaukee because of their knowledge and more of Jerry in his newspaper days, when he was a working stiff like them. Coming from a glowing session with John Riedl it was like diving into the cold water of reality to meet with Jerry. He held all the right opinions that Riedl held, but he had the Irish humorous sense of reality that very nearly borders on despair. He knew what lay behind public statements, he knew the skullduggery of any power bloc. He knew so much that he could publicly say things that would have been the downfall of Riedl. Much as we liked him, there was a German strain, a sense of right, in Riedl that even we could

168

not sway. We watched him helplessly as he stepped out and marched along the path that his enemies had set out for him. There were Jesuits and laymen involved in Riedl's fall, but that was a long way off when I went to Marquette. His enthusiasm fired even me, and along with Jerry O'Sullivan, Ben Drought, the dean of the Engineering School, John Hirschboeck, dean of the School of Medicine, and above all, Ed Drummond, the Vice-President, I had a phalanx of supporters. There were others, who had far more things to do, for building up a private university in an area where there was a plethora of them was a dire task, almost doomed to fail.

Within the Jesuit province there was Loyola University in Chicago, the University of Detroit, John Carroll University in Cleveland, Creighton University in Omaha. All of them had graduate schools, and where there are graduate schools the college pattern of higher education withers. Moreover they all had graduate schools that competed with one another, thereby debilitating the entire set-up, and costing far more money than if they came to some decision whereby one university would concentrate on a full graduate course in Chemistry, Biology, Philosophy, Linguistics, or Sociology, for example, and all doctoral programs and candidates attend the school that specialised in their subject. But this had proved to be quite unacceptable to the academic world, in private and state-supported institutions. The only way to accomplish this would be by FIAT, and then a howling intransigence, as dishonest as it is self-centred, would arise. There would be chaos, instead of the scattered and secondrate that is the norm under the present system.

The Catholic University of America could be a great institution if it was fully supported by the bishops, but they would rather have their own heaps to pay for and crow from. Some of them sent such a meagre contribution to what should be their national pinnacle, where learning and a great library could flourish, that the Catholic University is barely in the same ring as other Washington universities with far less potential for growth.

I realised all this before moving to Marquette. The lack of real cooperation between U. C. Berkeley and Stanford gave me an inkling of what worse lay ahead for me in Milwaukee. But it was time for me to move on from Stanford. I was ready for a show of my own, and there were advantages that to me overcame the hazards. There was no real effort to keep me at Stanford, rather a sigh of relief from my two senior colleagues, so deeply expelled that it ruffled my papers. The Library Board did give me a formal letter of thanks and appreciation, and wanted me to stay, but I had learned a lot, and wanted to learn and practise a lot more, something that I could only do if I was cock of the walk. Besides, Milwaukee was a good city to be in, and the surrounding Wisconsin countryside was Midwest at its best. Chicago was a short train or bus ride away and there were galleries and museums that put the West to shame. There were the Crerar and first class private libraries, and the Midwest Library Center under Ralph Esterquest was a bold experiment aimed at cooperative acquisition that was designed to enrich all members. The University of Chicago had a first-class and well-staffed library under Herman Fussler, and frequent meetings at the Midwest Center brought us all into a day together, ten or twelve times a year, and nothing beats those meetings for free for all talks and action.

Marquette had built a new library then, and was still staffed largely in the old way, with a library staff that were more like handmaids than they should have been. I was aghast at their almost bobbing curtsey-like treatment of the faculty, especially of the Jesuits, who numbered about half the teachers. There is a terrible condition called accidie which comes to people who by terms of their own will have forsworn the world and live in spartan and celibate community. Over the years the daily rote, the same faces, talk, communal devotion develops a dislike of one another's company, and this condition, to a greater or less degree, comes to them all, like the advent of old age.

Accidie spills over into their dealing with the world outside their walls. Like old age, it can come early or late. The Jesuits had their share of accidents, and besides turning in on themselves and their brethren of the cloth, they vented, subtly and otherwise, some of this venom upon a scattering of their lay colleagues and the library.

Lucky for me it was that I had Ed Drummond to run more than interference for me. He went further, and booted them out of my ken. But it was interesting if distressing to watch. Although this condition never was able to wound me deeply I used to limp a bit from it now and then, but "he jests at scars who never felt a wound," and a lay form of accidie is present here and there through the faculty of most universities, among the most liberal and godless of them. It is bound to be most likely among those members of the faculty,

170

the most of them, who do little else but teach their ten or twelve hours a week, attend committees, gossip, and regard research as something that brings even more time to idle and grants to do it in. Gossip, lechery, and idleness are faculty faults that need to be guarded against by all. The present and overdue attention being given to human rights by the liberal vanguard may soon topple the walls of academic tenure and rock the ivory towers so vigorously that the faculty bums will be flung out to face the chilly air as tattered and as bare without as they should have been within.

This is a digression. Another one that fits in here is the result of my work habits. For some reason I am an early riser, and more so since I have begun to write at length. The first draft of the day's writing I perform at home and "perform" is the right word.

14

The faculty, the administration, the library staff became more
to me as the years went by than just my fellow-workers, colleagues (how I hate that word!) or fellow labourers in the
vineyard of the Lord. They became my other family. I was
linked to them by all ties other than blood of kinship. Gradually I began to realise that the person I must care for the
most must be me if ever I was to love or expend myself fully.
You are flawed as an instrument if you do not realise the
singular importance of yourself; your life is necessarily limited, and must be husbanded to be spent to advantage. For
my wife and family they are an extension of myself. It be-
hooves me to realise that. Home has always been my haven.
Family life together has been the necessary sustenance that
I have always needed. The hardest things for me to accept have been the lonely nights in hotel rooms, from Kan-
sas, New Orleans, San Francisco to Bismarck, at conventions
and seminars that have been an essential part of the library
life and are exhausting, or they should be, a meeting and a
grappling with minds that are sharp, bright, and different yet
in the same game, on the same field, arena, or ring. Three
or four days at a good convention have always been as much
as I can take without beginning to limp or ache in my mind.
After a day of confrontation, of new horizons opening, of re-
buttals and sometimes plain pleasure in the company, it is
drear to go to one of those dreadful, silent, hotel rooms and
court sleep, often into the small hours.

Books like this one often skate over lightly or just ignore what it is really like to be one of a family. Robert
Frost said it best: "A family is where they have to take you
in. " A family is where you can shout, argue, and be at ease
as you can be nowhere else, take the mask off your face, the
shield from your eyes, the bridle from your tongue. All this
is within the kinship and the tribe. It is the other sort of

family, those among whom you work, that lacks these qualities, is more demanding of performance and cooperation. This working family is linked by reason of shared experiences, by plans that succeed or fail, or remain moribund in committee rooms, council and senate chambers, in diaconal quarters, in faculty meetings.

I have been part of a working family all over North America. Here has been my home for longer than my native Wales where I have only returned for brief visits for nearly forty years, and that I left for good in my early manhood in 1939.

As a result I can excoriate or bless my working family, from them all my friendships have come. I see them all, past and present, save few, through the glass of my vision, am as accidiental as any of them, perhaps even more so than many.

When I arrived at Marquette, I was lucky in getting a staff together soon to set the library rolling. Some of the original staff, like Cecilia Hauck and Virginia Soukop, for all their bobbing background, became stalwart members, in their own way, of the team that I was assembling. Peter Demery, returned from Abyssinia way after completing his draft Navy service, read my call for assistance in the Library Journal while he was coming back to the States. He and Mary, his wife, proceeded directly to Marquette and he became my friend and fellow, a strong right arm. He hailed from New York State, but graduated from St. John's near St. Cloud in Minnesota, and from the Graduate Library School of the University. He was lucky, and so was I, that his first real job was at Marquette.

Bob Haerthe left Philosophy to join me and went on to Library School to return at its completion. Bob questioned many of the tenets that he imbibed before, in Philosophy, and he always gave me a lift when he propounded them: he was a first-rate readers' service librarian to boot. I nearly had to boot Bob Miller out of History where he held a fellowship, and push him into Library School. He was another bright one, one that kept me on my toes all the way. Dick Matzek came back after graduating in Library Science at the University of Wisconsin and Neva White, after years in China, later taking time off to straighten out the Library of the University at Kabul, Beverley Pfeifer ... altogether we were a good team, and since it was the first one that I had assembled together, almost from scratch, it is well worth listing them.

174

I got a good team of invigilators also, starting with Mr. Francis, a retired railroad conductor. We were able to open up the second floor and shelve it with books within the first few months. It was a good library building, built on a patch of land facing on Wisconsin Avenue, the main city artery that led from the shores of Lake Michigan through Milwaukee and became the highway to Madison. Although there was considerable street traffic of all kinds the windows of the library were so well paned that there were no street sounds within the building. The entrance hall was floored with marquetterie, an appropriate form of very elegant and patterned wood work. Opposite the library on the other side of the street were a series of grand old homes, but the spread outward of urban sprawl from the city--the university was only twelve blocks away from the downtown centre--had resulted in a series of mean fronts being tacked on to them, and dry-cleaning stores, hair-dressing salons, and the like being established in them. I was to learn of this very soon from a long and pleasant afternoon I spent with Alfred Lunt and Lynn Fontanne who had their summer home at Genesee Landing, about twelve miles out from Milwaukee.

One of the first collections that I hoped to acquire were the papers and memorabilia of Alfred Lunt, who was a native of Milwaukee.

I am still being surprised by revelation of the number of famous and other well known people who hailed, in some degree or other, from that city. General Bill Mitchell's father had a grand house adjacent to the Public Library well-nigh across the road from Marquette. In my days it had been a good private club where the university used to entertain, Convocation lunches and such like. General MacArthur passed into West Point from a competitive examination held in Milwaukee, where the family were living between barracks quarters. Edna Ferber was a writer there, Pat O'Brien, Spencer Tracy, Hildegarde, Liberace ... the list goes on and on. My favourite is the showgirl played by Marilyn Monroe who is casually permitted by her playboy German Prince (Laurence Olivier) to listen to his plots at the coronation in London of King Edward VII. She warned the British of his scheming and his plotting was foiled. "But" stammered the prince in bewilderment, "you are an American! How could you understand German?"

Marilyn drew herself up haughtily and delivered the line: "I was raised in Milwaukee." Milwaukee, along with

175

Cincinnati and St. Louis were great centres of German culture in those days. The Public Library greatly benefitted from it.

Alfred responded to my letter that directly suggested that the depository of his papers be Marquette, with a long and most pleasant letter. He regretted that but a few days earlier he had acceded to a letter similar to mine from the Librarian of the Theatrical Collections division of the Berg department in the New York Public Library. He had sent off more than a boxcar load to them. Had he known of Marquette's interest, he wrote, he would most certainly have agreed to deposit them at Marquette, for he was born and raised in one of those fine homes across the street that now were in such a state of desuetude.

Several national magazines had made unavailing efforts to persuade the Lunts to be interviewed for an article, but both Lunt and Fontanne refused. Then a magazine, Country Beautiful, a well printed and set up national magazine, a short-lived venture from Milwaukee, approached them and suggested that I be the interviewer and writer of the article. They agreed to this at once. I spent a most pleasant afternoon with them at Genesee Landing; it was as good a summer house as anybody could wish for. I can still hear the country sounds around it.

"I was raised a Catholic, you know" said Lunt with a grin. "Without my parents' knowledge or consent. Our servant girl, Maggie, a lovely warm decent loving girl, was Irish, and every morning when she pushed me in my pram out for a fresh air perambulation she used to stop at Gesu, the great Jesuit church between downtown and Marquette, and wrapped up in a shawl I used to go to Mass with her. My parents never knew I was being raised a Catholic."

The first day I got back to England on my LIAP leave, in 1945, I had seen Lunt and Fontanne in O Mistress Mine, a play by Terence Rattigan. The Lyric Theatre in London was filled but the manager found one seat and three of us LIAP soldiers used it, one seated per act, while the other two stood with the ushers at the back. London at the time was being bombarded by a new kind of rocket bomb that hurled down silently on the city blasting whole city blocks. The civilians took it phlegmatically, but I was quite nervous about it.

The Lunts told me that after one performance they were

requested to attend upon the King, and a car called for them
after the show and drove them to Buckingham Palace where
they were honoured for their work in London and among the
Allies by George VI. Lynn Fontanne was English but I think
that Alfred Lunt was even more delighted. They were a great
couple. Few other great couples have graced the stage so
well and for so long.

Lynn Fontanne was telling me, I remember, about the
Provincetown Players and the O'Neill plays in which she
played the leading role at the first public performances.
They were both happy, proud even, to have known O'Neill.
He was, it seems, one of the most handsome of men, and
one of the gentlest.

This got me to reflecting upon the papers of Dorothy
Day who had been converted to Catholicism from a left-wing
socialism by her years with O'Neill. Her papers, correspondence especially, her writing, not only The Long Loneli-
ness, that is one of the best of autobiographies, but her
weekly column in the Catholic Worker wherein her diary tells
of her incarceration in the Tombs, of jail life, her daily comfort of the poor, and the skid rows.

Cardinal Spellman, who deplored her life, influence
and action, frowned upon her. Once, I recall, the Fire Department of New York City condemned her House of Hospitality on Mott Street as a fire hazard. She was ordered by a
local court to put in improvements that were far beyond her
means: her money came in and was spent daily on the destitute. Unless she was able to appear in court with funds sufficient to effect the improvements she would have to close
the House down as a fire hazard. This was a ploy often used
by the Establishment, using a subservient security force, to
silence opposition, without their being named as censors or
some other equally opprobrious word that might offend the
"liberals" of the Establishment. Mayor Daley used it with
great style in Chicago for closing down pornographic movie
houses and the like.

I remember Dorothy telling me this story at Marquette
where she was a frequent and respected visitor among the
students and many members of the younger faculty who had
worked with her for years during their university days.

Dorothy had an imp of mischief. She found all of us
soft who would not forsake our security and join her. She

and Ammon Hennacy, one of her long time fellow workers, I recall, opened a House of Hospitality in Denver that they called The Sacco-Vanzetti House.

Anyhow, on the morning of her court appearance, quite early in the morning, she had to push her way through a crowd outside who were waiting for food and welcome or who were thrusting their dollar bills to her to help for the court appearance. Among them was a blear-eyed shabby unshaven man who pushed an envelope into her hand and vanished, muttering something like "I'm sorry for your trouble." It could not have been quite that phrase; that is an Irish token of sympathy used to comfort the chief mourner at a wake, but it was something like that.

"Thank you, son" said Dorothy, and went on to catch the subway in order to get to court in time.

She had to tell the judge that she was nowhere near having enough money to pay for the installation required by the Fire Department. She was absent-mindedly opening a letter with her hands, the creased envelope that she had received that morning from the shabby stranger. There was a cheque in the envelope for $5,000.00. As she realised this she stopped the proceedings, to read out about this beneficence and to ask for a stay of execution from the court's order to vacate the premises. This was granted. Some court reporters picked up the story and it was on the national wires. Money poured in from all over the country, tens of thousands of dollars that more than paid for the fire safety regulation improvements, and the guests of the House were fed more often and in increasing numbers.... Dorothy took it as a matter of course after the first excitement. God's agent in the matter, it turned out to be, was the English poet W. H. Auden, who had just been elected to the annual appointment of Regius Professor of Poetry at Oxford, and the cheque must have come from an emolument included with the honour.

She looked so frail, yet somehow vigorous and cheerful, and she lived a long life.

I have spent these pages writing about her for she was one of the people who brought about and was an example to a rising tide of reform in the Church in America. It was no revolution, better than that, it was a gradual thing that has brought the steeples of the Old Church establishment tumbling down in a way that has not resulted from the education ex-

178

pounded from the older universities. It was the Catholic colleges, largely established firmly in the 30's, taught largely by seminarian priests, brothers and sisters, with a leaven of harmless laymen, who brought about this change unknowingly. The students, generally the first or second generations of immigrant stock, were the first of their families to get to college. The teaching generally was poor, athletics were extolled, but the students enjoyed leisure and began to read. It was largely from the books and company that they got their education. They began to write and in a civilised manner, often very comic, they and their companions brought a new element into American fiction and that world will not be the same again. I remember Harry Sylvester's great short story, "The Swede," a criticism of Notre Dame and its devotion to football. That appeared, with others, in the Collier's Magazine of the 30's, and his novel, Moon Gaffney, in 1948 appalled, distressed, and infuriated the Church Establishment so much so that the liberal Catholic magazine Commonweal felt it prudent to publish two reviews, one for and one against.

Too little has been done on this change in American mores. The best of the writers of this genre by far has been J. F. Powers whose stories many times began to appear in the New Yorker. Evelyn Waugh praised him in an article on American writing in Life magazine. His two books of stories of the 40's and 50's are classics: Prince of Darkness and The Presence of Grace. He won the National Book Award for his novel Morte d'Urban in 1958. All his stories are funny, not satirical but funny and the more sharply critical because of it. They were a new kind of story, about Americans who had never been written of before. George V. Higgins has followed him even more strongly in his novels Coogan's Trade, The Friends of Eddie Coyle and The Digger's Game. Higgins, I think, may turn out to be one of the best novelists of these times. Edwin O'Connor's The Last Hurrah received a good film treatment that starred Spencer Tracy, and his All in the Family is an indictment, almost in banter, of the cool Kennedys and other wealthy Catholic Irish families whose sons became big men on the campus at Yale, or even tried to be Hasty Puddings.

Dorothy Day's letters and papers are an essential part of any real study that has to be made on this, and without difficulty I secured her letters and papers for Marquette. Already studies are being done of these moving times, but the researchers are from the graduate schools, mainly of secular institutions, and the graduate schools, no matter where they

179

are, tend to be Teutonic, cautious, and dull. There are far too many graduate schools without enough good graduate teachers or students. It is the creative writers, like Sylvester, Powers, and Higgins, with many other good minor ones, who have been the true delineators, and in the novels of Walker Percy they have already begun to lap at the shore of Fame.

Marquette was a library that was built on traditional lines; technology was yet to come. I found excitement among the college students, more so than among the graduates, for the primary sources I obtained. Already, neglected and stored, the university had a splendid collection of primary sources in English literature of the twentieth century: the Furlong collection. It came to Marquette quietly, the result of an inheritance and tax benefits. It deserves far more attention than it has yet received.

Edith Mirriles, a grand teacher of English at Stanford, told me one day at a reception--she was recently retired-- that I should introduce my children to The Hobbit and I did so, with a success that surprised me. I had already become a featured writer in The Magazine of Fantasy and Science Fiction that had published my novella "Coo-Cullen" and my story about the Weerawannas, but I did not regard myself as a fantasy fiction writer at all. Fantasy stories meant to me The Worm Ourobouros by Eddison, Atlantis by H. Fowler Wright. The English always struck me as the fantasy writers par excellence, whereas my stories were all based more or less on truth.

Nevertheless I enjoyed The Hobbit as did some of my children, but when J. R. R. Tolkien's three-deck fantasy novel The Lord of the Rings came along, I was leery of its length and bulk. Leafing through it I was further put off by the footnotes and maps about folk who never were and a Shire that never was. In the early days of its U. S. publication the reviews were generally offhand and cautious, as they had been in England. The caution was partly due to Tolkien's high reputation as a scholar.

I left the three-decker well alone. There were hundreds of other books I wanted to read. There were articles to write, a library to run. There were excuses that followed excuses. I passed The Lord of the Rings on the shelves in the stacks every day. I swear that I believe the book was looking at me from the bottom shelf. It was in a red cloth

180

binding with gold lettering, and published by Allen & Unwin. The book, the three volumes of it, seemed not to be looking at me either balefully or hopefully, just looking, waiting.

Then one evening I picked the volumes up and took them home to read. I started in before dinner, absent-mindedly helped to put the children to bed, or something, and read all through the night, the whole book of it. I was dazed when I got through, as much as from the book as from lack of sleep. The same sort of thing had happened a few times to me before, when I had got so caught up in a book that I could not put it down until I had finished it. The Seven Pillars of Wisdom was such a book, The Story of San Michele was another. Strangely, a biography of Henry VIII was another. This nonstop reading through did not betoken any special virtue in the book. The Story of San Michele, for instance, I never think of again. All I remember of Capri was a clandestine visit that Sacha Carnegie and Johnny Langrigg and I made to the island on a vegetable boat when it was an American preserve, as Anacapri was ours. That, and the fact that Gracie Fields, a lassie from Lancashire, who had starred on the stage in Britain in the '30's, had a villa there. I have no idea why I was temporarily entranced by Hacket's Henry VIII.

But I was completely taken up with The Lord of the Rings. It delighted me, filled me with a sensation of the old that I had never known before.

Later, some years later, and the book's fame was slowly rolling to its popularity that reached avalanche proportions, I wrote an unsolicited and long review of the book and sent it to The Critic. They ran it opposite a more cautious review by Christopher Hollis who was, like Tolkien, a devout English convert to Catholicism. The Critic headed my review Pro and the other review Con.

I was pleased to have got my views of the book published. I regarded it then, and I still do, as a major work of art.

Later I received a letter from Tolkien commending me for my review, saying that it was one of the two reviews that he had read that seemed to understand what the book was all about. We began to write to one another and developed an affection that spilled over into consideration of C. S. Lewis, whose books of fantasy had already been very successful: Out

of the Silent Planet, Perelandra, and That Hideous Strength.
They were friends, both Oxford dons together, and when somebody asked Lewis whether he thought that Tolkien had been influenced by his success in the field he snorted in reply that
nobody, not even a bandersnatch could influence Tolkien, and
he was right. Charles Williams, an Oxford editor, the author of All Hallow's Eve, kindled the enthusiasm of Lewis to
such a degree that he and Tolkien saw less and less of one
another. There had been approaches made to him by several
American publishers for a suggestion for an author who could
write his biography. He wrote to me suggesting this, but I
turned it down, since while I was determined to write about
him I shied away from anything that could remotely suggest
hagiography. There the matter rested for years.

Tolkien had never been to America. He had received
an honorary degree from Uppsala and that seemed to be the
total of his travels, although he was regarded as one of the
world's great scholars.

I suggested to the English department at Marquette that
it would be a good idea to bring him over as a guest lecturer,
but they demurred, the chairman remarking to me that he was
too narrow in his field. I went to Ed Drummond, the academic vice-president among other things--he had taken his
Ph. D. in English from Michigan. Ed had a fox-like grin that
nearly split his face, but this time his face broke up entirely
into a guffaw. He told me to go ahead, to spare no expense.
I invited Tolkien and his wife to come and for him to give a
short series of lectures. He seemed to welcome the invitation, and we set a date. Within a week or so I was doing a
Sol Hurok on the deal. Harvard approached me, asking him
to give the Sather Lectures. I was flooded with invitations
that I answered charily. The only two that I favoured were
those from Harvard and Berkeley.

I waited with great anticipation for the arrival of the
Tolkiens at Milwaukee. Then, just before they were due to
sail, Tolkien advised me that the trip would have to be can-
celled due to the serious indisposition of his wife. Humphrey
Carpenter in his biography of Tolkien, explains this matter
further. It was a matter that he left unwritten in his subsequent
book on the Inklings. It was a sad affair, that has been revealed by Carpenter after they had died. However, the sudden
cancellation was more than a nuisance to me, and I had to do
an un-Hurok performance to get the sorry situation over with.

Tolkien wrote me a letter of apology. There was a

general note of near-anguish in the tone of it. He asked me
if there was anything that he could do to make amends. I
suggested that I buy his papers from him. The Tolkien cult
had barely started at this time and Oxford did not seem very
interested in acquiring them. We agreed on a price that
seemed fair to me at this time, and Marquette received the
Tolkien Papers. They are, of all the collections that I have
corralled, the most attractive for display and popular attention. All of the papers were in manuscript and the hand of
the author was well-nigh calligraphic in beauty. Many of the
pages have illustrations that he drew, like the early monastic
scriveners penned, to lift their spirits, drive away the devil
of accidie and others, to amuse themselves, or to rest their
eyes from writing.

The papers are not just of The Hobbit and The Lord
of the Rings but also of Father Giles of Ham and his other
children's books.

I think that Tolkien's lecture before the British Academy "Beowulf and the Critics, " is the most deserving of
praise of all the criticisms that I have read, yet the sensible
though slashing attack that he made therein on academic and
other literary critics probably cost him his election to that
august and most learned Society. He was quite a man was
Tolkien, a gifted and a learned man, one of the great teachers. Like most great teachers--they are very rare--he was
unaware of it. He was surprised at the crowds who came to
his lectures when he gave them.

Tolkien was the external examiner in English for the
University in Cardiff. This was long before his fame. Llewellyn, the head of the department, was talking to me about
him one day, and later when I visited Tolkien at Oxford, he
was talking about Llewellyn. They liked one another. Llewellyn had put himself through college by fighting as a professional
boxer. He was quite good, it seems, and mainly because of
his timing and quick reactions.

He was one of those rare ones who could move more
quickly than a fly. He would pluck them off his hands or
face or paper between finger and thumb, while we would be
swatting and missing, time and time again. Another man
whom Tolkien admired, for something of the same reason,
and some more, was Roy Campbell, the South African poet.

I remember both Llewellyn and Tolkien talking almost
with awe and certainly with delight about what a joy it must

183

have been to have seen Jim Driscoll in the ring. Driscoll
was born and raised in Cardiff. He was known as The Non-
pareil and was the lightweight champion boxer of the world.
His face was completely unmarked, so fast were his reactions.
He appeared at the first Tailteam Games in Ireland, in the
early 1920's, when Ireland, barring the Six Counties of the
North, had become a Free State, and he stood, fully clothed
in the ring, with his hands in his pockets and let all the boxing contenders, all rigged out for combat, try to punch his
face. With barely a move that was noticeable Driscoll would
react so quickly that never a one could connect.

I found in talking to Tolkien some years later that his
eyes really lit up when recalling Llewellyn and Campbell. He
was a bandersnatch of a man, and I am glad to have known
him, although I am at a loss to explain his glee. He walked
with a different step to those other dons: remote, some ineffectual, some majestic who rolled down the high, compact or
port, and with learning of a sort.

Altogether Marquette and Milwaukee were a pleasant
interlude in our lives. We lived there for seven years in a
house set on a small hill in Wanwatosa, opposite Jacobus
Park and near a splendid nine-hole municipal golf course.

We made many good friends there, of all kinds and
degrees. Mainly, to my surprise, they were extraordinarily
right-wing. I was strongly opposed to Joe McCarthy who
somehow or other was a graduate of the Marquette Law School.
Indeed I had been reported because of my speeches and writings as one who derided all that Joe held dear: Gene McCarthy, the senator of Minnesota, was my friend and remains so.

I have never been interested in politics, only in the
people involved therein. One Sunday, I remember, we had
a coffee party--there is a German name like Kaffeklatsch for
it--in order to drum up votes for Hubert Humphrey, another
favourite of mine. He was running against Jack Kennedy for
the Democratic Presidential nomination. All the people on
our block and for blocks around were aghast at our hosting a
pro-Humphrey party. Hubert was a liberal of the deepest
dye, and none of them came to our party. There was just
Abigail McCarthy and her brother, a few other party workers,
and our family. Meanwhile downtown the Kennedys had moved
in. The Schroeder and the Pfister hotels resounded to the
bands playing "When Irish Eyes are Smiling" and the Kennedy
clan was there almost in its entirety. They attracted thou-

sands as against our none for Hubert. Yet, and this is strange, our anti-Joe stand, stance, and reputation made absolutely no difference to their friendship for us. Charles Hanratty, an around-the-corner neighbour, Gert, his wife, and their family were among our best friends and remain so. When we were leaving Marquette Charles telephoned me. He was a successful lawyer and had just concluded a lucrative case. He wanted to give me thousands of dollars to help us get established in our new domicile. This he did with such tender consideration that he brought tears to my eyes and while I did not take him up on his offer it must seem strange that Charles was one of Joe's friends and admirers. Barring John Riedl there were few who shared our political opinions among our friends yet this did not make a whit of difference. This has been quite unique in my experience. Moreover, and this is revealing and certainly not widely known, it was the Catholic element in Wisconsin that finally laid Joe McCarthy low.

15

I grew to love the Middle West during the seven years we lived and I worked at Milwaukee. They were happy times for all of us. I watched the Library growing like a green bay tree with shoots like flame, with the addition of the special collections like the Dorothy Day Papers and the Tolkien Archive. But the University of Wisconsin had begun to expand into Milwaukee. The University took over Milwaukee-Downer Ladies College and, I wrote or sang somewhere, "Milwaukee-Downer's Virgin Malls Resounded to Male Wolf Calls." Peter Demery moved on to an editorial position at the A. L. A. Chicago headquarters. Bob Miller graduated from Library School and began to flourish in the acquisition department of the University of Chicago Library. Neva White came back from straightening out the Afghan Library Problem. Bob Haerthe was settling in as a fine librarian with the proper opinions.... I was getting the feeling that I would hang my boots up at Marquette. Seven years had been the longest time that we had as yet stayed anywhere. But I had a feeling that I was only now beginning to know how to field the ball, kick it, run with it, enjoy the contact sport of the Library Game and, deep down, I wanted to try out on a new field, in different circumstances, some of the ideas that were forming in my mind, to realise and implement the beginning of the new technological advances that were starting to lap at library shores.

One belief that I have always held, and never so firmly as I do today, is that the decay of the college system and the spread of the universities had been a calamitous development. There are too few colleges and too many universities. When a new college was suggested for New England, a college so good that its graduates would be accepted anywhere as graduate students, I believed that it was an idea that deserved our best efforts. Taking a cut in salary, leaving a greatly friended

187

company, we sold our house in Milwaukee and headed East where I had been invited to be a professor and Librarian of the new institution that was to open its doors at the beginning of the next academic year.

From the sale of the Wawatosa house which I sold for the price I paid for it, thinking thereby I was making a profit, since it meant that we had lived there for seven years rent-free, we sallied east by car. Leaving our household effects to catch us later, we went to Bridgeport, Connecticut, by way of Cardiff, Wales.

My mother was still lively and living, in her late seventies, in our Carlisle Street house with my brother Jack, who was a teacher around the corner, in the parochial school where he later became vice-principal. His uncle Charlie, my father's brother, had been principal there for years, and Annie, my father's sister, was principal of St. Joseph's, one of the best parochial schools in the city. My sister Nora was, until she died, after years of suffering, vice-principal of the Benedictine parochial junior school. Nearly all of these schools had cousins of ours on the staff or administration. I alone escaped the school teaching, which in those days was the sole means of escape from hard labour in the steel works or the docks for most of our kind. In the Spring of 1946 I was a qualified librarian with a good honours degree and an Oxford diploma in education, so I was offered jobs outside the parochial school set-up. I could have taught at one of the good grammar schools, Cardiff High School, for instance, that prepared boys for universities and professions. Luckily for me we decided against it, since these fine public grammar schools went, vanished utterly, and were replaced by comprehensive schools where there were no entrance requirements, no examination that would select the students. Comprehensive schools were established in each district, where all youngsters attended, whether they wanted to or not. This was done, said the planners, to give all students the same opportunity for education.

The reverse was the case. The private fee-paying schools boomed as never before and in this age of "enlightenment" parents beggared themselves in order to ensure a good education for their children.

The same calamity has been visited on the universities. So many new ones have been established during the past few decades, universities in the mist and rain and out of the blue, that the old universities have well-nigh been besieged by frantic applications, as over 90 per cent of the plum positions were filled by graduates from Oxford, Cambridge, London, Manchester, Durham, and other older universities.

It was necessary that we depart for North America anyhow. It was not only fair, but more than that. My wife needed to visit her family whom she had not seen since 1942, when she had sailed from Halifax to the war theatre as a Lieutenant in the Medical Service.

Far more tempting than the offers of employment for us both was the house my father wanted to give us. It was the house in St. Peter Street, my grandparents' home, which had been bequeathed to him upon their death. It was exactly as it was when I grew up in it, with all the fine handmade furniture, the aura of peace and quiet. My Aunt Annie had enjoyed a decade of happily married life there until she died peacefully in her sleep while we were at Oxford. We lived there for the last few months of our stay in Britain. My father and mother loved us being there, and a bond of affection grew between them and my wife. It was with real reluctance that we left that house behind us.

Now it was time to return for a visit. My father had died shortly after our return to my wife's country. She had never seen post-war Britain, or the length and breadth of my family connections, with cousins and other kinfolk from Cardiff through Aberavon to Swansea and even beyond.

There would be a house vacant just two down from my old home for all the summer, while the people in it went off to America to visit their children who had emigrated there or had become G. I. brides. For a week or so we had to live in a caravan on Fontigary Bay and we had a feeling of real holiday there. So many of the young cousins wanted to stay with our children that we rented a second one. It was a time none of us will ever forget. For the first time the children were taken off our hands. My mother more or less took over Nora. She used to positively glare at my cousin Paddy McCarthy, who came every Sunday morning to claim her and take her for a drive. Paddy was remarkably like me in appearance. Friends, library staff members and other who knew me well often mistook him for me. His own marriage was childless, and the baby Nora took to him in such a way that her grandmother was upset. Even my wife had difficulty getting her out of Gran's loving clutches. For my mother to have six American grandchildren running in and out of her house brightened her life.

We were able to leave all the children for the first time in our married life and take off on our own. We crossed the channel, I remember, to Weston-Super-Mare on our way to Bath, and aboard we got into a friendly conversation with a stranger who turned out to be a cousin of mine.

Wherever I went I was visiting bookshops and libraries. It was hard for me to believe, but Cardiff Public Library's only change that I would see was a patched roof where a bomb had fallen during the war and has exploded without penetrating the book stacks, killing two library staff members who were on bomb duty during the air raid. Another of the string of bombs cratered in the Public Market next to the Library. Mercifully the goldfish in the tank in the Gentlemen's Public Convenience survived, their tanks intact.

Lear's Bookshop in the Morgan Arcade supplied such good service for the library that I was building up for the new college in Connecticut that I used them extensively later, when I stacked the shelves with processed books in twenty new community colleges in Ontario.

The burgeoning University College had now a library of its own that was well worth the visits that I paid there. The Librarian was comparatively new to his position, was English, grew up somewhere around Southend where, as a boy, he had worked on the longest resort pier in Britain.

Wherever I went in Britain, save in a few of the older universities, I found conditions that would not have passed muster in America. There was a desperate shortage of U.S. funds available, so that their purchases from America were extremely meagre and, to my surprise, little or no private beneficence was available. The libraries were generally all too cramped and the hours of service were restricted.

The one saving grace was that the mail service was then at a standard of efficiency that permitted interlibrary loan service to do a splendid task. The National Centre at Boston Spa was well funded and organised and administered by Donald John Urquhart on lines that I believe were the most efficient in the world. Should a request by mail or telephone be delivered to the Centre early in the afternoon the material was shipped out in standard boxes by a fleet of trucks in time to

190

be loaded on the labyrinthine railroads by later afternoon, and generally was on the desk of the suppliant librarian by the morning of the next day. This service was more than 90 per cent efficient.

The centre was started at the Spa because of its location, and because of the vacant airport hangars there, hangars that were used by Bomber Command during the war and were rusting, rattling and greening over with desuetude.

Urquhart shelved the hangars, with a continuous roller belt running down the aisle. The books were numbered, along with the journals, and their numbers went up depending on their usage. More and more copies were added if the demand for the material mounted.

There was well-nigh continuous input and output. Urquhart and his assistants in this enterprise were scientists, or involved in the needs of the scientists, for current scientific information from all areas and sources. He was a senior civil servant of drive, energy, and imagination. His enterprise grew and expanded to include the social sciences and current material in the humanities from beyond the currency bounds of Britain. It was fortunate that the strong arm of Science was behind him. He and the enterprise grew together. The Library Association made him a Fellow and he served as President of the Association.

The time I spent with him at Boston Spa was a good time for both of us. He did not have a catalogue of the holdings. He saw no sense in one for his enterprise, and he was right. If the request for current material was valid it was already waiting delivery and if it was not there would be little delay before it was.

It was an exciting and successful project that could to some degree be operative on a state or provincial level, or in areas like New England and New York, but never to the same extent. Distances, weather, the vast continent that has to be covered militate against it, unconsciously or not. It does make sense to forget national conceits and set bibliographic economy to go every which way according to the need. There is bibliographic sense in sharing resources and action experiences along the West Coast, the Midwest, the Atlantic seaboard without considering national frontiers, state and provincial barriers. Surely, since all other forms of communication, information media, do not have to pass through Cus-

191

toms, the same situation should allow the book to cross over as freely, from one boundary to another? But it does not.

There is still a deep fear and dislike of the book. One of the most prized possessions that I obtained for a university library is a German Bible of the thirteenth century, written in a hand so miniscule that even with a magnifying glass it is hard to read. This book, a Bible, is small enough to fit into the palm of a hand far more easily than a baseball, or stuffed into a jerkin or a saddlebag without raising a bulge, yet it was dynamite that only needed the primer of the mind to explode away the obscurantism that power encourages and demands.

It was a welcome change for all of us, not only to become a part of a family, but to realise something of the meaning of Britain. The visit turned none of the family into Anglophiles, far from it: it made them more American, while engendering in them a liking for the British and some understanding of why I was the way I was, rather different in accent and approach to the fathers of their friends.

There is a digression here that goes beyond my power to control. One day we drove in our rented car up past Pontypool towards Brecan. We stopped for lunch in a country town where it was market day. We were all amazed at the power of the dogs. They herded cattle and flocks through the streets to the market street with hardly a bark, and with a skill and a patience that had to be seen to be believed. The shepherd or drover with his long stick walked behind, giving the odd thwack to a straying beast, but that was all. It makes me wonder why the herd dogs never played a part in the cattle drives in Texas and the West. Nor have I ever seen them operating on film with the sheep flocks of Australia.

One day the two eldest boys went for a climb and a tramp over the Black Mountains around Talgarth. Park, with some difficulty, had found a pair of climbing boots to fit him. Although he was still in his middle teens he had reached full growth, and needed boots that were two sizes past the regular. The boots that he found had thick, thick soles that added to his height, that was over $6\frac{1}{2}$ feet. He and his brother found that they had enough funds left to lengthen their stay in the country before returning by bus to Cardiff city. This was in Pontypool and, while they were standing outside a telephone booth discussing this, a Welsh miner passed. He did a double take for he was, like me, medium height for Wales, about

192

$5\frac{1}{2}$ feet. He passed, looked back, and retraced his steps.
Looking up at Park he said, puzzled and startled:

"Excuse me, sir, how tall are you?"

The answer and the talk he had with the two of them,
with their American accents, puzzled him even further and
he walked on, with backward glances, shaking his head.

The time in Britain went all too fast. We had accommodation on The Empress of Britain for the return voyage. While this did not compensate for the eastward journey
on The Seven Seas, a ship of about 10,000 tons that had been
fitted up for student travel and manned by a German crew,
it did help. Even now, it is not the voyage home on the
Empress that engages the family talk about the trip, but the
8-berth, windowless container in the bowels of the shudder-
ing, clanking, rolling vessel, eight stairways down from the
deck, that arouses the most comment by far.

When we got to Bridgeport, Connecticut, loads of books
came with me, before, or after me. The accommodation that
the administration had found for us was wretched, and it was
evident that the whole college idea had been brilliantly con-
ceived but was far from reality. There were circumstances
that militated against it from the start.

People of good will, faith, and hope persuaded some
of their children to leave colleges of good standing and established reputation to attend this new venture. The vice
president, the real promoter, with his aides from New Jersey, was anxious to fill the classrooms so that funds would
be available. The building was divided into two wings, but
there was a boy's high school in one wing and a girl's high
school in the other, awaiting new quarters. There was no
library building but only shelves made available in the school
library. The processing room was partitioned off from the
college's only recreation room. There was no shipping area
for library materials and the sound of students relaxing with
stereos, guitars, shouts, and worse was intolerable. All
this was part of the undue haste to get the college going long
before it was possible to do it with any chance of success.

Then, with the fall, there came a large number of
students who by college entrance sought to evade the draft.
The war in Vietnam was thickening up to all out combat and
college entrance was a way to avoid it. The original ideas

for the college perhaps necessarily went by the board. Had it not been for Dick Matzek who followed me from Marquette and shared the burden, Maureen Malone from New Haven who became a librarian with us, graduating from Cooper Union as she did so, things for the library would have been far worse. There were some friends on the faculty who were a help. Jim O'Connell, the college legal adviser, became a true friend. On our first meeting, when he realised that I had written The Great Disciple, one of his favourite books, we began to cement a friendship that has lasted through the years.

Under the new frantic enrollment and recruitment the original standards of the college declined. The build-up of the library, proper housing, staff, and processing were relegated to being of lesser importance. This had been the rooftree in the beginning and now it was being sawed up and whittled away.

I touched bottom. My enthusiasm for the college structure had voluntarily removed me from the mainstream of library progress. After a stay in hospital, and some intricate surgery that took a while to recover from, I began for the first time in my life to consider applying for a job. Then, as I was recovering and my optimism again began to flourish, a call came through from Canada, and I began the longest, happiest and most successful years of my life, as a librarian in Hamilton, Ontario.

Hamilton, Ontario? The Harvards and Yalies wrinkled their noses when they heard the town I was going to.

"What are you wrinkling your noses about? Cambridge, is that a town to live in or out of? As for New Haven, it sounds like a railroad station."

I said that before ever seeing Hamilton, and I am a great believer in a university being in a city and not out of it, on a well-treed and well tended park surrounded by faculty homes and gardens far from the madding crowds who paid for the lot of it.

It was good luck that got me to Hamilton, the home of McMaster University. With the 60's there was a great spurt in university development all over the country. Canada was in a time of great prosperity, and the ruling establishment thought that more universities were needed to stop the flow of graduate students across the border, and create centres of ordered and tranquil higher education for the young of their own kind and those deserving poor and others who wished to join them. In 1960 Ed Williams from Harvard, in the company of Emile Filion, S.J., had made a preliminary survey of library resources in the existing universities in Canada. It was a seminal report, and nothing has been the same since. In these years colleges that had before been denominational, privately endowed institutions, became state-supported provincial institutions. While conforming to the norms of provincial standards the old order of the college remained, a pleasing part of the turn-over. McMaster had been a proud and vigorous Baptist institution. It was fortunate to have had George Peel Gilmour as President during the turn-over; he had a hard time of it bridging the gap.

A new Divinity College was built, handsome and traditional, and the City had already welcomed McMaster from its crowded quarters in Toronto to a fine wide space of campus that was girdled to a great extent by the Royal Botanic Gardens, one of the best in the world. There are hundreds of acres of woodland, bridled with paths that are a backdrop to the playing fields. There is a bird sanctuary, a rock garden, an arboretum, a garden of roses, a large stand of irises.... I am no gardener, nor can I tell a peewit from a pelican at first glance, but I still marvel, after more than a decade of years, at the lilac dell in the Gardens. Lilacs are among my favourite bushes: they are, along with the berried holly, among my favourites in a garden. Until I got to McMaster and gradually, on our early morning walks, began to know the Gardens, I believed that there were about eight, at the most, different kinds of lilac bush. But at the Lilac Dell there are nearly 900! All different, from all over the world. My favourite is a delicate white lilac from France. My affection for lilac stems from the fact that it grows in the most unlikely places, in our back yard in Cardiff, in Winnipeg, in Minneapolis and Winona, where it survives the killing winters and blooms every spring when even the holly cannot flower its berries.

Besides the traditional liberal arts pattern of these converted denominational colleges, their beginning Science courses, schools of Nursing, and even some art teaching, there were several notable scholars among them. Northrop Frye was the product of a denominational college, and the classical historian, E. Togo Salmon, was in residence at McMaster as Principal of University College.

But all this is prelude, the past is prelude in this, for all this came later after I was appointed to McMaster as Professor of Bibliography and University Librarian.

The most significant and most promising future lay in the fact that the Chalk River Atomic Project, needing an academic base, was the fundament of Hamilton College. This, when combined under its Chalk River director Harry Thode, with McMaster made the university an institution to be reckoned with, and Harry Thode became the President of McMaster under the new order. Harry Thode is one of the Canadian Scholars, a scientist who enjoys world-wide renown. His pupils came from all countries and even during the hard times of the 60's he was not only a fine president but taught and did research as well. A nuclear accelerator and a nuclear reactor came on the campus during these years, making McMaster a unique resource for research in the field.

Then, to cap it, a federal grant was to finance the building and the establishment of a Medical School and Teaching hospital. John Evans, the dean to be, had already moved onto the campus and planning, nearly building, was on its way.

McMaster was also to obtain a graduate school of library service and a new University Librarian. Andrew Osborn had been chief of processing at Harvard, a vast task. He was a philosopher by academic bent, a professional librarian by education also, and he was teaching library science at the University of Michigan. He accepted this glove cast down; it was quite a challenge that he was picking up. Toronto already had a graduate school of library service at the university about forty miles away, but Metro Toronto was approaching a population of three million and more. The new University of York, just north of Toronto, hardly seemed the suitable place for this new graduate school, so the universities in council met and decided that McMaster should house it. The vote was 12-1 in favour of McMaster, but the one dissenting vote came from the University of Western Ontario.

When all the plans were laid for the graduate school to come to McMaster the University of Western Ontario opined that they would like to have the School at London. John Robarts, the premier of Ontario, came from London, so the school went there.

Andrew Osborn obviously had to go with the school as dean, but it left a gap in the administration at Mac, for he was to have been University Librarian too.

This left the Library Committee at a loss until Andrew suggested that they should approach me. He and I had known one another for years, had many talks about book collections, acquisitions, booksellers, and the like. He recalled that I had some Canadian connection, also I had been librarianating in America for at least two decades. He had been an Australian himself, so we had something in common. Anyhow he warmly recommended me, and I went up to Hamilton for a visit. Togo Salmon was the prime mover in library affairs. He was Principal of University College, the Liberal Arts wing then, and we took a shine to one another from the beginning. Educated at Cambridge he had previously done very well aca-

197

demically in Sidney and came to Canada in 1929. From 1930 he had distinguished himself as a writer, teacher, and administrator all at McMaster.

Our affection for one another grew through the good times and the lean times we shared together. They began almost at once. Cary Fox was about the oldest living alumnus, and he had been a most generous benefactor to the University, not just with money, lots of it, but with his loving pride and continuing interest in the place. An old classmate of the early 1900's wrote to him suggesting that his library and memorabilia become, along with himself, a part of the present McMaster. He wrote the letter on notepaper that was decorated with an arch whereon was written the name of his library, that included his own.

President Harry Thode brought it to Togo's attention who came across to the Library Office to talk to me about it. Obviously the matter deserved looking into, if only to assure Cary Fox that we had done so. We had barely moved into Hamilton and were still sorting out the furniture, but on the first Monday in August 1966 Togo and I drove down to see the would-be donor, having advised him that we should be there by about 11 a. m. His house was just across the river from Detroit; its fame lay in the glass-house tomatoes that were grown there. It was about 200 miles west of Hamilton, so we started off in a Volkswagen Beetle about 6 a. m. The roads were crowded with holiday traffic and we knew that they would be even more crowded coming back. We reached our destination about ten minutes before 11:00, and rang the bell. There was silence within, until, after a few minutes, the door grudgingly opened a bit and a little man, wearing a red silk dressing robe and black socks, peered at us angrily.

"You're early" he said.

"Come back at eleven. "

It was just about five minutes to the hour. We walked up and down the path, passing under the archway across it that gave his name and the name of the library and then, on the dot, we rang the bell again. This time the little man, dressed as a clergyman, opened the door and with no reference to our previous encounter greeted us graciously, inviting us in with a courtly wave of his hand. He led us into his lounge-library. The curtains were drawn so that the room had a dark, murky, and musty atmosphere. The only light was a spotlight on a painting of himself above the fireplace. It was not a very good likeness or portrait or anything else for that matter. Without further ado he went into a spiel about his collection. He went on until 5:30 p.m. non-stop, save for a break for lunch.

"I have reserved a table for us at a local restaurant. They serve excellent food there. I recommend it. Shall we go now?"

Then it was 12:30, and as we stepped out into the blazing heat of the day and blinked at the sunny brightness Togo and I almost wished for the dark, musty, cooler, almost chilly room.

The reverend old gentleman had donned a straw hat that he wore at a rakish angle. It gave him the appearance of a late Victorian transplanted masher. He led us at a fast clip, we almost had to trot to keep up with him. The hour and a half we had spent on our feet, me crouching down now and then, lying flat, standing on tiptoe to see and feel the books on the shelves, had left us looking forward to a leisurely and a comfortable lunch. Remember, we had endured about four hours of cramp in the Volkswagen before that, on a crowded, hot, and dusty road. Barring around Paris, that is called after plaster of Paris and not the Eiffel Tower, Montmartre Paris, the road from Hamilton to Bagwash was wide and well paved which made it all the more crowded.

We stopped at a truckers' drive-in called the Siwash Stop. Without a moment's hesitation the Victorian masher led us in. There was a noisy bar, and truckers by the score exchanging news, cheerful insults and dirty jokes at small tables where they were tucking into what seemed to be the main meal of their trip if they were driving a rig from Cleveland to Montreal. A jukebox was belting out some Western tunes, and the large room was warm and steaming over the hum of the air-conditioner.

Like an arrow our host led us through, and on the other side of a door there was a complete change. The room was large and long, suitable for dances, union meetings. It was completely empty save for a card table with a cloth on it and a meal setting for three. There were three collapsible chairs and other than that there was nothing. The air-conditioner was winning hands down in this room. The cold cut through to the skin and pierced it like a knife. It was so bleak, barren, and chilly, that a company of coroners would have found it too cold for autopsies.

The Reverend Bodmin slapped a bell on the table and a waitress appeared carrying our three lunches on her arm. They were all slices of meat loaf covered with gravy, with boiled potatoes smeared with the same. It was congealing even as she carried them through from the kitchen. When I went to pick up my knife and fork my fingers stuck to them, it was that cold. Our host ate the main dish with gusto and only some remaining shibboleth stopped him from sliding our barely touched food onto his plate and gobbling that down too. There was apple pie and ice cream to follow and coffee.

The waitress, a big awkward and unsmiling woman, presented the bill and while our host made a great play of going through his pockets, Togo with trembling fingers paid her. He told her to keep the change out of the four dollars he gave her. She nodded with satisfaction and began to clear the table for the autopsy or whatever was coming on next. Later I realised that it was an annex over the holidays for the funeral director of the town, for under a covering of dingy earth-stained cloth, on the way out into the warmth and noise of the public eating area, there were eight or more caskets stacked, and four insulated cadaver shipping trunks.

The Reverend wiped his lips elegantly with a paper napkin and called loudly to the waitress who was pushing with her rear into the swinging door that led to the kitchen.

"Mrs. Govern! Pray give the chef our compliments. It was delicious."

He turned to us. "Well, gentlemen, now you are refreshed we can return to our collection."

Togo and I looked at one another quickly. Neither of us liked his reference to "our" collection. We were cautious and on guard as we re-entered the dark and musty room. More and more the wily old one was realising the importance of Togo in the scheme of his, and so the lesser importance he was paying to me. Indeed he was eying me with growing suspicion, a suspicion that he kept hidden but not enough within him for a flash of calculating showing in bright jackdaw eyes. This time he switched the lights on.

"Consider, Dr. Salmon, this special supplement of the

Illustrated London News that appeared at the time of the marriage of Tsar Nicholas to Alexandra, the daughter of Queen
Victoria. See! See!" He flourished a coloured spread on
the centre pages. There was the young couple at the altar,
kneeling down for the wedding blessing of the Archimandrate
of Vladivostok. He had been the naval chaplain when the
Tsar was a young naval officer, and they had remained friends
ever after, if an archimandrate can ever be the friend of a
Tsar. Alexander showed him constant favour, and he ended
up as Patriarch of Omsk. This supplement of the Illustrated
London News somehow escaped the blood bath of the Revolution that engulfed him and the Tsar and so many other noble
Russians. I feel sure the Greeks and the Romans had a hand
in that, let alone the Swiss. "Regard, Dr. Salmon, the
splendid art work. It is so clear that you can count the nails
in the Tsar's dress Wellington boots."

Ignoring me, who was on my knees looking almost
open-mouthed at some of the bookyard junk--there were six
copies of The Manxman by Hall Caine on one shelf, I recall.
Larry Powell at U.C.L.A. had been sold a pup on a Hall
Caine collection some years before. The reverend stepped
over me and switched off the lights to put the spot on a recumbent houri, a painting that might have been daubed by
somebody beyond the hope of recovery. I could see Togo
actually flinch at the sight. Our host, if so he can be called,
was still wearing his panama hat at the rakish angle.

"Consider, doctor, the grace of the lady. Recumbent,
her face resting on her delicate arm...." He shook his head
in admiration and took his hat off to his houri.

So it went all afternoon. He was tireless. One of
his great treasures was a fireplace built of stones gathered
from all over the world. There was a framed postcard above
the fireplace signed by an eminent divine. It was typed.

"I regret that I cannot supply you with a stone from
Gordon's Calvary." It was signed hurriedly with a scrawl.
He pointed to it with pride.

"You see," he said. "I have aroused cooperation and
admiration from an eminence of the Church of Rome." Now
came the clincher.

"How fortunate it is that this collection and myself
are returning to my Alma Mater!"

201

I felt a real admiration welling for Togo as he picked up the deck and began to shuffle it.

"This has been a most interesting visit." Turning to me "Don't you think so, Professor? And what a time you must have had going through all those books!"

"Remarkable" I said. "Remarkable."

"You must have some ideas, some plans, for the disposition of the collection, sir." He bowed to the old and spry alumnus who Cary Fox, although McMaster was but a small Baptist school in those days, was unable to recall him, save that he remembered the name. The Reverend Bodmin began to play out the cards from his deck.

"What McMaster should obtain, and this is my desire, regardless of the priceless nature of the gift, is simply that they be housed safely and securely in a separate building, preferably one designed and constructed for the purpose. I have some plans here." He pulled out some drawings and papers from an inner pocket, but Togo smilingly waved them down.

"The design can wait. All of your projection, the collection, fireplace and all." He bowed. "I imagine your plans include the fireplace and the paintings?" He bowed in understanding at the reverend's nod. The old gentleman to me was assuming the look, especially around the eyes, of a Mississippi gambler. Togo continued in a voice and with a manner so mellifluous that Bodmin, if he were a movie-goer at all, should have seen the shade of John Carradine, at his very best, playing a gambler with such courtesy, such a long thin cigar, as a paddle steamer steamed out of Memphis bound for New Orleans, dressed so elegantly, his linen starched and spotless, that only a fellow gambler at the table would realise, without any sign of it, that there was a loaded Derringer beneath the flowered weskit.

"This, of course, will have to be submitted in your writing to the Board of Governors, who alone have any power to accept or to bequeath. But it would be well if you could voice to me your hopes, your ideas." Togo gave a little cough against the back of his hand. "And your dreams. You are thinking then, nay, proposing, that a separate institute bearing your name be established on the campus?"

The old gentleman nodded vigorously.

202

"Yes, to hold the collection and" he waved "this unique fireplace constructed of stones from Pompeii, Yokohama, Rome, Alexandria, Athens, Williamsburg, Cleveland and a Druid stone from Dartmoor along with stone relics from the Inca and Aztec civilisations that I acquired in Mexico City. The building should include modest quarters for me, and I would give a lecture every afternoon and more often by request on John Milton the poet. I would refuse any salary, save for an annual emolument for my material well-being, and sufficient travel funds for my summer peregrinations in enriching the collection. "

"There" said Togo, slapping his hands on his knees. He had sat down gratefully on a stool while the proposition was emerging.

"There. We have it then. The Professor and I will make representations of your offer, your most illuminating, indeed, enlightening offer to Dr. Harry Thode, our President, whose servants we are, so that when your far-ranging suggestions come from you for submission to the Board of Governors he shall not be unprepared. Now," looking at his watch, "It is nearing six o'clock and we have a long voyage home. So we must be on our way, and thank you, my dear sir, for such a frank and lucid presentation. It shall not be readily forgot, let me assure you of that. "

I made appropriate noises that signified nothing as we got to the door and wished the old gentleman well again before almost running out of the driveway to the Beetle that was parked under a nearby shade tree.

In case we could be observed from the Bodmin Library we kept silent and set faces until we got on to the streaming traffic-laden highway. Only then did we expel our breath. We felt relaxed, even in the Beetle. Togo drove and drove and we talked and talked, the words spilling out of us between groans, whistles, and laughs.

On the way back we made a detour out of Paris to a fine old restaurant and relaxed after our long day over a good dinner and two tankards of good bitter ale. Paris was but 20 miles out of Hamilton and it was barely 11 p. m. when Togo deposited me at the University Library where Vincent, following a call I had made from Paris, was waiting to pick me up.

The next morning we saw Dr. Thode, and Harry enjoyed the relation of our trip as much as we enjoyed telling it.

"Well, that's done. I'll tell Cary about it when I see him today. He assured me that there was no need to worry about hurting his feelings whatever we decided. But we had to know, didn't we? And I'll write to the would-be--what would you call him--donor? And that's the last of it. "

It very nearly was the last of it as far as we were concerned. There were some angry letters, mainly directed at me, but other schemes were already hatching down at Bagshaw and the result was that the old man won, or something. But that's another story, funnier and better than our own, and will have to wait.

Marget Meikleham, the retired librarian, went on to manage the Baptist Archive in the Divinity School, probably the best of its kind in the world, and out of the purlieu and possession of the University. Margaret was well suited for this position and she had earned a retirement from the rising hurly burly of the new order that was engulfing the university library set-up in Ontario. She had been a main influence in establishing a Telex communication between the libraries that was to prove invaluable and she, with Bob Blackburn, the University Librarian of the University of Toronto, had been leaders in the establishment for the first time of a union list of serials, two benefits that were of great assistance in our progress.

It is experiences such as the one that Togo and I shared on the first Monday in August 1966 that draw people together and reinforce or weaken their relations with one another.

Canada was going through a headlong time of university expansion, opening them where there had been no university service before, expanding existing institutions, developing the collections, building new housing for them.

Ed Williams in 1960, with Emile Filion, S. J. , a librarian who was also a guide, philosopher, and friend all over Canada, had submitted a preliminary study showing how lacking were the university libraries in books. Robert Downs, seven years later, submitted the Downs Report that was of inestimable value in furthering the cause of better libraries. In the days of economy and budget-cutting that were to come in the 70's, and carrying on through the inflationary patterns of the 80's, the Downs Report was a diving board for us to leap from after the big fish and the minnows of books that were to be had for the netting and the bait of dollars.

A staff seemed to grow around me during those days. Dorothy Davidson managed the processing and more. Narendar Passi began breaking surface and making a welcome splash.

Luckiest of all was I that from outside the library field completely I was to get two companions without whom I would have been sure to fail in some of my endeavours and adventures. Art Lawrence who, widowed, came from Cumberland, England, to live in Canada where his son, working for Stelco in Hamilton, was already settled, and Ken Tompkins who came over to me from the University Business Office.

It was Burt James, a senior administrative officer, who sent me Ken Tompkins. Burt was no book reader, neither was Mike Hedden, the Vice-President/Administration, but we struck sparks together. Never could one who was building up a university library system ever be so well supported as I was, although what I was doing remained a mystery to them. They would look at me puzzled sometimes.

"Why do you want the originals, Will, when copies would cost so much less?"

"You want $15,000 for eighteenth century binding tools? What for? We send all our binding out. Here...." Mike would wave a bill "Here's a bill for $20,000 for binding."

They both had desire and energy at least equal to my own. I would have been lost without them, and they were both great company.

We collected then, and nearly doubled our collection in the first year. The library, like so many others at that time, had been on the Dewey Classification System, and in switching the existing collection to the Library of Congress system, somehow processing all the new acquisitions, the staff did wonders. They worked long hours, often all for love and nothing for reward, or very little, anyway. It took me some time to straighten out the staff and salaries so that they made sense.

I talked to them all every so often in the auditorium

205

of the Divinity School. They were as imbued with the fire to match the library collections with the abundant funds as I was. The library buildings were positively humming with their efforts and idleness or scrimshanking of any kind were so impossible in that atmosphere that those who wanted either to idle or scrimshank just went some place else. Jobs were ten a penny in those days.

Alex Jamieson was my good reference librarian. She decided to go for broke, and via the Library School at the University of Western Ontario decided to take a doctorate at Maryland. She had already graduated from the Library School at the University of Western Ontario, and she had friends abundant in the library game who kept her au fait with the situation.

17

Bill Davis, the Minister of Education for the province, later
to become Premier, was responsible in 1969 for opening, as
with the stroke of an enchanter's wand, 20 Community Colleges: this was the best thing he ever did, although neither
he nor any of us realised the great flowering that was to
come from this planting.

They were all going to open in September 1969. Alex
Jamieson and some others realised in the early spring that
with all the rush to get an administrative staff together and
all the teachers, for colleges in Toronto, Thunder Bay, Ottawa, Belleville, Hamilton, Brampton, Windsor and the rest,
they had forgotten one essential ingredient that had to be
present for Opening Day--libraries.

This threw the Department of Education into a great
pother. They literally wrung their hands and went about recruiting library staff and finding buildings.

But what about the books to be put on the shelves that
they were seeking? How to process, how to buy them and
select them. Alex Jamieson had the solution to it all. "Get
Will Ready to do it." The startle of her words got back to
Government, and down to Hamilton came three deputy ministers or such like to proposition me.

I could not resist. Who could! With my McMaster
staff nothing seemed impossible to me then. Choice has already suggested the necessary basic library for the opening
day of a college library. I got Ken Tompkins right away on
field trips to California, New Jersey, everywhere that I could
see help in our effort. One thing I insisted on was that I
would do it alone, under no circumstances be answerable to
a committee and that funds be made available, $1,000,000,

to get the show on the road, and that this sum be made available immediately as I was leaving for Britain the next day, and would need the money in the morning to open an account that I could draw on for the thousands of books I would be buying for the colleges over there. They agreed, and the next morning, about 9:30 a.m., a courier arrived in my office with the cheque.

I did not want to deposit it in the Bank of Commerce, McMaster's bank whence I received my monthly salary cheque, nor in the Bank of Montreal where I had our family account, $317 at that time, plus a mortgage. So I drove downtown to the National Trust and got there at ten o'clock, just as they were opening. It was a blustery day, I recall, and I was wearing a puffy down parka, a knee-length coat, and a cap with ear muffs pulled down to stop the tingle.

There was a girl at the desk. She looked at me indifferently as I came in. After all, I was not much to look at.

"I want to open an account, a checking account."

"Yes" she said, eyeing me up and down. "Here, fill in this form." And she pushed across a form for me to fill in and disappeared somewhere in the back.

I filled in the form, name, address, and the rest, and waited for her return. I was still the only customer at the desk, and I was in a hurry. After all, I had a plane to catch at 5:00 p.m. I had to get out to Ancaster, a neighbouring town where we had our house, lunch, pack, and see the family before I took off.

I was left waiting at the counter. The manager's office was adjacent and the door open. I looked in. He lifted his eyes from that morning's Globe and Mail and queried me with them. He was leaning back in his office chair, taking his ease before the rush, if any, started.

"I'm waiting to open an account."

"The girl will be back in a minute. There she is now." He jerked his head at her as she passed and went leaning back reading his paper.

The girl took the form from me and checked it. It was in order.

208

"How much do you want to deposit?"

"A million dollars" I said, and passed the cheque to her.

"A million dollars!" She almost squeaked as she said it. She stared at the cheque. It was as copper-bottomed as a cheque could be. "A million dollars!" She stared at the cheque.

There was a crash as the manager came running out. He stared at the cheque that he snatched from the girl's hand. It was for a million dollars all right. A government cheque for a million dollars. He stared at me wildly.

"I want it in a checking account, and I'll be drawing on it from the Bank of Montreal in London, England, in about a week's time. Can you manage that?"

He nodded open-mouthed.

"Right. I'll leave it with you then. But remember, I'll be needing to draw on it in a week's time. Do you know Ron Pearson? He's a cousin of mine." He was, too, by marriage.

"He's a vice-president of National Trust. You can call him if you're troubled. Now remember, a week's time I'll need to draw on it in London." And I went out. Across the road I saw an office building of a national accountancy firm, Woods Gundy or something. I went across and asked to see a senior accountant. I was getting fairly well known about and around Hamilton by this time. That is one of the advantages of moving to a town like Hamilton. It was so variegated with the great steel works of Dofasco and Stelco in the east end, bearing towards the great Ford plant at Oakville and Metro Toronto, while to the north, past Guelph, world famous for its agronomy, animal husbandry and now one of the new universities, there was a road up to Tobermary on Georgian Bay where the Bruce Trail started and rambled all the way down to Niagara. There were deer running across our back yard nearly every morning, and above all there was McMaster University, semi-circled with the Royal Botanic Gardens.

I had been giving a lot of talks, meeting all kinds of people, reviewing books, writing articles for the Hamilton

Spectator.... I had no time to wait for the accountant. When I told him that I wanted the firm to keep an eye on the bills and ensure their prompt payment he agreed to do so, but fell out of his chair laughing when I told him about my depositing experience across the road.

It's a wonderful feeling, given to few, to build up a library from scratch, and to build more than 20 college libraries from scratch, while running a university library that was bursting the walls with its growth put the cap with a plume on it to top it.

A few days later I was in Blackwell's Book Shop in Oxford, in the same block as Balliol and facing the Bodleian Library. One wall was shelved and filled completely with the essential reference books that all the colleges would need, dictionaries, atlases, Oxford Companions, a good simple multi-volumed encyclopedia. The clerk, a gentlemanly fellow, who remembered me from previous visits, waited on me. Man and boy, I had had my own account at Blackwell's since I was in high school. They never dunned me even in those days, when I was like to owe them a pound or two for several months. Every quarter of the year would come a polite statement of my account. During my years at Stanford and at Marquette I had done a fair bit of business with them, and had supped with the Blackwells, father and son, here and there at conventions. Sir Basil, the old captain of the vast world-wide enterprise, was in his office above the decks of books. I took a deep breath; these, after all, were expensive books, costing more than a pretty penny, and there were hundreds of them. "I'll take the lot. Will you send them to McMaster University as soon as possible."

He made a note and bowed while writing.

"Yes sir, they will be packed and be on their way immediately."

"I want 20 more sets of what I have ordered. All to go to McMaster, as soon as possible."

I gave the order without a quaver, without a grin, although I had a hard time keeping my face and voice in order.

The book clerk dropped his order book and pencil; that was all the emotion that he showed.

"And send the bill to me. Or would you rather I paid you now?"

"Yes sir" the clerk dusted his knees. "One moment, sir." I could feel although I did not see Sir Basil looking down at me from the quarter deck.

There was just a few minutes conversation between the clerk and the manager: I suppose it was the manager. The clerk returned.

"I was just checking to see whether we have 21 sets on hand."

He smiled faintly. "Will that be enough, sir, 21 sets? We shall be sending them out before the week is over. Is there anything else?"

"No, that's enough for today."

He nodded, I nodded back and I made my way to the Mitre for lunch. Blackwell's did not ask me to sign, pay, or in any way bind myself to the contract. And the books arrived by sea and rail within a month. There was book-selling, and it explains why Blackwell's get so much of the business.

It was such a week of book gathering, such a week that I had never hoped for. And I was just in time. By the same time next year, the Downs Report for Canada, the days of affluence all over the U.S. were reaching a crescendo, a high note that was to crack in a year or so, but before that time books were getting hard to get, compared to the leisurely times of the past when librarians were getting used to the Grand Tour of Europe, picking up books in London, Amsterdam, and Paris before riding on to Frankfurt in a sedan for the world's great annual Book Fair.

What Blackwell's did for me in new books, Rota, late of Vigo Street and Savile Row, and now of Covent Garden, did for me otherwise. Bertram Rota who had set up the business in the Bodley Head in Vigo Street, had been an annual visitor to the States. His particular friend was David Magee who ran such a good bookstore of English literature in Post Street in San Francisco, almost above Warren Howell's bookshop, another rare Americana, father and son enterprise. It was people like these who made me wish sometimes that I had become a book-seller, but the feeling never lasted long enough to matter.

With the books ordered and pouring in I went home to Cardiff for a while. There, in the Morgan Arcade, was

Lear's Book Shop. They were already well known beyond
Wales and even more so within, as excellent suppliers of
good standard editions and they did well by me by sending
me the French, Spanish, and German early college texts
along with the English collected editions of the classics.

After some long talks with Mam, a few parties with
the family, with Jack at the piano in the front room, visiting
Aberavon, all the relations, wandering around the quiet dock-
yards and strolling down what was left of Love Lane and
Rhymney Hill, the pottery, our old football pitch at Black-
weir where we had, in 1939, given a Cardiff Rugby Club a
run for its money, I flew for home. Hamilton had become
home to us now, and was to remain so for the rest of my
working life.

The books were already piling up for the Community
Colleges. We had to clamber over the boxes of them to get
in to the library from the north-east entrance and exit. The
books from the States came in ready-catalogued and we rented
a place near Ryerson College near to the Toronto freeways
and exits and began to establish a Bibliocentre, as I called
it, to serve the community colleges. McMaster University
supplied the processing drive. We began to order the necessary journals to be delivered directly to the colleges who
were beginning to have lives of their own.

My cavalier, often headlong drive to meet the September deadline got the books on the shelves although many of
the journals were laggards. There were angry questions directed against Bill Davis as the progenitor of this all, and
about the set-up of the libraries without any committee, especially by a newly-come director from the States who seemed
to think that Dallas or Houston were in Ontario. Davis fielded
the questions like the politician he was proving to be, an heir-
apparent to Premier Robarts.

Harry Thode got some angry letters about my headlong
ways and his replies seemed to silence my detractors.

There was a good chance of a Union Catalogue, a
centre for processing, ordering, binding and the rest, but
the newly appointed librarians were restless and wanted to
run their own shows. I was sorely tempted to become the
Director of the Community College Library System; it was a
golden opportunity.

I have always believed that a library is a place for

books, readers and librarians, papers, book restoration and printing workshops, fine binding making and repairs, with library staff of all kinds, those skilled in the art of the book, archival staff, shelvers, shippers and most of all those who have the gift or aim to acquire it whose pleasure is among people.

All those who work, if work it can be called, in a library, belong to one scheme of things. They should meet and greet as fellow workers, as the garrison of Bastion Book because it is only by their efforts that the book will be saved, and themselves, out of existence. More and more certificates instead of less are being piled up, like sandbags to keep out the flood. More time, thought and effort goes into job descriptions that keep the people out who should be in at the job, but because they don't like either strait jackets or time-wasting workshops and courses, they have a hard time as yet climbing up the totem pole. But they are certificating.

When a new university was opening one of the old guard, a governor, a donor, someone who was a reader anyway, queried the ebullient president on the paucity of the library holdings.

"That's all right" said the president. "See that plug in the wall? There are dozens of them, in the floor, along the walls. Some of the desks even have them. All you or me or anybody else needs to get whatever you need for reading, anything, from anywhere in the world, is to plug into that thing and the book will appear on the screen before you. See? Every desk has a screen. There will be somebody at the desk who will call the number for you and there will be the print in front of you, like in the old microcard readers. But these new technologies don't need the cards to be here. Just dial a number for a text, a symphony, a poet reading, or a painting. They can all appear, the books with illustrations by Dali, Daumier, or Black. The pictures will be coming in full colour soon. And if you want a copy all you need to do is press a button and you'll have a paper copy of the book churning out of the machine. Who needs big old libraries?"

At Princeton, Princeton! a faculty man turned administrator, as more and more of them are trying to do, seeking the high ground, turned to the President as they were passing the Firestone Library:

"Well, that's off our backs, anyway."

213

The President, startled, looked at him, and Faculty
Dan went into a long spiel about how the new technology was
making the old idea of a library obsolete. Articles in popular and professional magazines encourage this fallacy; it
rouses the Yankee in us, the bad Yankee who is always fixing things so that eventually they will all fall down, or seize
up and die, but they will have saved time or made money.
Fallacy, fallacy, all is fallacy.

There is no easy way to anything that matters, in the
long run. Learning will always be hard, difficult and lonely.
It is a different process for everyone for from the moment
of conception and ever on: we are different one from another.
The Book has only had a short life, as we know the Book,
about 500 years, and in this new era, when information is
lauded, practised and taught over learning, it is in danger of
dying. This should be of prime concern to the librarians,
for, when the chips are down, they are the keepers of the
Book; yet, if you read the job descriptions that they have
concocted and made into their bargaining bible there are very
few jobs that seem to realise this or want to practise it.
They are beguiled by the machine, by technology: that's
the Yankee in us again.

We are certificating ourselves to death. I have taught
in three graduate library schools and compacted into two
years' hard work is an attempt at learning that should take
a lifetime. Certificates should be interspersed with field
work; certification, degrees, diplomas should only be given
after working on the job.

I remember once, passing Shevlin Hall at the University of Minnesota on a lovely spring day in May I began talking to a girl who was hastening along with me to Old Main.
I was on my way to give a class on some skullduggery or
other of the Angevin kings of Britain. I knew she wasn't in
my class so I asked her where she was going.

"303B, in that building over there. It's on philosophy."

"What are you in then? Are you taking philosophy as
a major?"

"No, I've got to take it for Pre-Mort" and she hurried
on. I was never much of a fast mover. The Infantry taught
me that: Take it easy. Rest your legs. Sit down whenever
you can. I saw her disappear around a corner. Pre-Mort?

214

I had to ask around as to what Pre-Mort was. It wasn't
Pre-Med, the humanities and science degree favoured to the
candidates to Medical School. No; Pre-Mort was Pre-Morti-
cian. There was a grab bag of courses for the Mortician
Diploma: that was what the girl was working for.

I remember another place when the dental technicians
wanted a graduation finale in Convocation style, with gowns,
organ playing, award of diplomas. It was arranged that they
take a special course in philosophy and a few other courses.
Then the President, the deans, senior academics would be
on the platform and they would be awarded their diplomas
just like degrees. Since it was a privately-funded university,
with a big dental school, the technicians got their way. That
night at a festival dinner, with all the dentists, the parents,
relatives, boyfriends of the technicians, was the valedictorian.
She lauded the dean of the Dental School and having looked up
his honours and awards she held out her hands in measure
like an angler.

"Girls" she confided, as it were, to her classmates.
"He has a Who's Who this big!"

At that moment, as the girls gasped, there was a
crackle and a flash and all the lights went out. It took
about five minutes for the lights to come on again, and then
the Dental Dean was eyed with wonder, respect and admiration by the graduating technicians. He was bewildered by it,
for he was a thin, scrawny little man and, until then, self-
effacing. But after that festival dinner, following the Convocation of his technicians, he commanded a new respect, and
the school was able to increase the fees and turn away more
students, some from as far away as Oregon.

There was one morning at McMaster when I was having coffee and one of the accountants sat down beside me.

"Will, do you know a writer called Dean Swift?"

"Yes, so do you, Bruce. He wrote Gulliver's
Travels."

"Oh, did he? Well, I was at a wedding reception in
Toronto last week and I met an old gentleman there who used
to be principal for years at John A. High School. I was a
freshman there in his final year. He had a nice big lot north
and west of Yonge, but, he was telling me, his family grown

and gone away, he and his wife were living in an apartment
in Mississauga, and he did not know what to do with his
Swift books. His children, all married now, did not want
them. He had given most of his books away when they had
moved out of their house in Toronto, and the booksellers
had bought some from him, but these Swift books he had ...
he'd like to see them placed all together. When he found
out I was working at a university he was wondering if I could
tell him what to do about it. I've got his name and address
and telephone number if you like. Do you want it? Good.
Then I'll tell his nephew, who was best man at the wedding,
that he may be hearing from you."

I called the old gentleman--he had been retired for
many years--and arranged to visit him and see his Swift
books. A few days later I was in his apartment and was
surprised at the near totality and quality of the books. I
bought them then and there, and with Art Lawrence who was
waiting for me outside, we loaded them and they were added
to our already growing collection of 18th-century books. An
Institute of 18th-century studies was developing at McMaster,
members of all the faculties were involved, and there was a
particular interest in Anglo-Irish books of the period for that
century saw Dublin flower in elegance, learning, and with its
own Parliament House. I recall that the second edition of
The Tale of the Tub was the only Swift copy we were lacking
after my trip to Mississauga.

Whenever I went over to Britain on a book expedition
I always included a trip to Ireland. The National Librarian,
Paddy Caughey, and Denis Roberts, then Librarian of Trinity
College and later to become the National Librarian of Scot-
land, had become friends of mine. They introduced me to
a great bibliophile who had a splendid collection of Anglo-
Irish literature to dispose of. He lived in Naas, near Dublin,
and he had a good wine cellar also. He had served in the
Inniskillings during World War I, so we had a lot in common,
tales mostly, of soldiering and the like.

There was one in particular that we relished. The
Inniskillings were always known as a shiny, smart, regular
regiment, but in common with all the other Irish regiments
they had a great affection for the Connaught Rangers. They
were really untamed lads from the West Coast of Ireland,
hardly broken to boots, let alone drill--wild Irish soldiers.
They could hardly parade for their own officers, and most of
them spoke Gaelic. They loped, not marched, and on the

216

Diamond Jubilee of Queen Victoria they brought up the rear of the Honour parade, wondering what in the name of God they were doing in London. They were rarely allowed even in Cork City as a unit, and then only when they were coming or going to serve a seven-year stint in India or the Barbados. Still, they made the most of it, and the officers were running around them like sheep dogs keeping them together as they loped past the Queen.

She was a grumpy old lady by the time of her Diamond Jubilee, and as she sat on her throne, her feet on a cushion, in Hyde Park, she kept turning to Field Marshal Lord Roberts, an Irishman himself, asking what them soldiers were who were parading past her.

"Them's your Royal Life Guards, Ma'am."

"Hm." She snorted and took another drop of her medicament from under the tent of her handkerchief.

"Who's them?"

"Them's your Bengal Lancers, Ma'am."

There was another grumpy snort from the old Queen, who kept dozing off until the blare of the bands of approaching regiments, the clash and flash of weapons raised or lowered to salute her. The parade was miles long and it took hours to pass her throne.

At last Lord Roberts could bend to her and say "That's nearly the last of it, Ma'am. Here comes the last of it now." To scattered applause the Connaught Rangers came loping by, their heads turned right towards her in salute, but a salute of a such a friendly puzzled kind that the old lady stirred herself and sat up straight--

"Who's them?"

Lord Roberts, his eyes softened by the looks of the omadhaums, said proudly and affectionately "Them's your Connaught Rangers Ma'am."

The Queen looked back, more and more lively than she had been all morning and afternoon. She said to her Field Marshal, "Jasus, them's troops!"

It was with stories like that that Barry Brown and

217

I enjoyed one another's company, that, and talks about his books. It was a great collection, but he'd just about exhausted the field. Besides, books that he had paid a few pounds or even shillings for in 1922 or '3 were now costing much more. His house was groaning, literally groaning like a living thing with the weight and the life of them. His wife, a lady whom he had met in Switzerland when he was still recuperating--he had been buried alive for hours when the regiment was charging through a shell barrage--was most anxious to get the books safely away. There was so little room to move around in even to climb the stairs, that they were thinking of moving to a nearby house that Barry also owned and let the books have this one for their own.

The booksellers knew of the situation and had been courting Barry for years. He had caught some peering in a window at the books. Several were sending him Christmas presents--of books!--and a few had been able to talk business with him. They wanted to buy some and leave others. They were cautious in their prices. One or two had driven him to lunch in Dublin, and book business had dominated the conversation.

I had a good bookseller friend in Hanna. He was not an antiquarian bookseller at all, although they had some book shelves of dusty old books in their store. Hanna's was a bookseller firm who did most of the school and college business, and had displays of modern books. He was the fourth generation of Hannas in the book trade. Their shop and office were across the road from the wall around Trinity College. I often used to drop in on him for a chat and I went out now and then with him of a Sunday to watch the small boats sailing in Dublin Bay. He knew how to pack and ship books fast; that was an important part of the Hanna business.

One day, after lunch with the National Librarian and Barry Brown and talking it over with Denis Roberts at Trinity, we decided that since they had all the books already that Barry Brown had collected, it would be well to let the books go to McMaster where they would be plated with the family crest of Brown and inscribed with his name.

"Barry" I said. "I can think of no better disposition. You'll be glad of it, the books will be housed together in fine quarters. They will be studied and read. I like the feel and heft of them. If it's agreeable to you I'll give you a cheque now for £25,000, and have them packed and on their way across the ocean by next Thursday."

218

Barry sighed with relief. There was no havering about it, and the next day a large pantechnicon with some good packers of Hanna's, including Fred himself, were there and they rolled off towards the shipping lines with Fred to see them through the customs with all the bills of lading that he gave me the next day.

Mrs. Brown and Barry were delighted. It was one of the best collections that I ever encountered. We had established a rapport over the years. There were friends we trusted and who knew the book game, the contents of his library that was already in the holdings of Trinity and the National, and preferred it to go to a place that needed it, would care for it, and plate the name of Barry Brown therein. It was an ideal operation from the beginning and had a happy ending. There turned out to be more than 11,000 books in the collection, all eighteenth century, neither foxed nor mildewed, but as they had come from the auctions and the booksellers, maybe thirty years and more before. Often the bill would flutter from the pages at a perusal, and books now impossible to obtain for any money, Barry had obtained for more or less than just a pound.

There still remains with me a belief that there are many more books in Ireland, often well-nigh mouldering on the shelves. The days of the Big House are gone, but the stories of Somerville and Ross have bathed them in the light and the dark, the sun and the moon, the dilapidation, the driveways overgrown, the unpeopled residence of a brilliant society. Around Baltimore, west of Cork, there is such a society still in residence. Admiral of the Fleet the Earl of Cork and Omery would call it home. The True Charlotte, a novel yet to have its due, was written there by a woman who was dead, according to the one remaining of the duo, Oenone or Martin. The Earl of Halidom, when his roof's leaking letting in too much rain water for the house to bear, calls in the roofers, and to pay for the lead, the ladders, and the men, he sells another shelf of the books in the library.

The papers in whatever muniment rooms there are, the letters, maps, thousands of them, are crumbling and decaying over there. Booksellers are generally sent around to the servants entrance, aggressive librarians are neither understood nor welcome. Is it any wonder, then, that I frequented the selling up of a Big House whenever I was able? The quays along the Liffey offer food enough in books, but they are well picked over, and the antiquarian booksellers, like all the other antique shops, were doing a whale of a business when last I was over. Dublin is one of my favourite towns in all the world. There is still enough Georgian architecture standing, sufficient concern to preserve it and make it better, such libraries and colleges, such good theatre, and Dubliners galore, that it was with a wrench that soon I parted the west to a sale at Cabra, yet it seems often only like last week, and maybe it was, when I reflect on how we are discovering that the past may be now or in the future. If this is so, and we press the right button or say the right word, I'd like to be in Cabra today, maybe, but this is asking for too much perhaps, in time to bag that oil painting of Swift.

The Earl of Wicklow had a castle in Ireland that I went to that was later turned into a hotel, but the silver tableware was too heavy to lift; the place was not meant for a hotel at all. I wondered what they would do with all the heavy stuff, not knowing then how the sales would bring the dealers swarming. There were Muscovy ducks there who used to nest in a gutter of the roof that overlooked the west lawn of that castle, and when the ducklings were big enough to learn to fly the mother used to push them with her beak down a water drain-pipe. They rolled out at the other end onto the soft grass, and learned to fly from the ground up, which is the proper way.

There is a bookseller in Wales who lives in a sixteenth-century house. He too kept Muscovy ducks. The drake used to save the eggs and flip them at the postman with his wing, from the next above the small keep gate. He was a real Roger, that drake, and used to try and mate with the young ewes on Cowbridge common, causing such alarm, anticipation, and despondency among both the sheep and the commoners of Cowbridge, that the bookseller had to get rid of them. Now he has a goose that will live to be seventy and grazes on the common.

The Big Houses are going, going one by one. There was one in County Cavan about fifty miles out of Dublin. There was a book sale there, winding up the whole auction of the effects. The household effects were being auctioned off earlier on the same day, and there were furniture dealers in bowler hats from London, and precious boys with suede high boots and gay scarves knotted under their left ear or earrings, clawing at the fabrics and the lovely bibelots.

What was left of the Ascendancy in the neighbourhood, arrived in their Land Rovers and, perched on their shooting

220

sticks amid the debris of another Big House going, they bid for Chippendale and portraits of Green-Jacket colonels, their friends and relations at Hunt Balls, family pictures in huge gilt frames ... there was a fine painting of a Dean Swift that was sold before the sale. I bought the daub of the Dean there, done by a peddling artist that somehow has life in it, especially since it hangs among his books at McMaster.

There were books galore, musty, dusty, and with mould here and there from the attic rooms as well as the morocco bindings from the shelves in the library, bindings full of poor editions of Bulwer-Lytton and Thackeray. But there were good books amid the moulded, the foxed, and the breakfronts, that brought the book dealers bidding all the way from Europe--it was muttered that one was all the way from the States--and one that was from Kilkenny. There were clergy, bibliophiles, there too, and all knew the values of a book both for itself alone, for the market price, and as an investment. Better than investing in the new Scottish School of Painting books are, especially eighteenth-century books and there was Swift, Sheridan and Goldsmith. If the catalogue was read aright, it would have English departments crowing and moisten even the lips of some of them.

Suburbia was here in force as well, trying to buy a tapestry or a chair that they would put in view from their front window and refer to as having come from the Castle. Drovers in their dunged gum boots and thwacking sticks, wandered around too, getting a lumpy down pillow or a counterpane to remember the old place by, and for a song too, since most of the things they wanted were not of dealer value.

Castle Cabra is an old manor house, castellated and mock-Gothicked through the centuries, with even a holy wishing well within its demesne. But the hundred or so castle acres were now being subdivided by the Land Commission, into small holdings, or afforested.

The day of the sale was of a sort that is common to Ireland, with the sky so low that you could touch it, and everything so damp, save within the castle, where the walls had been built and plastered so rightly that although it had not been lived in for years it was as dry as a bone, though chilly. The rain came down. The damp, green turf around the castle and soft pelt of the rain deadened all sound, so that even the cars starting up did so with a hushed sort of cough.

The sale went on all day long and the bidding was fierce. The priests there in force, book time; they knew their books, and the prices they would bring before the auctioneer knocked them down. But the prices the books brought were more than expected. The books, the Pope, the Scott, the Edgeworth, the Gibbon all went at soaring prices. Here and there were bargains. A fourth edition Richardson's Clarissa (in seven volumes, published in 1751) went for £50, and the 1960 London edition of Pope's Works, (nine volumes) for $75, for example. Swift's works (the nine volumes of the Dublin 1735 edition) went for about $40, a bargain, but Loss's Topographical Dictionary of Ireland and his Dictionary of England brought far more and so did Carey's Atlas, about the same price. It was books of travel, with illustrations and maps and prints, that brought the dealers. There was an Atlas of Rare Skin Diseases (1830) with coloured plates that brought $250. It would bring $2,500 now.

It was good to be there. The books all seemed to go to the dealers because their method of bidding is so rapid and expert that a tyro is lost in the flickering and nodding, the nose stroking, and the winking that signify bids. One thing that it did show, you should hire a dealer to bid, send one on your behalf, or hide behind the arras.

Sales are the most saving and economic way of building up resources. Besides, it will get the librarians away from hardware for a while, and back to books, which remain the only reason for being beguiled by hardware in the first place. It is ironic that just when librarians, after generations of colleagues like Downs, Cronin, and Larry Powell paving the way, are beginning to get accepted by the academic community as peers, they are slipping off the rock like Gollum in search of a bright shiny thing.

When I was leaving night was falling over Castle Cabra, over the County of Cavan, over Ireland, all the Western World. I had a few books under my oxter, some in the pockets of my Burberry, all paid for, and a load in the back of Hanna's estate wagon that he had bid in for me. As we lurched and swung and bumped over the track, past the Saint's well, down the boreen to the road, there were a quackle of Muscovy ducks perched on the boughs of a vast arbutus, and the drake of them all was flying easy in the sky, bulky, black and white, a dazzle against the louring sky of the coming moonless night; Leda McComb was dawdling, ignoring her mother's call from the cottage where the candle in the window was guttering for her return.

The book collections that we amassed were the light of my life, but they were light beacons, that light the way towards better library service. I always flinch within when references to me appear as a book collector, a book collector, period. Nearly all that collecting was a matter of luck. I just happened to be there at the right time, and because I knew that university library service depended above all, on primary sources backed up by books, I was willing and able to acquire them for service.

18

The libraries everywhere are stirring. Everything about
them is changing faster than I can imagine. The greatest
change that I have seen is in the nature and the quality of
the staff. There was a time in my library life when many
of the staff were there, often placed there, because it offered a haven to the shy and the insecure. This fostered a
jocular and avuncular attitude among those rascals of the
faculty who objected to the rules, who thought of the library
as their preserve. Students who used the library deserved
less service than they did, should abide by the rigid rules
that allowed the teachers their peculiar privileges.

It was the rising sense of their own importance among
the students that helped to bring about proper reform in library service: it would have been far more difficult to effect without their vociferous demand for more than their just
deserts.

It is hard for me to believe that when I first got into
librarianating on a managerial level the faculty were allowed
to take books out for months, for years at a time, with no
penalties invoked against them if they did not return a book
that others needed. Journals, even the most current, they
tucked under their arms and took off, and generally returned
them when they remembered to. They had rooms of their
own for study in the library, besides their faculty study rooms,
and they howled, one actually did howl, when they were
brought under the same library rules as others. When fines
were levied against them there were Chicken Littles among
them. This was common through university library service
everywhere. Some of the loudest cluckers had never even
borrowed a book: they may have read one, but their previous
privileges that they had fashioned over the years were coming
to pieces in their hands.

The whole university structure is coming to pieces: all of us are beginning to realise this, and we are at a loss. There is one blessing that I am thankful for. I have graduated from one graduate library school and taught in three of them and, with all their faults, and I could drive a team of Clydesdales hauling a wagon load of beer barrels through them, they are the reason for a library staff emerging that will cope, will even belly their sails with the winds of change. The library schools, thank God, are changing. They are more and more becoming a part of the structure of higher and further education. They are already more a part of professional education than they ever were in the past. They are becoming islands to leap to or from in the lifelong learning that we need. Over-certification is assuming a babu stigma, and the development of the technical schools, the introduction of courses in the business schools, the computer workshops, the mingling of all the talents, this is the way to go, all the way, all the time.

The university of my past is as dead as the dodo and is beginning to lie down. I remember, as I write, Adam Smith's excoriation of Oxford, Balliol in particular, I regret to say, and while his dour Scots and earnest way and faulty philosophy were endemic, protesting against the free and easy ways of the English university as compared to the gruelling programmes of his own dour Glasgow, his excoriations were of little account, common slings hurled by the earnest non-conformists every generation against that home of lost causes, that Bastion of Privilege and nursery of the Establishment. Beneath the profligate veneer there has always been the hard core that governed Britain, the statesmen, the judges and the administrators, a caste more rigid than the Brahmin.

As the common people rose to a degree of leisure and a degree of affluence that put chickens in every pot, a car in every garage, and campers and cataramans within the reach of many, there arose also a demand for higher education, better schools and avenues of advancement that did not lead to the mines, the blast furnaces, and the forty-hour working week. The Establishment satisfied this inchoate yearning on both sides of the Atlantic by enlarging and developing local universities, the land grant colleges and provincial institutions, by making high school education well-nigh mandatory, and creating and unloosing on their world the Monster Sham. Suddenly, and it was suddenly, a post-war phenomenon, there were unloosed schools and universities where none had been before. They created a teaching body of men and women hastily processed to serve as faculty. In doing so they did not realize that despite all their efforts, silent and subtle though they may have been, they were participating in their own demise; they were joining the dodo.

They had been caught up, with their gulls, in the talons of an idea whose time had come.

After the first joyous and intoxicating embrace of the new generations by high schools and universities it began to be realised that the old orders of privilege and promotion were stronger than ever. The clamouring horde who had been to claw at the halls of ivy had been given halls of their own, an arriviste faculty that promoted one another as their olders and betters had done for centuries. A groundswell of unrest that culminated in the storms of the students of the sixties whirled through the whole educational set-up. They would not accept the second-rate; they deserved the best, and they have begun to get it.

Le trahison des clercs is a term that must remain French; the nearest that we can come to it in English is The Betrayal of the Intellectuals and that is not good enough, but will serve.

What had happened to the Catholic church in the States, following the new and "suitable" colleges of the thirties, now rattles the fabric of the new and swollen universities. They have begun to rival and then to beat some of the older institutions that had never welcomed them in. It is a painful time, this, like a new birth, but from this squalling infant is arising a pattern of education that is altogether different and better than the old.

Within the span of a few decades scientists and scholars of world renown think twice about settling with their talents on the eastern seaboard. The University of Illinois at Champaign-Urbana houses the papers of H. G. Wells and a great collection of Milton. The state University of New York is growing annually in its great services, faculty and library, available at Binghampton, Buffalo, Syracuse and points north, east, south and west. Together they share one of the great libraries of the world. Boston Public Library is embracing surrounding areas, and with its resources has become the basis for higher education, an education that is not timed to be through in three years, but to continue for a lifetime.

McMaster University in Hamilton, Ontario, established

there during the past few decades, has far more "mature" students enrolled from the city and surrounding areas than they do regular, full-time students. The faculty has agreed to serve them. They will have to do a better job.

The faculty was reluctant everywhere to accept this new pattern of education. Often there was not room for them at the parent institution, and courses began to sprout in public libraries, high schools, church basements and the like. My own favourite course on Writing was held in a local branch library, near downtown, across the road from public transit and a donut coffee shop. Later, because of the growing needs of the community college, various clubs, talks, and film shows, I was unable to get regular hours and evenings there. Then, out of friendship, the local Jewish synagogue, Temple Anshe Shalom, gave me the Board room in which to hold my weekly evening class, and this was by far the best room I ever had for my classroom workshop and seminar.

The mature student still does not get full service. Most of them have worked a full day. This has to change. There must be time off at full pay for classes: it will prove a great economy. Many of the shrewder or more enlightened firms are realising this, but there is still a long way to go. The faculty are often unwilling or unable to handle this new learning process, and give the identical lessons that they give to the young regular students. Some of them still have the casual habit of missing classes, of turning up late, of substituting audio-visual programs or graduate students to fill their time for them, while they take off for travel trips or worse, claiming this truancy as "research." Many times they do not even meet the students or even comment on their work. The government is reluctant to support this new learning and the mature student is less well publicly funded, has to use quarters that have been in use all day, lounges that are dirty with spilled dixie cups of coffee, empty coke cans dripping and rolling around, and garbage cans that are filled and worse. The libraries diminish service after 10 p. m. , and generally close by midnight. There are no good departments that are dedicated to their needs, nor any discussion areas where they can meet, talk, and organise.

Gradually, as most of them are learning the hard way --and there are more of them--they are assuming a role in university affairs that is far different from that propounded by the garlanded Uncle Toms among them. Here and there are some enlightened faculty and administrations that realise

228

the coming power of the have-nots, but most of the fat cats,
like the opulent nations, think that by donating glass beads
and spills from their abundance they can contain the growing
wrath of the far more fiery and numerous peoples, nations,
who have been denied the basic needs for living by the likes
of us.   There is an inexorable drive upwards throughout the
world: It will require heroic action for us to share our gains
and goods with them.   This is not an heroic age: we gorge
in Consumer Country while babies of the Third World die by
the million every year.

This sound-off has little to do, it might seem, with
the state of libraries, but libraries are involved even more
than the formal teaching programs.   All that libraries need
are more paths to the doors, more co-operation, more room
for readers, realistic service.

Librarians of this new generation, which is not my
own, are no longer the line of burros led by Gabby Hayes.
There are still some Gabby Hayes around, of all sexes,
smartly dressed, shaven, powdered, pomaded, and coiffed.
They are in their element at conventions, with their membership and committee ribbons fluttering, their plastic bags of
bumf and their clip boards under their oxters, greeting their
like in phrase and pitch that are identical to the outsider, to
the good grey working stiffs among us.

I still find it hard to believe, after all these years,
that of the forty or fifty thousand new books that a university
may annually acquire, most of them are in languages other
than English.   The thousands of learned journals are, the
majority, also in other languages.

The great number and essential nature of these books
and journals tend to give a very good business to booksellers
involved in this library trade.

An entrepreneur, by his very nature, adds to the cost
of the business.   I decided to visit some of the great book
centers of Europe, where much of the foreign acquisition
originated.   Generally once or twice a year one of the representatives from the great European booksellers paid a visit
to the campus, but it was less of a working visit and more
of a state occasion, salesmen who knew the going prices of
books, what the traffic would bear, but were not bookmen,
as booksellers rarely are, save in the antiquarian ranks, and
they generally know more about the value of an edition than
they do of the contents.

I visited, after my well-nigh annual trip to British libraries and bookshops, Amsterdam, Paris, and Frankfurt, timing the trip to coincide with the Frankfurt Book Fair. This annual event was growing too large and too important even for Frankfurt to contain, and Frankfurt has been large enough and sufficiently well organised to manage nearly all the business fairs of Europe.

There was talk of moving the Book Fair out of Frankfurt, even to Blackpool in Lancashire, during the holiday off season. This startled me until I went to the Frankfurt World Book Fair. It was a wonderful experience to me, with all the fun of the fair.

There was a one-eyed shabby veteran peddling a needle threading kalamazoo in the foyer of Halles 5-6 that housed the book stalls and exhibits from Canada, the U. S. , and Britain. A cold rain kept the people huddled in the foyer waiting the roundabout fairground train, the sort they have in all fairgrounds of any size, and the veteran was doing well out of the wait and the wet. This gadget was the sort spielers sell at every fair; by the time you get it home the skill is gone from it, all back in the hands, eyes, and mouth of the wide boy at the fiar. But this poor veteran could not even make the little plastic needle-threader work at the very sale point, and what was he doing there at all, anyhow? He must have had a concession for all fairs at this vast Frankfurt walled market place; there were some publishers and booksellers buying it anyhow, as a puzzle they could work at during their slack times at the stalls.

But the thing was, above all, that there was no slack time at the stalls, no leisure either, nowhere to relax. It was Business, with a big B. There was a Benjamin Franklin restaurant nearby Halles 5-6, a vast armoury, drill hall of a place, with a cafeteria in a half of it and table service in the other. It was jammed, queued, steaming, and inadequate for the book merchants who wanted food and drink in a hurry to get back to their trading. The Federov restaurant for the Soviet bloc was just as crowded and so was the Asian Li Po-like one, and, anyhow Chinese kind of food was not what the Dutch, German, British, and their ilk were looking for; they wanted bulk to stay their stomachs, not tantalizing mandarin duck to arouse appetites rather than to quell them, and appetites that would have been for more than food also, for love, contemplation, and reading. Reading was far from the minds of the hard-faced men and women who were handling one of

230

the big export businesses of the world; they could just as easily have been selling tractors or rubber goods. Books were something that they had to move, merchandise, and they were in on the biggest bonanza that had ever struck print.

The great question--it was on everyone's mind there-- was where to go from here? There seems to be one of two alternatives: the Book will start to die out, like horses, and the Anti-Bookites will be right, or it will keep on growing, as people do. If death starts to set in, then Frankfurt can contain the Book Fair for years to come; if it does not, they will need to take over a city to show the bookware, a closed city like Blackpool in November, cleared, all the shops out, stalls, hotels, pier establishments, a Book Wakes week. Or Miami the same way in July; Blackpool in November even rather than that. But at the rate the books are growing there will be nowhere soon to house a fair of them. There were more than 10,000 stalls alone at Frankfurt when I was there; there are millions of books to start, and books are all prime and current, coloured, fine for export. Whoever or whatever first scrawled or cut the first symbol, sometime after we had shed our pelt, learned to use our hands, is making the sorcerer's apprentice look like a piker. All this has come upon us in so brief a time that it is almost within the memory of the living when books were for the few and the many could not read, less than a century, or half a century ago. Most people still cannot read, and many who can, don't.

Some of the Arab countries had spent their oil like water to make books that looked like a jeweller's front window. The Turks and Koreans had displays that rivalled Ireland's. The Scandinavians lacked the schmalz of the Swiss: they took the cool just a little too much for their elegant and angled show. The British were the best: Rolls-Royce engines, the Grand National, Carnaby Street, the Old Vic all rolled into one, somehow, Shakespeare. A Nonesuch pageant of their books came up from their stalls; books are among the top earners in their export drive. They seem to know the book trade, like their blunt Brummagens know electrical transmission, yet they present an illusion that publishing is rather a gentleman's game: dress like Guards Officers off duty, or shandy quaffers at tennis with Joan Hunter-Dunn, even though many of them are mere ringwraiths of the Thomson Empire (it's Kraus-Thomson Reprints now).

The Americans had a gusto, an attractiveness about

their bookwares; smacking them on the flank to show how good they were--and good they are. Some of their stalls literally shone and gleamed with the health of their business and the jackets covering the Kennedys, the Grand Canyons, the Couples, and the picture books were alluring and provoking. But not to touch--that was the trouble throughout. The books were for show. "If you want to buy a watch, buy a watch; if you don't want to buy a watch, get away from my window. "

The Canadians--in Frankfurt it is "Kanada," like a different country--had a stall that showed a good clean picture of us like a mirror, a mirror we had adjusted to show us like we think we are. Nearly every title had the word Canada in it, showing our narcissism like a drooping slip, as though the answer lay within us and not beyond. The French-Canadian books seemed to have pride of place, as well they might--why not? they are turning out good books from Quebec these days--but it is a fallacy to believe that because they are written in French they might enjoy a better relation than the Canadian books written in English. English is far more of a European language than they would have us believe: it is the Urdu of the world, even if it often has a Hindu-Welsh, American, or chop-chop accent. The technical qualities of the Canadian books showed up well, especially in the school texts, although there seemed to be, so everywhere, a decline in the quality of the production of the cheap paperbacks.

The cheap paperbacks, the really cheap, expendable paperbacks, were everywhere, and there is where the future lies. The remedy for the plethora-sickness of the Book is in books so cheap that they can be thrown away. This is a coming solution. While most of these cheap books now seem to be about topless Chinese beauties hanging from hooks awaiting the evil mischief of a blonde Fu Manchu, these books have taken over most of the market, like paper has replaced linen; pressed sawdust, wood; plastic, silver. This was a fact like an iceberg.

The coffee-table books, at the other end, were more in evidence than ever. Every publisher on the planes, the airport buses, hotels, shared taxis, had one or more under his arm, a disguise of the real vulgate of the book. These art books, fine photographs, illustrated histories are no more books than a landau is transport. They are a part of the travel expense account economy of the world we live in, and the publishers will drop them in the gutter--just as some of

them would render their own mothers down--when the buck
beckons in crude paperback, but they will remain money spin-
ners while the dollar lasts.

The children, above all, are well served by the books
in the Fair. The text, the illustrations, the general sense
of the books made for them is a vast improvement. A whole
change of mind has come over the schoolbook makers. But
they are still too solidly constructed: more of them should
be giveaways, even throwaways.

There were some recalcitrants gathering around the
entrance to the Fair--Cohen-Bendit was expected--to protest
against the annual Book Fair medal going to the President of
Senegal for his poetry. His poetry may be all very well,
but he disciplined some students at the University over there
in Africa, so there was to be a march against him, slogans,
banners, and all. But the wind was cold, the rain was driving, the students were shivering, the gates were guarded,
passes were needed to get in, and the student attack fizzled
out with the quick grab-arrest of their leader by the police.
The business of the Books clicked on like computers just as
if it was a paper sale, which it was, but it was a sale of
paper with the marks, some of it, that could blow up the
world or make it live again.

Death and resurrection was in the Book Fair, and it
was all for sale, more profitable than tractors. Somehow
the Fair shows both the best and worst in man. The deal
of the business showed up free enterprise as a go-go-go concern.

The trouble with Mao and the Russians, the Albanians
even and their ilk, is that they took the Susie Wongs right
out of the books and made forced-feeding out of paperback.
That is where the free enterprise system has the edge. There
will always be something bad or rotten about some of their
book-making, enough to make the good books sell, along with
the bad. There has to be corruption for there has to be
growth. The earnest will always lose in the long run, and
if all the fun is taken out of books, who will read the rest
of them? That is another argument in favour of moving the
Fair to Blackpool--they can have the illuminations on, and
the Fat Lady can perform at the Pier. A Book Wakes Week
--wouldn't that be something? Better than old Frankfurt any
day.

What with my library trips to Britain and Ireland, to

233

Europe, and Latin America, there has always been a tendency to regard me as a librarian always on the run, a book collector rather than a university librarian. We have garnered more than seventy collections of primary sources at McMaster. I have been in at the beginning of the acquisition of many collections to whatever university where I was librarianating at the time. The Tolkien Papers and the papers of Dorothy Day I regard as prime sources, essential for research. Primary sources are essential for all the areas of research in the humanities and the social sciences, and these include the history of science and of art. During my early years at McMaster I had to devote more time to collecting than in the later years, when a team of experts developed under my roof. Few of them devoted their full time or near it to the collections game. That is as it should be. The collections should be part of a librarian's concern, not all of it. They must cast on all collections a cold and calculating eye. My staff got so good at it that following my kickoff I could leave the field and become the non-playing captain. Often the faculty participated. Had it not been for them many good collections would have got away, the Samuel Beckett collection for instance, and the Guatemala archives. There are so many stories to be told about the adventures, mishaps and successes of these acquisitions, that improve in the telling, that it is impossible to relate them all, or nearly all. Yet this purports to be an autobiography and a brief note about the acquisition of some of the collections is needed to get the record straight and remove some of the gilt from the gingerbread.

19

Following a lead given us by Dr. John Browning of the Department of Romance Languages, a cordial invitation to visit Guatemala City by the then archivist was offered to me. Arthur Lawrence, my butty and business manager, flew down with me to become acquainted with the situation.

The trip started to thicken up a little from the time we were waiting for the plane at Mexico City. There was a bishop in a long white habit and a soup bowl black hat with a red rope around it sitting near us in the embarkation area. He was surrounded by disciples, priests, nuns, and laymen, obviously a group of the new reform group within the Church, dedicated to bringing some social justice to the town and country poor. This was in 1970, and around this group were scowls and mutters against them by well-dressed fellow travellers and uniformed officers of the junta that was in the saddle at Guatemala following a sudden coup.

There had been little or no news out of Guatemala in the U. S. media, and none at all in the Canadian, save that there had been a military overthrow of a more liberal government. The National Archivist who had been so well-disposed and very much in favour of our visit had been replaced, but that was about all we knew, save that there was a great treasure of archive in Guatemala City. Lima and Mexico City, the other two centres of Spanish colonial government, had the archives in good shape, but not Guatemala. Millions of documents extended back as the General Archives of Central America to Spanish colonial days, nearly 500 years ago.

In these troublous times of violence and counter-violence, it would be well for all the world of learning if they were calendared and recorded and open for research. Also, if it were permitted, it would be a great relief if they were filmed.

The Donner Foundation of Canada gave me $30,000 to start the project if I could, and it was by hook and by crook that we eventually managed to secure a filmed copy of the entire Archive.

We were well under way in the air, flying over rugged mountains when our Guatemala venture really started. I was dozing in my seat when Art Lawrence nudged me awake. With a twitch of his whiskers he directed my eyes outside. The plane was jettisoning fuel at a great rate, and only the fact that we had both, at different times, been veterans of the Guns of Navarone in WW II kept us from breaking into loud and public prayer or something. The plane banked steeply and, fuel pouring from its wings, high-tailed it back to Mexico City. Armoured cars, no ambulances, raced along the tarmac keeping pace with us. No sooner had the plane stopped than heavily armed military leaped aboard, rushed down the aisle, and hustled off three well-dressed and even smiling passengers who were going down to Guatemala to start something like a smuggling ring or a bomb factory.

That was a good start to our expedition. The plane refuelled and took off again, arriving hours late, when it was dark.

Guatemala City is a mile high. We landed between three active volcanoes that were belching smoke and flame.

The city was under martial law. All traffic other than military was forbidden after dusk. Unauthorized traffic was shot at; the occupants liable to arrest or worse. We did not know that as we went racing through the streets in a taxi whose driver was obviously a moon-lighting military, for we arrived at our motel in the fancy suburb just outside the city with no incident. There was a sense of danger in the air, and I hired Jorge and his taxi as our personal car for the extent of our visit. Jorge slept in his cab somewhere around the motel and while he was a gaucho at the wheel, we felt secure with him. We had plucked a good one.

I was awakened next morning by the sound of gunfire and bombing. The students at the University were protesting against the government, were holding out at the campus. Their protests were being discouraged by dive bombers and crackling musket fire.

Jorge drove us down fine wide boulevards towards the

236

City Square. Trucks of heavily armed soldiers proceeding slowly and much too alert for my fancy, protected the morning pleasure ride on fine blooded horses of high-ranking officers and their friends. Many of the friends were really well-kept beauties as groomed as the nags.

When we got to the Government Building, that occupied a palace on one side of the great colonial square, it was under heavy guard. Somehow my transparent innocence allowed us through, and we were conducted to the office quarters of the Minister of Education with whom I had corresponded while back in good safe Hamilton.

The Minister was out at the University, but his deputy, a tall thin Latino with a drooping mustache treated us with great courtesy. He deputed a guide to take me to the Archives. I would have felt more expansive and easy if it had not been that the Minister's deputy carried in his rear trousers pocket a hand grenade that was nearly falling out. He was wearing a gun belt that held a revolver and bullets that looked ready for use at any time. He seemed to be a graduated gunman of a politico.

The Archives were housed in a new solid building. A severe earthquake earlier had brought the old building tumbling down, and the papers were in a far better condition than I had hoped for. The man running the archives was a civil servant who had replaced the real archivist, who I hoped had fled to safety. But we had made contact and while it took up some months and further visits by Mac staff, in times of civil disturbance and earthquakes, we eventually got the show on the road by establishing a good relationship with a Mormon missionary, a Harvard Ph.D., who was working for his Church on the enormous task of microfilming the birth records of all Latin America.

The task took us many years, but it was worth it. The library staff and library benefitted from it. So do the scholars who are using them more and more as Latin America becomes of greater concern, will continue to loom, for better or for worse.

Art Lawrence and I enjoyed the trip; it was a change from our daily rote. We saw the Quetzel everywhere, the parrot bird that is the national emblem like the eagle, visited Antigua that was the old capital until it quite tumbled down by earthquake. It is a beautiful place, the only place in Guatemala that I would like to visit again. Jorge nearly got us over the tiles to a cock fight, but decided against it. We saw the plight of the Indians, a great understatement that, but all the more powerful because of it. I dare not say more without destroying any form to this book. The Indians are the losers now: they will be the keepers when all this is over. We visited their market where they sold furniture fashioned out of scraps of wood that had been torn from crates and boxes that imported the goods and bounty of the wealthy.

The secretary of the Canadian Embassy was arrested or kidnapped while we were there. Only the fearless and timely intervention of the ambassador saved her, and got her on a plane for home. A few hours before the leader of the liberal opposition party had been gunned to death by the military right outside the office of the embassy.

The only time that Art Lawrence and I were in danger was when we were sitting in an outside cafe waiting for Jorge, Art telling me an amusing story or something, when we noticed that everybody was outside the cafe standing at what passes there for attention. The marimba, the national musical instrument, was playing something else: it had been tapping a tune all the time that we were there. We both realised at the same time that the reason for the standing, the silence, and the staring was that the marimba was playing the National Anthem. Some potentate, some governor or the president was due to arrive at the hotel behind the cafe. Art Lawrence and myself immediately stood to attention, quivering, out of apprehension as well as out of an old military drill, and this saved our day and maybe more.

The next morning early Jorge drove us to the airport. Late that same day we arrived back at Toronto. I had bought some souvenirs. Among them was a kind of lama toy in bright colours and a paper baby black bull with golden horns. Somehow this survived, that and the lama, and look at me in my bookroom this very day. I would not have missed the trip to start our acquisition of the Guatemala Papers. There is more to the tale than this, but so there is to all the collection game, enough for another and more fun book--I actually have to pull my pen off the page to stop telling of John Coulter and the canoe in the storm, Anthony Burgess with his stick with the horse's head handle....

238

20

Most times when I am introduced to give a talk, receive an award, both in library circles, on social occasions around a campus and even beyond, my connection with the coming to Canada of the papers of Bertrand Russell is referred to. Indeed, most people who know of me at all in the world of books, associate me with that coup to the almost total exclusion of everything else that I have done. This is one collection that I must include in my autobiography, not only because it is expected of me, but because I want to. It was the most rewarding event, for all, in my life as a library collector, and put me at the top of the pile, but I wince within whenever I am introduced, which is almost invariably with no mention of my other library deeds which altogether, to my mind, were more important in aggregate to the obtaining for Canada, for North America, for the whole world of learning and beyond, of the Russell Papers.

On my way back from Oxford, where I had been meeting J. R. R. Tolkien, among other things, the train to Reading stopped at Didcot, as it always did, before linking up with the main line that ran from London Paddington to Cardiff station. It was a Sunday, and I picked up a Sunday Times there and started reading it on my way to my Cardiff home. This was in the fall of 1967. I read an article about the Bertrand Russell papers that were coming up for sale, probably the most extensive and most valuable archive of a single individual that had ever been.

The article related that there were hundreds of thousands of pieces, letters, films, tapes, manuscripts of essays, articles and books, some unpublished.

The memorabilia included his Nobel Prize medal, the Order of Merit, regalia and dozens more of such items and

239

commendations, including what appeared to me to be the Order of Chastity, third class (Morocco).

The material was being transported, at this time, from Earl Russell's home in North Wales in a fleet of armoured trucks, to vaults and safekeeping in the city of London.

It was estimated by the Times reporter that the price for this collection would be about £1,000,000. This was based upon the generally held conclusion that Russell was the most significant Englishman of the century. This assumption had been recently confirmed by a BBC poll which listed him far above even Churchill as the man of his times.

He had preserved his papers for posterity from an early age, so that they spanned nearly 90 years of his life.

I returned to Canada a few days later and suggested that the federal government should support the universities in an attempt to acquire this great archive because of its enormous research implications as well as for the fame that would descend upon us were we to obtain it.

It would put Canadian libraries in the forefront as holding a great collection to which scholars necessarily would come in ever-increasing numbers from all over the world. The reputation and fame of Russell was growing all the time.

I held forth on this topic with force at a meeting of the Ontario Universities Librarians in November, 1967. In the midst of a tremendous storm that swayed the building, they unanimously decided to approach the Canada Council for a grant that would enable the Ontario University System to acquire this remarkable collection.

(The University of Toronto had already been privately prosecuting an attempt to acquire this archive for as long as I had known of it. There was a considerable pressure led by the Dean of Graduate Studies there, to obtain the Russell collection for Toronto, but they fell short.)

It was proposed by Dr. Blackburn, librarian of the University of Toronto, and seconded by Dr. Talman, librarian of the University of Western Ontario, that McMaster should attempt to acquire the collection, and OCUL unanimously agreed to support our application for funds.

This request was despatched to Canada Council by

Donald Redmond, librarian of Queen's University, and within a week or so I received a telephone call from Canada Council advising me that as a result of my plea and that of the Ontario Universities, and subject to expert opinion and advice, they were prepared to assist McMaster in obtaining for Canada, this collection, to the tune of $150,000.

They suggested as the two experts Dr. Brough McPherson of the University of Toronto, and myself.

We arrived at the headquarters of Continuum, the firm that was handling the sale on behalf of the Russell Foundation in London, on Boxing Day 1967.

Both of us were so impressed by the importance and scope of the archive that had already been handsomely catalogued, that we wrote individually to Canada Council recommending the purchase. I met with the agents and gave them to understand that I anticipated no difficulty in raising sufficient funds.

I wrote to Lord Russell advising him of our interest and beseeching him that whatever happened to the archives they should finally be deposited in a place where they were both secure, intact, and available for scholars of all creeds, nationalities, color, or condition.

During my letters to the earl, I described McMaster as well as I could, pointing out its high scientific stature as well as its record in the arts, that our principal of University College, Togo Salmon, was a distinguished Cambridge scholar, and that our president, Harry Thode, was a Fellow of the Royal Society and altogether a most distinguished man of science.

I pointed out that there was also at McMaster Fellows of the Royal Society including my friend Dr. Bertram Brockhouse who was not only a famous physicist but a philosopher to boot. He wore a Hobbit name. (This makes McMaster unique in the Canadian world of learning.)

His letters back were cordial and sounded promising to me, and the agent for the sale of the papers came over to visit us.

He was sufficiently impressed to report to Lord Russell that McMaster would be an excellent depository for his collection, and it was especially fortunate that I, the librarian, was one of the few in Canada, who besides his professional library graduate degree, had post-graduate training and a diploma in archives and archival management.

Cyrus Eaton, an illustrious alumnus, became most enthusiastic, especially since Lord Russell had been one of his counsellors in the establishment of the Pugwash Conference.   He sent me a cheque for $25,000 and an earnest pledge of his intentions to support us to obtain the papers.

Moreover, I received information about this time that both the University of Chicago and Massachusetts Institute of Technology were trying to acquire the papers, along with many other institutions and, of course, a veritable swarm of booksellers.

They, however, wanted to split them, so that MIT would receive the mathematical and Chicago the philosophical content.   There were many other American universities trying to get the papers, but I realised that Texas, with its abundant funds and aggressive acquisition policy, was the one most likely to succeed if it was just a question of money. Fortunately it was not.

To begin with Lord Russell would not have liked his papers to go to Texas, and since the Russell Foundation had been the mainspring of the Stockholm Peace Conference that had recently met, where Lyndon Johnson had been condemned as a war criminal, it seemed unlikely that Texas was to succeed or even to wish to.

There were rumors mixed with truth regarding the great hunt and prosecution for the papers that was going on throughout the world.   Time magazine had a story of twelve or more representatives of great institutions, of wealthy individuals, bidding against one another in a closed room, and how all the eyes widened with surprise when, the bids being opened, McMaster University in Hamilton, Ontario, had been given the nod.

There were tales of an Arabian sheik who had been anxious to buy the collection.   Meetings around the Mandelbaum Gate; tracks of camel pads in the snow of Snowdonia....

One university really tried to help me obtain further funds, and that was Waterloo.   They had tried to raise $150,000 for me but failed.   The University of Toronto would have been more willing to help if they could house the collection.

The Laidlaw Foundation approved a grant of $25,000 toward the purchase. The deadline was fast approaching, and I was on the verge of parleying with other universities who might share the burden of the cost and thereby break up the collection, when the secretary of the Atkinson Foundation, Mr. N. A. Folland, came to see me.

The Atkinson Foundation had been generous to McMaster in the past. They had previously given funds that helped to cover the cost of the construction of a nurses' residence. I received Mr. Folland pleasantly but with no great anticipation.

After all, there was a great difference between helping to fund the cost of building a nurses' home and the sort of money that I was wanting if I was to throw McMaster's hat in the ring. However, he warmed up to my description of the collection. I must have reared back with that Welshy hwyl that can be so Pentecostal, and finally he held up his hand to stop my flow of words.

He asked me how much money I needed to enter the ring with any chance of success. I replied, "two hundred and twenty thousand dollars. " He produced a guarantee letter from his the trustees, said "American or Canadian?" and filled in the amount for $220,000 U.S.

We went across to see Dr. Thode and after a cordial greeting there, Mr. Folland hurried off to catch Mrs. Hindmarsh of the Atkinson Foundation for her signature before she flew out of Toronto International Airport that afternoon. The next morning I received the Atkinson guarantee which gave me altogether something more than $500,000.

It was with this amount that I went to England. By this time I had such high hopes of acquiring the collection that the university lawyer, Mr. Frank Weatherston, Q. C. accompanied me.

Richard Robinson, our English solicitor, was with me when we received the news that Lord Russell had agreed to our offer, and that the train from North Wales coming in would bear the contract signed by the earl. It was April 2, I remember, one of the birthdays in our family. I was too

243

anxious to sit still and wait for the news. I was wandering up and down the Burlington Arcade when I saw from the other side of the street Frank Weatherston and Richard Robinson smiling at me and waving.

The transaction successfully concluded, Lord Russell invited me to celebrate over tea with him the next day at his house in Penhryndeudraeth. Alas, when I awoke early in the morning I called up my old home in Cardiff, Wales, to hear that my dear mother had died during the night, and that as a result a wedding within the family that was to take place the next day was being postponed.

Faced with this fell situation, and as the head of the family, I wakened Frank Weatherston and asked him to go to Penhryndeudraeth in my place while I proceeded to Cardiff to arrange the wake of my mother and the wedding of my sister.

From there I flew home to the plaudits and congratulations of my friends and colleages at McMaster.

In the meantime Frank Weatherston had had a singular experience. Somehow or other Lord Russell, who by this time was almost 96, was not aware that it was not I who was taking tea with him, and he addressed himself to Frank Weatherston as if it was to me, asking him diverse library, bibliography, and archival questions that Frank was at a loss to reply to and that Russell and I had previously discussed in our letters, some of which had been quite acerbic.

Therefore, he put on a wise look and bowed his head slowly before replying to the earl's rather mumbled questions with a "yes, my lord."

Lord Russell was considerably baffled about this, and many times afterwards related that Will Ready, in the flesh, over the tea cups, did not seem the same man with whom he had conducted correspondence in the past.

The booksellers in particular were rather cross about our acquisition. They could have formed a ring to purchase the collection and it would have been worth many millions to them broken up and sold in bits and pieces.

Letters similar to hundreds of Russell's were even then bringing prices of between $500 and $800 each on the market. The Whitehead correspondence alone, regarding the

Principia, the enormous file of letters from Lady Ottoline
Morrell, Russell's hand-written diary of his trip to Russia
in the early days of the Soviet, were well-nigh priceless
items.

The vast collection of the Amberley papers--Lord and
Lady Amberley were Russell's parents, both of whom had
died when he was a child--were worth a fortune alone.

Their value, like that of all the archive, has greatly
increased since.

Russell was so concerned that the papers would receive good housing and treatment, that they would be kept
together and used for research in a good university library,
that I had been fairly sure, once I had received the generous
financial backing of the Atkinson Foundation, that we would
be able to acquire them.

Cambridge had treated Russell so shabbily in the past
--dismissing him from his fellowship for pacifism in World
War I--that it seemed unlikely that that university would become the depository.

The British Museum, which normally would have been
more interesting, was at this time a place of great confusion,
alarm, and despondency, since there was a threat of moving
this great library institution into a converted railroad depot
at Euston, where it would be known as the British Library.

They were courteous, but rather distracted, and did
not pay much attention to me when I advised them that I was
hoping to acquire the Russell papers.

In any case I am sure that they thought they would
still remain British, as Russell did, for Canada has remained
to them over there a place singularly remembered by them
as an extension of the Island.

Russell, himself, a true blue Englishman of an earlier
generation, still thought of Canada as British, I am sure.
So I had many things going for me.

Nevertheless when it was announced that Lord Russell
had signed the agreement there was a great shock in the land.

Questions were asked in the House; learned societies

protested. There were letters to The Times. The booksellers whom I used as packing agents were hauled to court
and fined for some breach in the Board of Trade regulations.

McMaster became known throughout the length and
breadth of the world of English, and there were literally hundreds of newspaper items and articles about us. There was
a comedy of errors in the shipping of the first consignment,
although I did not think it was funny at the time. I was concerned that the shipment should arrive directly in Canada,
and not go through the States, just in case the customs there
might embargo them as material un-American.

I insisted that Air Canada be the carrier and not BOAC,
whose freight planes make a landing first in New York before
proceeding to Toronto.

However, unknown to me, about Maundy Thursday
BOAC went on strike.

Air Canada took over their freight traffic and so the
Russell papers came to us through New York anyhow, but
without being stopped or inspected.

I knew that the papers had been put aboard the plane
on Thursday in London; I had a cable confirming this. Yet
when Good Friday came I was unable to locate them at Toronto airport.

It was the Easter holidays and there was nobody at the
Air Canada office who could help me. They were all on vacation.

The papers were not there in the warehouse at the
airport, I was assured by a Russell enthusiast who was working there.

On Tuesday morning, when the Air Canada office staff
returned to work, there was still no trace of them until finally the Russellite in the warehouse discovered that they had
been sent by train to Hamilton. We found them in the CNR
station on North James Street in Hamilton.

This was probably my worst experience of the whole
project. My raven black hair, my one redeeming feature,
began to grey at the seams.

When the papers arrived and were opened they more

than met our expectations, and gradually through the summer all of them arrived.

Kenneth Blackwell, who had been working for Russell organizing his library and cataloguing it, later worked at Continuum filing and cataloguing the papers.

He was a Canadian, a graduate of the University of Victoria, British Columbia, who had obtained a Canada Council grant to study Russell, and had spent his time in England working on a bibliography. He knew so much about the papers that I hired him to help in the packing and to fly out with the last consignment, perched on one of the boxes, to become the Russell archivist at McMaster. When, in the course of his research on Russell, he had called on the Master at Penhryndeudraeth, his home in North Wales, he was told that Lord Russell was not receiving visitors, but as he trudged away, downcast, he was called back and became a general factotum, helping with the first holograph catalogue and afterwards.

There was a great deal of comment when it was finally realized the extent and the significance of the papers that had left England, and the rows that built in the papers and elsewhere increased in volume until they reached such a pitch that I received a call from the London Observer questioning me as to what action the Canadian government would take if Britain demanded the return of the papers.

This sounded as if the reporter was trying to stir up some gunboat diplomacy, with HMS Daffodil sailing down the St. Lawrence showing her colours.

I replied perfunctorily and cursorily and paid for it, since I discovered later that he had reversed the charges and that I had to pay for his telephone call.

Once the papers arrived here further difficulties began. Mills Library was undergoing the necessary trouble and turmoil of construction, a project that was to double the size of the new extension. As a result of this, all of the books and staff had to be packed into an area that made moving difficult.

The Russell papers and my office became one behind a wire enclosure on the second floor on the east side, while the area that was to become the archives and my own office were taken over by processing departments and reading areas.

Once, during this time, the roof above us began to leak and the rain broke through the tarpaulins about 2:00 a.m.

We received the news from the security people just in time for a rescue, and by sweeping and pumping we saved the papers from inundation and soaking, but as long as the papers were there they were hardly in an adequate state for any research to be done on them. Nevertheless during that time, using a rather antiquated microfilming machine that we borrowed from the department of engineering, we managed to microfilm the major part of the collection so that when the building project was over and we were able to move into the excellent new quarters the papers were in a good state for the research and the study of them to begin.

The research began soon after the Russell papers were in their proper quarters. Blackwell has been an enthusiastic curator and between us we must have given about twenty talks on Russell and the archives during the next two years.

I wrote a paperback on them, Necessary Russell, that included a biography of the carl as well as a description of the collection. This was published by Copp Clark in 1969. I also began the publication of McMaster Library Research News that has world-wide circulation among the universities, and in 1971 we began the Russell newsletter.

This has a paid-up circulation that more than amortises the cost. The amount of gifts that we have received has been both surprising and touching. By exchange we have acquired much more.

The market in single Russell items is prohibitively high, aimed at jackdaw bibliophiles, rather than at scholars, so we have acquired only by purchase complete collections.

The most significant of these by far is the collection of Lady Constance Malleson, more than 1,000 letters of Russell, among other items: She was one of Russell's dearest loves, and we have not been idle in filling in crevices elsewhere among the papers.

Blackwell has a single-minded devotion to the Archives that can be frightening at times, to me anyhow. Nevertheless without him the archive would not be what it has become. During the growing and settling years he had a staff of nonqualified archival assistants who did much to bring about our present good state.

Ruth and Paul Sharrett, who married during their employment in the archives, were clerks and assistants who did remarkably well, impressing visitors with their helpfulness and know-how. (They also served in Guatemala.)

While they were working in the archives they not only wed but completed their degree courses at McMaster and this, combined with their years in the archives, got them speedy admission to graduate library school at Dalhousie university.

The last member of the quintet was Liam Francis Ready, a relative, who not only contributed to the Russell newsletter but became a searcher, copier, and something of a bibliographer during his two years there before reluctantly moving on at his father's insistence to a sterner and less attractive academic program.

Schools frequently request tours of the archives. John Slater, chairman of the department of philosophy of the University of Toronto, an eminent Russell scholar with a private library that complements our own first-rate collection of Russell first editions, is a constant visitor.

Patrick Rosenbaum, a Bloomsbury scholar from the University of Toronto, was another enthusiastic supporter. The archive is remarkably rich in original material relating to literary figures of that period, Lytton Strachey, J. M. Keyes, the Woolfs, and others. (I find the Joseph Conrad letters particularly touching and endearing.)

Among the visitors was Ronald Clark, who wrote a best-selling biography of Russell wherein he refers to me as being, among other things, a devout Churchman. I am not: I am a cradle Catholic. (His biography of Einstein won not only scholarly acclaim but was also chosen by the Book of the Month Club.) His biographies of scientists, of the Huxleys, of J. B. S. Haldane, of Sir John Cockcroft make most illuminating and refreshing reading.

Victor Lowe, of Johns Hopkins, the biographer of Alfred North Whitehead, N. Z. Alcock, Director of Canadian Peace Research Institute, faculty from many universities including such scholars as Duram, Eames, Bortessa, Fish, Smiley, Lackey, Leavitt, McEwan, Morton, Pitt, Alpers and

Cook, and many more, are more or less constant visitors and correspondents.

Morton, for instance, the distinguished Canadian historian, author of The Kingdom of Canada, found original material for his coming biography of Lord Monck in the papers.

These men represent diverse fields of scholarship. They are coming to McMaster more and more as they realize the wealth of the collection, which, frankly, is hard to believe.

21

I think it well to give this informal account of a literary and archival expedition that has meant so much to us here at McMaster and throughout the world of learning in Canada. Many books have been published already, which are credited to the Russell archives. There are at least a dozen, major manuscripts that give acknowledgement in prefaces to the singular strength of materials and the splendid service that they had received in the archives of McMaster.

Besides the many McMaster faculty members who are engaged in research among the Russell papers there are Ph. D. candidates and an increasing number of M. A. candidates using the papers as prime resources for their dissertations.

Distinguished professors have already begun to come to McMaster to lecture, to join as visiting scholars, and there will be more of these along with the permanent appointments as time goes on. It is well to realize that all of this came about through the enthusiasm and the generosity of government, industries, universities and business.

The Atkinson Foundation above all deserves the thanks but it is remarkable how many individual gifts in money and in kind continue to be received to further extend the scope and the extent of this great collection which has made Hamilton the centre of all the world for Russell studies.

The acquisition of the Russell Papers marks a milestone in the library life. John Evans, who was then the dean of the new medical school and health complex that were to come, was in Britain and elsewhere recruiting medical and allied staff. McMaster had been until then remote or unknown to many of the people he was interviewing and Hamilton as a city wherein to settle and practice was unknown. The news about McMaster suddenly changed and they had all heard about it. It was in the newspapers, in conversation, even was it talked about on the BBC.

But, coming home, there was building abundant all around the campus. Bulldozers and the like made a cacophony of noise day after day, week after week, month after month. Trees were uprooted, lawns torn up. The sunken gardens vanished under concrete. There families from all over the city had come in their finery for wedding, graduation, birth and get-together pictures.

An addition to the main library had been planned for years: it takes years to get government approval and funds. This edition was designed to become a part of a previous addition, that already dwarfed the original library building, the Memorial. The new central library of the university would be able to contain far more volumes, give more space to readers, and bring nearer a Science Library that was long overdue. The Health complex had a library built into its plans. All this was before I arrived at McMaster.

As usual the designs of the architect were good and strong. The entrance mall had won an architectural prize. But, as the Empress Josephine said when shown the red brick dull solidity of the new Keble College in Oxford: "C'est magnifique, mais ce n'est pas la gare."

I felt the same way about the planned addition. The inner stairwell was most impressive and promised to be more so. The lofty ceilings added class, and let the sun pour in to the addition of an entire new level. C'est magnifique mais.... The central stairwell ate into the heart of the library. Where there should be books and readers was the noble stairwell expanse planned, along with the high ceilings. I persuaded them to abandon the interior stairway, construct an architectural excrescence on the outer wall and build instead the sort of stairway within that makes the gallery in the theatre a place for gods with wings. That was a hard-fought battle but, with that under my belt and having made more room for books and readers, I proposed that the ceilings be lowered on the entire floor and that an addition to the outside wall, by cladding if need be, an additional floor be added upwards. This caused a sort of pandemonium in building circles on and around the campus, but the addition of so much more material was coming in that with faculty

252

support I got approval and the work got under way. Then, to complete the deal, to strike while the iron was warm, I got them to lower the basement and construct a mezzanine floor. I pulled out a theatre and levelled the slope therein and added more room that way, putting in a locked series of stacks and beginning to store in austere shelving our lesser used books.

Then, I will never forget the day, it was a louring afternoon, I got the grave news that the provincial government had arbitrarily forbidden the going ahead with all university capital structures that it had approved: there were to be no exceptions. Reasons for this were manifold. The boom Ontario train had come to the end of the line. Economy, not go-go became the order from above. The universities, new, reconstructed, heavily and more than generously financed, had not turned out to be the citadels of conservatism that the Conservative Government, long in power, had hoped. Instead they became centres of unrest, vociferous opponents of the government that had financed them.

That was all very well, and reasonable enough as politics go, but I was waiting for the Science Library, realising the need for it and marvelling inwardly at their patience: their library situation was barely to be borne.

I remember Harry Thode and I stopping outside the Memorial Library as dusk was falling on one grey day. He was coming or going to a student remonstrance meeting in the Union.

He had spent days in the corridors of power, a suppliant for permission to go ahead with the Science Library for which McMaster had been waiting so long. There was no hope. We lacked the clout of other, older universities. Queen's University had a tradition that extended back over a century to federal service. After all, the first Prime Minister practised law in Kingston; his support came from the University to an extent; it was a part of the Establishment, and where it counted the most, in the permanent civil service. Deputy Ministers, in the long haul, see their Ministers come and go at elections, but they remain, the mandarins of government. In the same way, but with double barrels, the University of Toronto staffed the higher civil service, both at the nation's capital and at the provincial level, at Queen's Park, in Toronto, that was rapidly becoming a Metro complex of three million people and more. To some degree also this was true of the University of Western Ontario at London, which was one of the powerhouses of national financial interests. Where was McMaster in all this? After all, Hamilton was Steel Town, with a new university that was only first-rate in the arts and sciences: it lacked even a law school.

Yet somehow, over the next decade, by administrative financial know-how, by the generosity of its alumni, McMaster managed to raise five million dollars. By this time however capital building was needed badly by the burgeoning School of Business Administration and the departments of Social Sciences were in dire need of space. Somehow we three had to present our case for capital expenditure and the Library won. Neither Social Sciences nor the Business School had any advantages to be gained from a new science library. Yet when I presented the need, we three, the deans of the two schools who needed space for their own departments, and myself, just the three of us around the table with the president, the two deans, gave the nod to me for the Library and we started on the building. We adhered completely to the government's rules for building costs so that if ever the ban was lifted on capital building expenditure we could request the funds that we had been promised before the ukase.

The faculty was so hungry for a library, had been waiting so long, that they were actively, even daily, involved in committee meetings about its structure. Fortunately I had chosen Harold Siroonian, a graduate in Science from McMaster who had been Science Librarian at CCNY under Bernie Kreissman, to be the Science Librarian. He attended all the meetings, understood the need, the minutiae of the demands, and the building was reared and opened on schedule in 1978 at a savings of more than one million dollars over the estimated cost.

I managed to get some of my ideas built into it. There is a whole, pleasant, working level below ground. The preoccupation with gleaming windows gave way to a fine rounded rear brick wall that was a buffer to the throughway traffic, and we gained 15,000 net square feet for library book storage.

My one great failure on the building was its location. Instead of squaring off the green-treed, beflowered centre mall, a controvert faculty member aroused a student protest

254

that put it amid the science buildings, diminished its aspect and prospect, so that it has to be sought for rather than nearly on the university close to the heart of the matter as is the new sunken Pusey Library at Harvard or the new underground library at Yale or Illinois.

Every university that I visit has built already well-nigh the perfect underground storage area for its collections. All it needs is to make the campus traffic-free, save for constant circling public transit. Cars must go. The underground parking lots are ideal for book storage. They require little or no improvements or additions save for the shelving. Lighting need be no problem. The libraries are too powerfully lighted now. These long silvers of neon tubing strung into the ceilings are far too powerful. They offered an immediate advantage of making of the library a clean, well-lighted place but, believe me, they are far too light, far too hard on the eye of the reader in any long haul.

I believe that libraries should be maintained for the benefit of all. Nearly all the readers that I know are bewildered by the plethora of books that they are confronted with where all they seek is just one book. There should be bibliography practised around the library shelves, librarians to take the big word bibliography and change it by their action and skill into a working tool. The books, numbering in their millions in many libraries, should not get equal shelving. The shelving is far too good for them. I am obviously not in favour of near-caging good old dotards in the subterranean tunnels, as in the old British Museum, the old Bodleian, but I am in favour of making over an underground parking lot. There, donning hard hats with lights in the front of them, and garbing the readers so even to the extent of giving them a suitable coverall too, the readers can browse under guidance among the hundreds of thousands of books, even be left to their own resources. Then the parking lots can be used as part of the university, the very heart of the university can pulse away there.

The car must go, the car must go. Students who march in protest against any rise in the living cost are already getting too much for nothing anyhow, and at the expense of those who are denied, were or will be, their advantages. Every student deems it an essential part of his equipment that the ads proclaim as essential to his needs, a car above all. Now it costs about $1,000 a year at least even to maintain a car, and generally being in hock for the

purchase of it raises his monthly payments for something that
is quite non-basic and unnecessary to more than his book and
food bill. Moonlighting results for altogether wrong purposes.
The living quarters are cleaned and swept for the students.
This entire maintenance task should be theirs, and the sweeping, the cleaning of the whole university should be part of
their task, the policing, the collection of garbage, the growing
of crops. Somehow they are being raised to benefit anybody
but themselves and the commonweal. This cleaning and pedestrian approach should be part of their education. They are
fed packaged and frozen food by international combines that
have taken over the corporate feeding of hospitals, schools,
prisons, and universities. I suspect most of the meat is
zebra, and it has been frozen and dead for decades. Every
university should feed itself, clean itself, be an institution
peculiar to itself. That way the students can pay off some
of what they owe and, under guidance from their betters in
the field, learn what work really is about.

I have always maintained within a library as free a
traffic as I can of the staff, so that those in Special Collections know what goes on in the Shipping Room, the Processing
Department, behind the circulation desk, and how different is
a library at night, week ends, and early in the morning.
Personal desks, niches, closed shops are anathema to me
because I believe it is against true library economy, and
economy, as opposed to waste, is of prime importance to
any organisation. When a rising young librarian gets a desk
of his/her own, with a name plate, there tends to be a sigh
of relief, and the skill of the trade begins to atrophy from
that hour. Any university librarian who seeks a private office as a reward, as a shelter, is not going to realise the
potential within. It is a tragedy, a cutting off of lines of
communication.

Every so often I break out into song, song that comes
unbidden. It can be a cause of consternation or pleasure.

Some time ago I was giving a talk to the Military History Club on the Victorian soldier. The genius of Kipling
caught that poor man well in the Promethean despair of Mul-
vaney, in so many other pages for those who read and care
about the human condition. Once this Irish soldier is Krisna,
outside the arch of the temple of Prithi-Devi in Benares, and
Kipling knew and wrote obliquely about the life of single men
in barracks far from home. His poem Danny Deever is an
irresistible work of art to those who care and feel. The sol-

256

diers had little, yet somehow they know. Of all the writers of the
British soldier it is Kipling alone who is held aloft by the enlisted
regular soldiers of the past. They quote him ceremoniously in
the sergeants' messes on guest nights, poems like Gunga Din,
Tommy, and, most of all: Danny Deever.

"What are the bugles blowin' for?" said Files-on-Parade.
   "To turn you out, to turn you out," the Colour-Sergeant
   said.
"What makes you look so white, so white?" said Files-on-
Parade.
   "I'm dreadin' what I've got to watch," the Colour-Sergeant
   said.
      For they're hangin' Danny Deever, you can hear the
         Dead March play,
      The regiment's in 'ollow square--they're hangin' him
         today;
      They've taken of his buttons off an' cut his stripes
         away,
      An' they're hangin' Danny Deever in the mornin'.

     Now this seems far away from the topic of this book,
and meandering by a writer can, when it is well done, be a
refreshment to the reader. Yet, deep down, there is no meandering here. It gets down to the very function of the Book
and, the keepers. A book is a launching pad, above all, and
when its emanation engages with the planet of the mind it can
properly be shelved again and cared for; if it is a great book
this is very much the more so. That is how I came to break
into song in my lecture. It has never happened before, through
all my years of teaching and lecturing, but it will happen again,
I feel sure. The Book contains more than print; it is an
amalgam of print, sight, and sound. Suddenly in my lecture
as I was talking about the Victorian soldier and his sorry lot
I suddenly thought of the poem from Barrack-Room Ballads:
"The Screw Guns." I had read this before, had served as a
gunner myself, had heard it sung and recited by regular time-
serving soldiers who had spent their time in India. The Royal
Pack Artillery were strong big men who carried on their backs
the screw-guns, carried up hills where the mules or horses
could not be the beasts of burden. Then when a group of
them assembled at the crest they would screw the pieces of
the gun together and have a weapon beyond the power of the
tribesmen to counter. It was with all this and more coming
into my mind, with my audience fully attending me, that I
suddenly began to sing "The Screw Guns." The startled look
that came over my listeners, who were nearly all professors,
was a tonic. They liked it; the trouble was that I sang it

through for several verses: one would have been enough.
But only could this lecture have been given so well had I
not been suited so very well for that occasion.   There are
hundreds of such occasions and not in the form of lectures
either, and they all are recorded for the final, and most recent, launching.   It is a marvellous pattern.   It is an essential part of our heritage that is contained in the Book.

SCREW-GUNS

SMOKIN' my pipe on the mountings, sniffin' the mornin' cool,
I walks in my old brown gaiters along o' my old brown mule,
With seventy gunners be'ind me, an' never a beggar forgets
It's only the pick of the Army that handles the dear little pets
    --'Tss!   'Tss!
For you all love the screw-guns--the screw-guns they all
    love you!
So when we call round with a few guns, o'course you will
    know what to do--hoo!   hoo!
Jest send in your Chief an' surrender--it's worse if you
    fights or you runs:
You can go where you please, you can skid up the trees,
    but you don't get away from the guns!

    I have always been so concerned with the aspects,
prospects, and futures of those who would be librarians that
once, years ago, I took up my pen and wrote a brief essay.
I posted it in to the Toronto Globe and Mail next day.   This
is as near to a national newspaper as Canada has ever had.
The whole thing, from pen-up to type-down, took only about
an hour.   It was with surprise and satisfaction that the editor
of the centre page called me later in the week to congratulate
me, and to tell me that he was going to publish it.   That was
early in June, and every morning after my wife or I would
turn right away, ignoring headlines and world events, to seek
my essay on the centre page.   It was never there.   We gave
up.   Then, when I was teaching at Dalhousie University on
November 12 it did appear.   Halifax was a town where the
Globe and Mail was not easy to come by, and reading it over
the other day I was reminded of this.   Rarely does a writer
enjoy reading his own writing, or at least admitting to it, but
as I read this over, while I was writing this book, it seems
clear enough and fresh enough to include here.

    It raised little interest when it appeared.   There were
a few librarians who wrote to me, protesting that I was taking

the profession too lightly. A law librarian wrote to me scornfully that I should get my facts correct: there is no Cocklecarrot who had written a book on Torts.

STACK WALKERS

Lithe, lissome and bounteous are those librarians who walk the stacks by night and day. Alas, only the larger or well-endowed libraries can contain their services, so that it might require an expedition to Trent for the unsatisfied reader in Lakefield to appreciate library service at its bobbling best, and the daily visitor to the Grimsby Public Library might well hie to Hamilton before it is too late. These sprigs and aspirants are the ornaments of their ancient profession. Every spring and early summer sees their ranks refreshed as the doors of the graduate library schools clang behind the best and most dexterous of them. Those will never dance and skylark, lollygag again, and cavort as once they did around the lecterns piled high with atlases and commentaries, or clamber up the side of a bookstack with a python's rippling grace to dislodge a snaggled volume of Cocklecarrot on Torts. They are as different from their senior and more sedentary colleagues as were the flowering wands of the Celtic abbots from the wooden hooked sticks of croziers that the Roman bishops used to beat them down at the Synod of Whitby in A. D. 664. These supple librarians are the sherpas of the book trade. They ply through the stacks with the easy grace of a Venetian courtesan cruising along the waterways of San Marco. They plunge and grovel like gollums restored to goodness and beauteous human kind as they enchantingly snort over the richness or desiderata that are often sequestered around the fundaments. Sometimes they stoop half double to read the third or second shelves from below. They swan among the stacks of books for hours daily. Even in a medium-size library such as McMaster's, there are more than four miles of books and there they go, the stack-walkers, in gaily colored trews or skirts, seeking the book that is missing or misplaced, that has the bubble reputation, that needs repair, or has been hidden behind another by a provident and evil reader.

The reader often detests the library, for the book desired is never in, but out, lost, stolen or destroyed. The gentle reader often fears those miles of books, stretching in solitary aisles, silently before and after, above and below. It is with a sigh of relief that borders upon gratitude that the reader sees a gaily-clad librarian come vaulting silently over the nine-foot stacks upon rubber spring heels, wearing the polka-dot hard helmet at a slant, with the miner's lamp set in it, shooting beams that dance off the dark corners and the ceilings. These librarian sherpas look all too often as if they have found the Fountain of Youth that Ponce de Leon sought on Bimini.

A walk through the stacks is a necesary part of the librarian's trade. It is no mere stroll either. At least a mile of the way must be crawled on hands and knees, with a miner's helmet to guard the skull from books falling from the upper shelves. No mere construction hard-hat will serve, for the helmet has to have a headlamp, in order to read the titles on the bottom shelves. There are some traditionalists, who prefer a Davey lamp and an old infantry steel helmet. The Davey lamp illuminates the book titles well enough to read through a magnifying glass, and also warns of any noxious gases that might be emanating from the goatskin bindings, or from those rare Central American treatises bound in the skins of iguana. Since we have realized that the daft and happy smiles and subsequent behaviour patterns of several of our colleagues come from having been beaned by a tumbling volume of Parliamentary Debates, more and more of us are turning to the steel helmet rather than favoring the more rakish lines of the polka-dot hard hats. The steel helmets are available at any good Army Surplus store and the polka-dots can be rented at any entrance to the stacks, or they should be.

22

This is the best of times, this is the worst of times for the Book.

Information replaces culture in our civilisation, yet books keep growing as they are decried; today they are better and more numerous than ever. No library can hope to house them all. Their numbers increase in so headlong a fashion that the serious reader is often late or lost. Besides, the reader often requires access to facts that are not in the books, or even in print form, so that a welter of information media are ousting the Book save in its popular or learned style. The seer-scholar McLuhan, with his usual reason, has declared this era as the end of the book-contained culture. The recording and delivery demand for information has already gone far beyond the capacity of the Book, and this is just the beginning. There are many who agree with McLuhan, including information retrieval experts, and all kinds of librarians who are concerned with library science and economy. Transmission and transmutation of the new learning that ever growing information sprouts can only be managed by the delegation of the Book, and its replacement by some other means of making information compact and available.

Desperate times demand desperate remedies, that to future generations often seem to be the only rational solution. Communication provides the power these days. We must fashion it into a library tool.

Communication is achieved through symbols. Words are a combination of symbols. The use of the printed word is a recent development. More and more the word is being ousted as a communication medium. The computer, by manipulating machine-readable symbols, compacts, sorts, and transmits information on a scale undreamed of by Gutenberg, yet he was a visionary engineer.

There is something in the nature of a book that defies analysis, that cannot be transmutted to any other form of communication. The book is but a link in the chain of knowledge. It contains thereby, along with its own dynamic, a quality that remains intrinsical, and cannot be abstracted by other more modern methods of communication that are based on computer technology. These more modern methods of information retrieval, analysis, and communication cannot be neglected if learning is to expand and survive. Yet too much dissection, both physical and psychological, can reduce a book to its component parts, as modern medicine tends to do to Man. As we seek a solution to the library's present and future problems, the computer has come to the fore, but as there is something intangible, irreducible in the earth, in Man, so there is in the Book, and the solution eludes us and always will.

There is something in the earth that makes a people. It is, for example, the soil of France that forms the soul of it. Were all the present French to pass away, or emigrate to Quebec, and a new barbarous people inhabit the land, speaking Tartar, or a clicking African tongue, German even, or Urdu, within a generation or so those people would grow French, and shrug and save, as like as any Frenchman of today. Remove a body from its native ground, its mother soil, as did Hercules with his wrestling enemy Anteus, and there is a diminution in the strength, even of his foe, whose mother was the earth and the sea his father.

The people who chaffer in the market places of Athens are very different in appearance from those ancient Greeks, who drove their bargains there, but Aristophanes would find them just the same, grist for the mill of his humour.

Likewise, in every American north of the Rio Grande, there is Yankee. Yankee know-how has survived and taken root, seeded and flourished in every wave of migration that has flooded over the original nutmeg swindles of Connecticut, and the gin mills of Eli Whitney. North Americans are happier tinkering with a gadget than with reflection of the mind, like reading. Even their writing has a tinkering quality about it, a preoccupation with the ways things work out, be they live or mechanical.

Most librarians are not readers in the old, traditional sense. They would much rather switch-on than read, turn a screw rather than a page. They have been turned-on by the

262

glitter, the whir, and the shine of the new machines and electronic devices that are changing the libraries, revolutionising them. University administrators welcome the new library computer age also, assured that it will relieve them of the burden of supporting the vast numbers of books that accumulate, without, it seems, ever being read at all, just stacked in any way that can form a statistic, that may enable them to increase their grant from the provincial or local legislatures.

Computer Science is a major course in the library schools. The deans of some of them are engineers of this new and surprising method of controlling learning. Let any librarian write lovingly about books that he or she has read or wishes to read, and the professional library magazines will suspect the submission is from a nonprofessional. Library journals give information about how to buy and process books, but contain little that is not "library literature."

Some anticipate the day when, lying on a divan, they can read the Purgatorio, with Dali illustrations, projected on the ceiling, and drop off to sleep on a mattress wired for nocturnal learning, so that they will awake in the morning all fed in the mind with the Second Law of Thermodynamics, or the contradictory criticism of F. R. Leavis. Even a judgment value may have been transmitted into them which will depend on the whim or creed of a programmer who died last week of a forgotten anklet.

Eyes light up, cheeks flush, tongues are loosened, an air of light pervades some library professional meetings now as never before, because the participants have been freed from the shadow of the guilt that haunted them in those B. C. days when they were expected to read more books. Now they are engaged in a vast confidence game with the salesmen of the machines, with the administrators who believe that their institutions can now do without a library, with the educationists who are daft on resource centres that do not contain a book, but only ephemera, and are filled instead with films, records, photocopies of information that, in many cases, is better, more conveniently, and far more cheaply, available in a book that has been displaced.

This is not to denigrate the use of the machine. We are living in an age of technology. But we will be doing our own kind and the Machine a disservice if we surrender. All of the learning and the wisdom that we amassed from the

263

times past, present, and to come, are contained within a book that remains the most convenient and cheapest way of conveying information and can give wonder and delight.

The data bank of Everyman becomes a secondary and timid transmutation source. Out of the dust of the ruins a modern Sauron, who began as Man becomes a Board of Control, that conjures up visions of a future when there is no bloody sweat, no tears, no chasms--only broad sunlit uplands. All will be accomplished for Man's pleasure through the power of Information, but at the cost of the deliverance of freedom to the Board, computer-oriented Board, clean and shining Board, information-powerful-beyond-all-the-measures-of-ordinary-Man Board. If Sauron has his way, there will be only one Board; it is mustering, not in the shady cover of Mirkwood, but in carpeted, unbugged or bugged conference rooms, tapping behind walls of vinyl.

Computers can be of great library service. Resource centres can further enrich the scope, depth, and treasure of our libraries because film is Book, discs are Book, so are slides and magnetic tapes. They can serve well the future that began with Gutenberg. Indeed, in order to control the plethora of information, in order to produce a new right form, even of the Book, we will need computer data banks and all technological aids. Moreover, in most academic libraries, even in Bodley's, the computer is beginning to play its part as an aid in getting some sort of order out of the library chaos that has developed over many years. But the learned library must and will remain Book to the core and there must be few of them, and fewer still will be their readers, if learning is to remain free.

More and more academic libraries, with the covert or overt wish as may be, and with the hopeful anticipation of the administration, faculty and students, are putting more and more of their budget into controlling and programming what they can't have enough of, the Book. No single library can ever satisfy the reader. This brings libraries closer to sharing their resources: but it must be Fair Share, and a rationalisation of collections with a network. A return to special libraries of special collections is in the offing.

Academic library budgets all over North America show a diminution in the amount of money spent for books, offset by the greater proportion of the budget spent for technological aids to control the relatively dwindling mass of them and this seems inevitable; hence the Library Machine. I do not deny the essential virtue of the computer as a bibliographic tool and as an information source. It has released librarians from many hours of paper work and made immediately available facts, figures and other data that before were dormant or neglected. There is no aspect of library work that cannot be but improved with ready and general access to a computer terminal.

Library schools are turning out more and more computer-oriented students, impatient experts. Many directors are courting them in a way that they never have courted book people.

Beware, lest we neglect the major for the less. It will be a long time, perhaps never, before anything so convenient, so compact, so portable, so possible to steal, hide and print in a small, poor place, will be discovered that will better the Book. Above all there is a danger to Freedom, that first essential quality of a university, if we depend upon one of the great technological centres for our information, or data, or synthesis, or retrieval, rather than upon books. Books are harder to destroy than any film, any tape, any central reservoir of information data on discs. Moreover, books can be passed around, even if need be, surreptitiously, whenever freedom is threatened. A hand press, as Resistance and Underground history shows, can do more harm to Sauron than bullets or barricades. After all, it is a battle for the minds of men that we are involved in, and books remain our surest ammunition, our basic ration for the mind that is under fire.

Books are going up in price, and they will cost more, so will their care, but every transaction that is greeted with a wild huzza, whereby pages are sent through the electronic media, cost generally far more than the price of the book in the first place. Acquisition, care, maintenance and repair of books should be the prime concern of academic libraries. All else should be ancillary, including the desires and dreams of the librarians who would be happy to be Yankee and Not Brahmin. There must be Division, subordination, a rationale for acquisitions. There is a tide against this flow.

Dr. Louis Wright of the Folger Library, and Dr. Gordon Ray, President of the Guggenheim Foundation, voiced at the Washington, D.C. meeting of the Association of Research Libraries in October 1976 some of the reflections that Lord

David Eccles, Chairman of the British Library, vented on February 25, 1977, at the opening of the new library building at the University of St. Andrews.

> The twin technologies of automation and telecommunications could make the library as we know it obsolete.
> In my view the technologies will revolutionize beyond recognition one half of the library's work, and could disembowel the other half, unless we understand why and how we must intensify the traditional methods of using a library. I am not suggesting a campaign against the use of computers. Mechanical storage and retrieval should be employed for all they are worth.
> But suppose that you are also interested, as the Greeks were, in understanding people, in achieving some order in your own thoughts or at least in learning how to put up with life. The data-bases and on-line terminals will not be of much help.
> You will want to share the experience, recollected and ordered in their writings, of poets, dramatists, theologians, historians and novelists. Literature does not copy the world. It selects and designs patterns which you cannot see at first hand because you are too entangled with reality.
> This kind of knowledge is best pursued by handling books and manuscripts in your own time at your own pace.
> We are beginning to sober up from the orgy of social statistics and technological discoveries. The unanswered question is whether academic libraries are going to put as much effort into re-thinking their presentation as they were bound to put into enlarging their computerized information services.
> (The Times, (London), March 4, 1977, p. 3A.)

It is remarkable and encouraging how these three scholar-bookmen urge caution in the use of the Machine when it is given the go-ahead in humanistic studies that must remain, after all, the heartland of the universities. Science, Medicine, and Law all need to be subject to them, and they are based on the Book.

Nothing can be more tedious to read than facts, facts unadorned with opinions, suggestions, conclusions, or relations. Facts are the boot camp of any form of learning or

266

profession. I have always been struck that in the Military the hardest and most rigorous boot camp is that of the U.S. Marines. It results in casualty rates in combat that are about one-third of those boot camps that are more leisurely and easier to bear.

Facts must be studied and observed to make sense out of opinions. The facts can be persuasive and embraced the more easily if they are new, popular, and in the groove of current thinking.

One of the most dangerous, probably the most dangerous opinion held in current library philosophy and practise is directed against the Book. The Book must go if it is not needed, if there is no proof of its usefulness, and one central storage area for the region established where there will be a store of little-used books--most books in foreign languages and books that are expensive, rare, and difficult to maintain.

This lessening of the individual library's purchase and processing policy has much to commend it, on the surface. Library automation is the prime culprit in this fallacy as well as being the most useful of tools. There is no doubt that the use of technology has improved library service dramatically. Now, for the first time, a union catalogue that can be adopted to bring a bibliography of the books of the world is becoming a reality. The use of a bibliography to locate and identify the books makes all my years that I have devoted towards any form of union catalogue worthwhile, and the facts show results beyond my most roseate of dreams.

Yet, at the same time, it threatens the use and the being of the Book. The idea is fostered by any form of union catalogue that the individual library can ease up on its collections. This can be calamitous, and experience shows it to be so.

I believe that in any library space must be used to the best advantage. That is why I want the library to be allowed to expand into the underground parking lots and the cars thrown out. For most of the world, save for the few temperate zones, those blessed plots set often in the most unlikely positions, like Truro, Fishguard, Sligo, Freemantle and Nanaimo, the rigorous temperatures, the great extremes in weather, mean that an equable mean temperature of about 50° F is desperately needed if books are to be collected and preserved. No amount of air conditioning, so subject to the vagaries of power and the expense and artificiality of an induced climate, comes anywhere near the benefit of a natural climate that an underground facility can bring.

This reservoir of books on the campus is a nuisance in itself. I noticed that after choosing hundreds of thousands of books for this adjacent facility I had recourse to books among them several times a week, just for information perhaps, but information that led me to reading on the spot by the light of my hard hat. It adds thirty minutes or so for the finding and the return of the book to the comfort of the main reading area or the circulation desk. And this is for a book within the library area. A book listed in the bibliography as "readily" available from a central source that serves many libraries generally takes a minimum of a week to become available. The universities of Ontario, before the advent of a union catalogue, but with the advantages of Telex, knowledgeable interlibrary loan librarians, and a link-up with the province of Quebec, provided its own fleet of trucks that make daily pick-up and delivery service to all subscribing libraries. This has greatly facilitated inter-library service and saved money by making packing and mailing of the books through the postal service unnecessary. This good service, however, takes a week or so for delivery service and that is for two closely knit areas that are rich in resources. Distant libraries for many materials that seem unlikely to be popular, do better to buy the book. This is a problem that will grow worse as more and more information becomes available through national, computerized bibliographies.

These previous few pages have been an attempt by me to sugar the stick, to present the facts easily, with my own conclusions drawn. There is much more that can be said, but I am not the one to say it. Although technology is necessary, I was never able to grasp its inner workings, which to me were often magical. I could never make a lecture or a talk out of it, any more than I could ever explain an artillery piece. One thing I will repeat: we must not neglect the major for the less. I believe this. My life has been the Book, and the People; computation and machinery has been for others. The report which an adjutant wrote of my time as a gun sergeant has struck a chord throughout my life:

> This officer showed an ability to command and to inspire enthusiasm, but was unable to master any knowledge of the equipment.